Spanish popular cinema

Edited by
Antonio Lázaro-Reboll and **Andrew Willis**

Manchester University Press
Manchester and New York
distributed exclusively in the USA by Palgrave

Published by Manchester University Press
Oxford Road, Manchester M13 9NR, UK
and Room 400, 175 Fifth Avenue, New York, NY 10010, USA
www.manchesteruniversitypress.co.uk

Distributed exclusively in the USA by
Palgrave, 175 Fifth Avenue, New York,
NY 10010, USA

Distributed exclusively in Canada by
UBC Press, University of British Columbia, 2029 West Mall,
Vancouver, BC, Canada V6T 1Z2

British Library Cataloguing-in-Publication Data
A catalogue record for this book is available from the British Library

Library of Congress Cataloging-in-Publication Data applied for

ISBN 0 7190 6282 9 *hardback*
    0 7190 6283 7 *paperback*

First published 2004

13 12 11 10 09 08 07 06 05 04   10 9 8 7 6 5 4 3 2 1

Typeset in Sabon with Frutiger
by Northern Phototypesetting Co. Ltd, Bolton

Printed in Great Britain
by Bell & Bain Ltd, Glasgow

Spanish popular cinema

MANCHESTER
UNIVERSITY PRESS

Inside Popular Film

General editors Mark Jancovich and Eric Schaefer

Inside Popular Film is a forum for writers who are working to develop new ways of analysing popular film. Each book offers a critical introduction to existing debates while also exploring new approaches. In general, the books give historically in-formed accounts of popular film, which present this area as altogether more complex than is commonly suggested by established film theories.

Developments over the past decade have led to a broader understanding of film, which moves beyond the traditional oppositions between high and low culture, popular and avant-garde. The analysis of film has also moved beyond a concentra-tion on the textual forms of films, to include an analysis of both the social situations within which films are consumed by audiences, and the relationship between film and other popular forms. The series therefore addresses issues such as the complex inter-textual systems that link film, literature, art and music, as well as the production and consumption of film through a variety of hybrid media, including video, cable and satellite.

The authors take interdisciplinary approaches, which bring together a variety of theoretical and critical debates that have developed in film, media and cultural studies. They neither embrace nor condemn popular film, but explore specific forms and genres within the contexts of their production and consumption.

Already published:

Thomas Austin *Hollywood, hype and audiences*
Harry M. Benshoff *Monsters in the closet: homosexuality and the horror film*
Paul Grainge (ed.) *Memory and popular film*
Julia Hallam and Margaret Marshment *Realism and popular cinema*
Joanne Hollows and Mark Jancovich (eds) *Approaches to popular film*
Mark Jancovich, Antonio Lázaro-Reboll, Julian Stringer and Andy Willis (eds) *Defining cult movies: the cultural politics of oppositional taste*
Nicole Matthews *Gender in Hollywood: comedy after the new right*
Rachel Moseley *Growing up with Audrey Hepburn*
Jacinda Read *The new avengers: feminism, femininity and the rape-revenge cycle*
Aylish Wood *Technoscience in contemporary film: beyond science fiction*

Contents

Illustrations

Acknowledgements

We would like to express our gratitude first to Mark Jancovich, who supported and encouraged this project. The volume would not exist at all without him. A collection such as this brings together the contributions of many people, not just those whose names appear within its pages. For that reason we would like to thank the following who have made their presence felt in many, varied ways. We would especially like to thank Peter Evans, Pepa Ibáñez and Chicho Ibáñez Serrador (for giving us some of his time to discuss his films), all of those at the ¡Viva! Spanish film festival, Manchester, in particular Lorraine Rolston and Linda Pariser. We would also like to acknowledge the help and support of Matthew Frost and all at Manchester University Press, and Manolo and Ana at the Filmoteca de Zaragoza. We are particularly grateful to members of our respective departments, Hispanic and Latin American Studies at the University of Nottingham and Media and Performance at the University of Salford, and to The Institute of Film Studies at the University of Nottingham. Antonio would like to thank Donna Fitzgerald for the many films watched together and for the exhilarating walks back home (many more to come). His list of inspirational people further includes Celestino Deleyto, Paco Collado and Peter Evans. Andy would like to thank Perveen Hussain, Joanne Hollows, C. P. Lee and Núria Triana-Toribio.

A note on film titles. For the most part the editors and contributors have, where available, offered commonly used English translations after the Spanish original. When there is not a commonly used translation we have left just the original to avoid confusion.

Notes on contributors

David Archibald is a freelance academic who lives in Glasgow. At the moment he is completing his PhD on 'Representations of the Spanish Civil War in Cinema' in The University of Glasgow´s Department of Theatre, Film and Television. He also works as an arts journalist and has provided articles for numerous Scottish and British publications, including *The Guardian*. In addition he is the manager of the hit theatre show *Bright Colours Only* by Pauline Goldsmith, which is currently touring internationally.

Federico Bonaddio is Lecturer in Modern Spanish Studies at King's College London. His research interests include Spanish poetry, drama and film. He has published articles on the poetry of Federico García Lorca, the plays of Luis Riaza and has, more recently, been working on Spanish cinema. His publications include 'Lorca's *Romance sonámbulo*: the Desirability of Non-Disclosure', 'Sensing the Stutter: A Stammerer's Perception of Lorca' and 'Servants Who Would Be Masters: The Inscription of Complicity in the Theatre of Luis Riaza'.

Peter William Evans is Professor of Hispanic Studies at Queen Mary, University of London. His recent publications include, *The Films of Luis Buñuel*; *Subjectivity and Desire* (Oxford University Press); *Women on the Verge of a Nervous Breakdown* (BFI) and (ed.) *Spanish Cinema: The Auteurist Tradition* (Oxford University Press). He is currently working on a volume for Paidos on *Jamón Jamón*.

Esther Gómez-Sierra is Lecturer in Spanish at the University of Manchester. Her research interests focus on Medieval and Golden Age writing, the politics of the literary canon and film adaptation.

Daniel Kowalsky earned his PhD in European History in 2001 at the University of Wisconsin, where he studied under Stanley G. Payne. He has taught at Wisconsin, Washington University in St Louis and is currently

Assistant Professor of History at the American University in Cairo. He is now completing manuscripts on the Soviet intervention in the Spanish Civil war for Editorial Crítica and Columbia University Press.

Antonio Lázaro-Reboll is Lecturer in Modern Spanish at the University of Kent. His main research interests include cultural studies, film studies and reception studies, and art-horror in Spanish visual culture. He has published on Spanish horror cinema in the 1960s and 1970s and is the co-editor (with Mark Jancovich, Julian Stringer and Andy Willis) of *Cult Movies: The Cultural Politics of Oppositional Taste* (Manchester University Press, 2003).

Candyce Leonard's research centres on the socio-political and cultural inscriptions of the image as represented in film and theatre. In addition to extensive publications on twentieth-century Hispanic theatre, she has recently co-edited three volumes of contemporary Spanish plays. Leonard teaches at Wake Forest University in North Carolina.

Steven Marsh teaches Media Ethics and Cultural Theory at New York University in Madrid. He is a researcher on the AHRB (Arts and Humanities Research Board) international collaborative project, *An Oral History of Cinema-Going in 1940s and 1950s Spain*, and joint editor (with Parvati Nair) of the forthcoming volume *Gender and Spanish Cinema* (Berg, 2004).

Alberto Mira is Reader in Spanish at Oxford Brookes University. He has published widely on Spanish, British and North American theatre, with a special interest in translation. He has also researched the history and articulations of homosexuality in Hispanic literatures. He is currently working on an edited volume on Spanish cinema for Wallflower Press.

Philip Mitchell is Principal Lecturer in Media Studies at the University of Glamorgan's School of Humanities and Social Sciences. His teaching specialism is in international media, and his research has focused on national and regional media in Europe, with a particular emphasis on Spanish broadcasting, cinema and journalism.

Chris Perriam is Professor of Hispanic Studies at the University of Newcastle upon Tyne. He has published widely in the field of Spanish literature and film and his latest book is *Stars and Masculinity in Spanish Cinema: From Banderas to Bardem* (Oxford University Press, 2003).

Andrew Willis is Senior Lecturer in Media and Performance at the University of Salford. He is the co-author (with Lisa Taylor) of *Media Studies: Texts, Institutions and Audiences* (Blackwell, 1999), co-editor (with Mark

Jancovich, Antonio Lázaro-Reboll and Julian Stringer) of *Defining Cult Movies: The Cultural Politics of Oppositional Taste* (Manchester University Press, 2003), and editor of *Film Stars: Hollywood and Beyond* (Manchester University Press, forthcoming).

Eva María Woods is Visiting Assistant Professor of Hispanic Studies at Vassar College. She is currently working on a project entitled *White 'Gypsies', Folklóricas, and Stardom: Racing for Modernity in Spanish Musical Films, 1923–1954*. She is the co-editor of a collection of essays entitled, *Seeing Spain: Vision and Modernity, 1868–1936* (Berg, forthcoming), and is one of the authors of *An Oral History of Spanish Cinema-Going in 1940s and 1950s Spain*, funded by the British government and headed by Jo Labanyi (University of London).

1

Introduction: film studies, Spanish cinema and questions of the popular

Antonio Lázaro-Reboll and Andrew Willis

Current and past methodologies of Spanish film studies have remained primarily aesthetic, auteurist and nationalist in their purview. The increased critical interest in Spanish cinema in recent years has been paralleled by the academic respectability gained by courses offering Spanish cinema as their focus of study; gone are the days in which the study of film was treated gingerly, its choice and use justifiable only in terms of serious art / high cultural prestige and subordinated within language, literary or cultural modules. This introduction and the chapters that follow are an intervention in the area of Spanish film studies. In their interdisciplinary approach to the study of an important part of twentieth-century Spanish culture, film studies are expanding and contributing to changes in the map of modern peninsular Hispanism. The book partakes theoretically and methodologically of the turn towards cultural studies that has taken place over the last decade in Hispanic Studies departments across the UK. The turn towards the intellectual project of cultural studies derives in part from the important work undertaken by academics such as Helen Graham and Jo Labanyi (1995), Labanyi (1999), Paul Julian Smith (1999) and Jordan and Morgan-Tamosunas (2000). Graham and Labanyi have argued for an approach heavily informed by the thinking of Italian Marxist Antonio Gramsci, whereas Smith looks to French sociologist Pierre Bourdieu. Such continental thinkers have had a significant impact upon the development of cultural studies in the UK.

One of the main turning points for the development of Spanish cinema studies in Hispanic departments in the UK was the publication of John Hopewell's *Out of the Past: Spanish Cinema After Franco* (1986).[1] However, this development also needs to be understood in the wider context of academic interest in cultural theory and cultural history in the 1980s, as well as another important factor which was the availability and commercialization of films on video.[2] Since the publication of Hopewell's study, much of the academic work produced has focused on general introductions to Spanish cinema (D'Lugo (1997), Jordan and Morgan-Tamosunas (1998), Stone (2002)), the auteurist tradition (Evans (1999)) and a narrow number of established auteurs (D'Lugo (1991)) and individual directors, namely Almodóvar (Smith (1994), Vernon and Norris (1995), Allinson (2001)),[3] and numerous articles on a relatively small number of canonized films. These dominant critical perspectives have generally bypassed Spanish popular cinema in a rather alarming fashion. Whilst there have been recent publications on Spanish popular cinema, they are fragmented and scattered.[4] This collection aims to provide a resource that will encourage the wider analysis of Spanish cinema, specifically to include works that fall broadly into the category of popular cinema, something that is not always easy to define. The objectives are twofold: firstly, to shift the emphasis towards more popular forms of Spanish cinema, and, secondly, to engage with a variety of theoretical and critical debates around popular film. An important strand running through this volume is the critical engagement with genres situated at the margins of mainstream cinema, thus challenging the status and place of popular films within accepted histories of Spanish cinema. Whereas dominant critical perspectives have mainly focused on the properties of the film text and questions of production, issues of consumption and mediation have been neglected. Our aim is to place Spanish popular film in a political and cultural context, showing how large sectors of the population were, and still are, consuming an aspect of culture which has been largely overlooked by critics. If popular film with its inherently ideological tensions is not reducible to easy chronological divisions and ideological categories, Spanish cinema, as many of our contributors argue, is more complex and contradictory than it is often purported to be, if only because of the political events that have marked the history of Spain in the twentieth century. The overthrow of the Second Republic (1931–36) by the military uprising of General Franco in July 1936 which ended in the Civil War of 1936–39, General Franco's dictatorship (1939–75) and the country's transition to democracy after the dictator's death on 20 November 1975, endorsed by the elections of 15 June 1977, affected the film industry and shaped the narratives.

It was never our intention when writing this introduction to offer merely a chronological account of the place – or lack of place – of popular films within the accepted history of Spanish cinema, singling out genres or films as representative examples of a specific period; this has been done elsewhere (see for example D'Lugo's (1997) historical overview of Spanish cinema). Nevertheless, for the sake of clarity and for pedagogical reasons, we will offer a general chronological overview of trends and sub-trends of Spanish popular film. More central is a concern to highlight a series of questions: How is this history written? How are canons constituted within it? What is at stake in the 'popular' in Spanish popular cinema? In pursuing such questions our interest lies in examining what the consignment of popular film to the marginal category of 'sociological interest' has neglected, and in exploring through Spanish cinematic institutions and practices the discursive structures through which popular film has been produced, controlled and consumed. These questions point towards a more productive framework for the study of Spanish film by situating any account of it in the intellectual project of cultural studies. What follows is by necessity wide-ranging but nevertheless committed to understanding popular Spanish films produced at specific historical moments in a variety of production contexts. Before focusing on the specificities which characterize the local cinematic regime, let us turn to a general overview of notions of the 'popular' in film studies.

Film studies and questions of the popular

Whereas the turn towards the analysis of popular culture in Hispanic Studies departments in the UK is relatively new, the shift to the popular by scholars working in disciplines such as literature, sociology, psychology and history, and more significantly newer interdisciplinary areas such as cultural studies, developed from the 1960s onwards. In the field of film studies the shift began around the same time and since then has strategically opened up the field. Writers sought to break new ground with what had been considered illegitimate objects of study in a range of the above disciplines and to question the politics of those who claimed dominant culture. Within film studies there was a desire to take popular products, most often Hollywood, seriously. In the late 1950s this took the form of elevating film directors to the status of individual artists like novelists or painters. The development of the auteur theory in France, and its export to the USA and Britain, gave those wanting to take film seriously a seemingly legitimate way to do so. Their positions drew widely on literary approaches, such as those of F. R. Leavis, which advocated close textual analysis as the most productive way to understand texts (for more on theories of authorship see Caughie, 1981). The influence of these approaches can be seen in such landmark texts within film studies as V. F. Perkins *Film as Film* (1972). The late 1960s and 1970s saw a shift away from a focus simply on auteurs and a move towards a consideration of the industrial contexts of film production; a move typified by the rise of genre theory in the 1960s and star studies in the following decade.

However, some of the most influential work in film studies in the 1970s emanated from the British journal *Screen* and writers closely associated with what has become known as '*Screen* theory' (see Jancovich, 1995). Rather than champion the study of popular cinema, *Screen* saw the products of these industrial contexts as ideologically reactionary, unprogressive and flawed. Instead, they championed avant-garde practice as the only real way to resist the ever-widening influence of Hollywood and the national cinemas that closely followed its model. The influence of '*Screen* theory' on film study in the 1970s meant that scholars were not encouraged to consider popular cinema from within these other national cinemas, such as that of Spain, unless they were using ideological and psychoanalytical approaches to reveal the problematic and 'dangerous' ways in which these films were working on (predominantly working-class) audiences. Today, much of their anxiety regarding mass culture seems close to the concerns of the Frankfurt School forty years earlier and subsequent theories which address the negative effect of mass culture on the viewer. The 1980s saw a move away from the dominance of these positions as the influence of cultural and media studies began to be felt by film departments. Interdisciplinary approaches began to challenge the dominance of textually driven methods of analysis and once again approaches to popular cinema began to be reconsidered. Central to this was a questioning of simplistic notions of popular cinema and its relationship with audiences.

Raymond Williams suggested two different, and conflicting, notions of what constitutes 'the popular' (1976: 198–9). Firstly, he argues there is a tradition of the popular referring to something that is organically produced from within social groups or communities, whereby the popular is something of the people. This definition usually involves setting an organically produced popular against products, such as films, that are not produced from within and are therefore by definition not of the people. This position also suggests that there is something élitist about material not produced from within, and that these forms are foisted upon ordinary people, usually via commercial means. Such definitions involve a struggle over the meaning of 'the people'. Here, popular refers to materials consumed by small, often very locally specific groups. In this version, popular culture has clear links with communities and lies in opposition to materials produced by social, cultural or economic élites. The position of mainstream cinema in this version is clear: it is produced by a powerful economic group to be predominantly consumed by a less powerful one. This has led to the denouncing of forms like mass culture products because they are destroying more organic popular forms such as folk festivals. Graham and Labanyi (1995) have noted this distinction in writing about popular culture in Spain: Williams' distinction between organic and mass produced cultures would fit their categories of *'cultura popular'* – pre-modern rural culture made by the people – and *'cultura de masas'* (1995: 8) – modern urban culture provided by the culture industries for a mass audience. However, cinema and its relation to the popular is not always as straightforward as this. In their introduction to *Popular European Cinema* (1992), Dyer and Vincendeau note the 'productive messiness of the term' (1991: 2), acknowledging that any '"pure" notion of the popular is wholly untenable' and that 'there can be no understanding of popular film without reference to the market, because popular cinema has only existed in a market economy' (1991: 2).

Perhaps Williams' second version of popular culture would seem more significant for us. He argues that it refers to something that is enjoyed or consumed by large numbers of people but not produced by them. This links cinema to the market and identifies films as commodities. However, any understanding of these popular forms must accept that mediums such as cinema do not operate simply within society; rather, they form a complex set of relations between production, distribution and exhibition, and consumption. As some of our contributors suggest (Woods, Gómez-Sierra), the filmgoer may use popular films in ways that do not correspond with the intentions of their producers. This potentially creates a blend of Williams' versions of popular culture – both organic and mass-produced. The advancement of audience-based film and television studies (see for example Jenkins, 1992) also suggests that mass-produced texts can achieve another status when they enter the realm of consumption.

Another definition that must be considered refers to films that may be conceived as popular, meaning that they are aimed at a large mainstream audience, but for a number of reasons fail to reach them. In a rather contradictory way, popular here may prove to be unpopular. Such films remain popular because they use the codes and conventions of mainstream cinema rather than those associated with 'art' cinema. However, these films are neither popular (organic) nor popular (at the box-office), but they remain *popular* in both their conception and the production techniques which they utilize. However, the status of films within these categories is not fixed. Some popular films through their elevation to the canon of film studies, or Hispanic Studies, may migrate from the realm of the popular to become more widely 'accepted' by cultural élites. Berlanga's 'classic' *¡Bienvenido, Mr. Marshall! / Welcome Mr. Marshall!* (1952) is, like the films of John Ford or Alfred Hitchcock in Hollywood, a case in point – the status of the film increasing as the medium became more respectable and reflecting the changing nature of the canon. Using Pierre Bourdieu's categories (1996), films such as this are able to shift from 'popular' to 'middlebrow' dependent upon the taste formations of those watching. This change often reflects the broad historical shifts in the cultural status of cinema. The appearance of a book such as this one, devoted to various types of popular Spanish cinema, shows that what had previously been seen by writers working in the field as inconsequential and unworthy of attention now must have a more central role within Spanish film studies. It may also assist in reconsidering some of the perceptions that are currently held about Spanish cinema in general and Spanish popular cinema in particular.

Smith's (1999) call for a more eclectic approach to Spanish popular culture links with more general shifts in film and media studies in the 1990s. These approaches have advocated studies that acknowledge the importance of those involved in production, distribution and exhibition, combining what has traditionally been labelled a 'political economy' approach with those that advocate the study of consumption as well as textual analysis (for example see Kellner, 1997). This relocates the work of the academic in a much wider cultural field than simply film or media or Hispanic Studies, the cultural field understood 'as the space of interaction of texts, producers and institutions' (Smith, 1999: 11). The chapters that follow therefore variously address issues relating to production, distribution and exhibition, as well as the consumption of Spanish popular cinema at a variety of historical moments, ranging from the 1930s to the present. They also draw on a wide range of critical and theoretical approaches indicating a number of potentially rewarding avenues that may be pursued by those interested in studying Spanish popular cinema.

Spanish popular cinema / Spanish popular genres

Genre is widely accepted as one of the main points of entry into the investigation of the production, distribution and consumption of popular film. And when it comes to a discussion of Spanish popular genres and sub-genres, the term *españolada* crops up again and again. It is used by critics and audiences alike. Although often used pejoratively, the term can be used positively or endearingly in relation to Spanish popular films. In its more general sense, the term refers to any action, show or literary text that exaggerates the Spanish character, thus connoting excess.[5] And in its general filmic use, the *españolada*, as the film-maker José Luis Borau (1998: 321) reminds us, accounts for a large part of the national production. Furthermore, the excessiveness of the term cuts across generic boundaries: the thematics (bullfighting, the lives of bandits, gypsies and singers) and the aesthetics (*costumbrismo*) associated with it appear throughout the decades in musical dramas and religious dramas, historical narratives and comedies. It also trespasses across national borders: at the turn of the century, the *españoladas* referred only to those filmic products made in France and Hollywood that offered a stereotypical (and exotic) image of Spain (mainly derived from nineteenth-century French novels and travelogues), but then it was appropriated by the Spanish themselves in order to define a local product. In histories of Spanish cinema the more specific use of the term is reserved for the folkloric *españolada*, 'a hybrid genre of romantic comedy and / or melodrama incorporating regional, primarily Andalusian, song and dance' (Vernon, 1999: 249). Worthy of praise or object of derision, the *españolada* forms part of the critical and popular vocabulary of historians, critics and audiences. The following section maps out the development of different popular genres and cycles cultivated in Spain in the different decades. The main purpose of this overview is to familiarize the reader with a 'tradition' of Spanish popular cinema – films, directors and stars – in order to lay out the terrain for the discussions that follow.

Early Spanish cinema had a distinct popular, that is, folkloric, quality. As D'Lugo (1997) and Talens and Zunzunegui (1998) have noted, the Spanish popular cinematic tradition is rooted in cultural traditions different from other European nations. Although not focusing strictly on popular film, their work emphasizes the preference for local popular forms, themes and styles rooted in the theatre, in particular the *sainete* (light, folksy operettas) and the *zarzuela* (comic playlets featuring recognizable types and archetypes), during the early decades of Spanish cinema and the first years of Franco's dictatorship. Such pre-cinematic popular forms were re-inscribed, allegedly, in the narratives of popular genres such as the Andalusian musical comedy films of the 1930s. In the words of Vernon, the *españolada* 'constituted an element of cultural continuity between the Republic and the Francoist period' (1999: 251). Popular themes and popular stars became the main ingredients in the productions of Filmófono and Cifesa (*Compañía Industrial Film Español S. A.*), the latter straddling the period of the Republic, Civil War and the first decade of Francoism. With a system of production à la Hollywood, the films of the director Florián Rey and the star Imperio Argentina provide an example of the commercial popularity and success of the folkloric musical during the decade. Films such as *La hermana San Sulpicio / Sister Saint Sulpicio* (1934), *Nobleza Baturra / Aragonese Peasant Nobility* (1936) and *Morena Clara / The Fair-Skinned Gypsy* (1936) were produced in Republican times, whereas co-production agreements with Germany allowed Rey and Argentina to film *Carmen la de Triana / Carmen the Girl from Triana* (1938) and *La canción de Aixa / Aixa's song* (1939) in Nazi Berlin during the Civil War. Their films remained audience favourites during the first years of the dictatorship. The other director associated with the *españoladas* of the period was Benito Perojo, whose major successes were *La verbena de la Paloma / The Fair Virgin of Paloma* (1936), *Suspiros de España / Longing for Spain* (1938) and *La niña de tus ojos* (1939), the latter two Italian-Spanish co-productions filmed at Rome's Cinecittà.

In the context of the régime's policy of economic and cultural autarky, such generic forms became the officially sanctioned cinema.

For the next two decades the 'official' cinematic culture produced three autochthonous types of film: *cine de cruzada* (crusade cinema), *cine con cura* (missionary film) and *cine con niño* (child centred narratives) (Stone, 2002: 39). Heroic deeds, whether military or religious, and 'national Catholic' moral and cultural values are the organizing principles of the narratives of crusade cinema and missionary films. Although lacking the commercial success of the Andalusian film comedy, they were the staple diet for contemporary audiences. Titles such as *Escuadrilla / Squadron* (Antonio Román, 1941), *Raza / Race* (José Luis Sáenz de Heredia, 1941), with a script by Franco himself under the pseudonym Jaime de Andrade, *¡A mí la legión! / The Legion's for me!* (Juan de Orduña, 1942) and *Los últimos de Filipinas / Last Stand in the Philippines* (Antonio Román, 1945) focus on the militaristic; whilst revelatory titles such as *Misión Blanca / White Mission* (Juan de Orduña, 1947) and *La mies es mucha / Great Is the Harvest* (José Luis Sáenz de Heredia, 1949) were part of the religious propagandistic arsenal. These cinematic models celebrated the heroism of the nationalists, extolled the virtues of an imperial past and, ultimately, served the régime's interests in projecting homogeneous definitions of national history and identity. Recent scholarship (Labanyi, 1997) has claimed that genres like the missionary film and the folkloric film musical whilst certainly serving the régime's interests also allowed space for subaltern groups to rework dominant discourses. Thus the simple idea that all cinema under Franco supported the régime until the late 1950s when alternative voices appeared is challenged.

Towards the end of the 1940s and well into the 1950s, there was a continuation of the generic forms that had been popular before the war; for instance, the folkloric film musical (*La Lola se va a los puertos / Lola Goes Off to Sea* (Juan de Orduña, 1947), *Lola la piconera / Lola the Coal Girl* (Luis Lucia, 1951), *Un caballero andaluz / An Andalusian Gentleman* (Luis Lucia, 1954)) and the heroic costume drama, this time taking the form of a cycle of historical epics produced by Cifesa (*Locura de amor / The Madness of Love* (Juan de Orduña, 1948), *La duquesa de Benamejí / The Duchess of Benamejí* (1949), *Agustina de Aragón* (1950), *Pequeñeces / Trifles* (1950), *La leona de Castilla / The Lioness of Castile* (1951), *Alba de América / Dawn of America* (1951)). Indeed, Cifesa's productions had become the vehicle for the transmission of the régime's identity values – 'the régime's ideological standard bearer' (Evans, 1995: 215).

Musical melodramas were still showing in Spanish cinemas in the 1950s: new stars like Sarita Montiel in *El último cuplé* / *The Last Couplet* (Juan de Orduña, 1957), new takes on the long-established *zarzuela* tradition ¿Dónde vas, Alfonso XII? / Where Are You Going, *Alfonso XII?* (Luis César Amadori, 1958). Another cinematic tradition which continued was the religious melodrama. The themes and narratives of the films of Rafael Gil (*La señora de Fátima* / *Our Lady of Fatima* (1951), *Sor Intrépida* (1953), *La guerra de Dios* (1956)), José Antonio Nieves Conde (*Balarrasa* (1950)), or Antonio del Amo (*Día tras día* (1951)), although more oriented towards social issues and presenting a more liberal tradition of Spanish Catholicism, reinforced the dominant social values.

Within already well-established cinematic traditions was the child-star film, one of the most popular forms of the *españolada* in its wider sense. These hybrid products, melodramatic plots punctuated by songs, were the vehicles for the child prodigies of the moment. Spanish cinema produced its own child-star system in the 1950s and 1960s; musicals, melodramas and comedies launched the careers of Pablito Calvo and Joselito in the 1950s and Marisol in the 1960s. Pablito Calvo became internationally renowned through his role in *Marcelino, pan y vino* / *Marcelino, Bread and Wine* (Ladislao Vajda, 1954), whereas Joselito's voice, the so-called, nightingale of Spanish cinema, was commercially exploited by Antonio del Amo in *El pequeño ruiseñor* / *The Little Nightingale* (1956), *Saeta del ruiseñor* / *Song of the Nightingale* (1957) and *El ruiseñor de las cumbres* / *The Nightingale of the Peaks* (1958). Similarly, Marisol, perhaps *the* female child prodigy of the early 1960s, starred in films directed by Luis Lucia: *Un rayo de luz* (1960), *Ha llegado un ángel* (1961) and *Tómbola* (1962).

The policy of economic self-sufficiency and of cultural isolationism, as Franco and his ministers were soon to realize, was no longer viable in post-war Europe. The need for industrialization, the modernization brought to Western Europe by the Marshall Plan, and the development of a capitalist market economy made Franco change economic policies in an 'attempt to "integrate" Spain in the booming world of advanced Western capitalism, particularly in the European market' (Carr and Fusi, 1993: 54). In order to gain approval from European governments, the Spanish image abroad had to change. Cinema, of course, was a useful medium to that end. Filmmakers Juan Antonio Bardem and Luis García Berlanga were well aware of the power of cinema and the function of film in society. They represented the emergence of a dissident cinema which drew upon popular forms and local and international cinematic traditions in order to articulate a critique of Francoism. Indeed, many academics have become interested in popular forms because directors occasionally seem able to use consciously their codes and conventions to include what might be considered subversive elements. In the context of Spanish cinema, Bardem and Berlanga are often identified as directors who managed to work within popular forms and, almost despite them, still create significant, socially and politically relevant works.[6] John Hopewell has observed how Berlanga's *¡Bienvenido, Mr. Marshall!* is in dialogue with the mythmaking of the *folklórica* films, whilst Marvin D'Lugo argues that 'the familiar stereotypes and cliched plots he derided remained an irresistible formula for commercial success' (1997: 14). Wendy Rolph sees the film as 'marking out the possibilities of working within comedy as a way of outmanoeuvring state censorship' (1999: 11). Certainly, these comments indicate that film-makers began to use the popularity of particular formulas to criticize existing social structures. These possibilities were taken up by others, most notably, directors Marco Ferreri, Fernando Fernán-Gómez and scriptwriter Rafael Azcona, who utilized the popular comedic tradition of *esperpento* to create films that contained criticism of the state and its values. Hopewell goes so far as to claim that *esperpento* is 'the only authentic Spanish film tradition' (1986: 60).[7] Popular cinema had the potential to be about more than simply entertaining audiences.

The *Nuevo Cine Español* of the 1960s was promoted and heavily subsidized from within the Francoist administration. Directed against foreign film, the impact of television, the decrease in national cinema audiences, as well as the new position of cinema within the leisure industry, José María García Escudero's policy as Minister of Film (1962–67) was aimed at restructuring the economy of commercial cinema as well as improving the quality of Spanish cinema through the production of artistic or cultural films (*Cine de Interés Especial* (Special Interest Films)) intended to promote a liberal image of Spain abroad. Many of the names associated with the so-called New Spanish Cinema (Carlos Saura, Angelino Fons, José Luis Borau, Manuel Summers and Miguel Picazo)[8] were formed in the *Escuela Oficial de Cine* (Official Film School). Critical and metaphorical in their approach, their films were widely acclaimed in international circles, critically and institutionally supported but never particularly popular with home audiences.

Writers and directors in the late 1960s and 1970s continued to strive to find ways of making political and social commentary, even if, necessarily, cloaked in popular forms and genres. Thus directors such as Vicente Aranda and Gonzalo Suárez 'combined uncompromising political reflection, formal advances and censor-evading techniques best summarized as a resort to diffusion. *Fata Morgana* and Suárez's *Ditirambo* (1967) distract attention from covert political implication by the use of stock film genres, the sci-fi thriller and the *film noir* respectively' (Hopewell, 1986: 69–70).

Some film-makers working in this period felt they had little choice but to embrace popular forms. This fact is reflected by the work of other film-makers in the 1970s, such as Eloy de la Iglesia, who worked with thrillers (*El techo de cristal / The Glass Ceiling*, 1971), horror (*La semana del asesino / Cannibal Man*, 1972) and science fiction (*Una gota de sangre para morir amando / Clockwork Terror*, 1973), before moving on to more politically explicit social melodramas in the late 1970s and early 1980s.[9] Indeed, it is possible to see a number of thrillers and horror films made in the 1970s as politically subversive, from Bardem's *La corrupción de Chris Miller / The Corruption of Chris Miller* (1972) to Jordi (Jorge) Grau's *No profanar el sueño de los muertos / Let Sleeping Corpses Lie* (1974).[10] Commercially popular forms offered some directors a freedom they were unable to find elsewhere. For this reason, it is important that these popular films are reclaimed from the critical neglect that many of them have fallen into.

The economic failure of the New Cinema proved costly for the industry. With the industry in crisis, 'only a few forms of film-life survived and festered in such an economic climate' (Hopewell, 1986: 80). The survivors were the genre or sub-generic forms, the most commercially successful being the Iberian sex comedy and the horror film.[11] During the late 1960s and early 1970s, westerns, thrillers, comedies and horror movies became the *españoladas* of the moment. The autochthonous versions were the *paella* western, the *cine policíaco* (urban police thriller), the *cine sexy celtibérico* (sexy Iberian comedy) and the *terror hispano* (Spanish horror). The most commercially successful were the Iberian sex comedy and the horror film. Indigeneous comedies and horror films were as successful as American films: comedies such as *Vente a Alemania, Pepe*

(Pedro Lazaga, 1970), *No desearás al vecino del quinto* / *Thou Shalt Not Covet Thy Fifth Floor Neighbour* (Ramón Fernández, 1971), or *Lo verde empieza en los Pirineos* (Vicente Escrivá, 1973) topped the box-office lists together with horror movies like *La Residencia* / *The Finishing School* (Narciso Ibáñez Serrador, 1969) or *La noche de Walpurgis* / *The Werewolf's Shadow* (León Klimovsky, 1970) to name but a few. Both genres created their own repertoire of films, actors and directors. In the case of comedy, the actor Alfredo Landa gave his name to a phenomenon called *landismo*. Horror cinema was the domain of many film-makers (Javier Aguirre, Carlos Aured, Jesús Franco, Enrique Eguiluz, Jorge Grau, Narciso Ibáñez Serrador, León Klimovsky, Amando de Ossorio) and iconic figures well-known to contemporary audiences such as Paul Naschy (Jacinto Molina), widely known as the Spanish Lon Chaney Jr. Comedy was only for internal consumption since it addressed a series of issues related to Spanish society of the period; the horror genre was for both internal and external markets and competed with other European productions. Following a late 1950s policy, it was common practice that Spanish audiences saw a censored version while another more explicit version was destined for international consumption.

Both comedy and horror in their multiple combinations of sex and nudity, titillation and repression could be considered as the precursors of the 'cine de destape' (nudity films) that arrived with the end of dictatorship and the lifting of censorship, which followed in 1977. In fact, some of the directors (Carlos Aured, Ignacio F. Iquino, Jesús Franco) who worked in the genres mentioned above moved into the pornographic film industry that flourished in Spain between 1977 and 1984. The permissive experimentation in the press, television and film, the sexual catharsis of the nation enabled film-makers, actors and producers to bring explicit sexuality to mainstream culture.

Spanish film comedy, in all its variegated forms and ideological alignments, has been one of the most dominant, popular and commercially successful genres in Spanish cinema (see Jordan and Morgan-Tamosunas, 1998: 63–86), and it has been particularly rich in the democratic period. Spanish horror, on the other hand, had disappeared from the screens until very recently; contemporary Spanish horror is enjoying something of a revival in cinemas thoughout Spain, and is receiving acclaim in international circles – an important factor for exportability – and, in terms of conventions is prompting original takes on the genre, among them Jaume Balagueró's *Los sin nombre* / *The Nameless* (1999), Álvaro Fernández Armero's *El arte de morir* / *The Art of Dying* (2000) and Alejandro Amenábar's *Los ótros* / *The Others* (2001). Their use of generic conventions is part of a wider trend among young Spanish film-makers in the 1990s that engage with popular texts as well as other cultural and sub-cultural artifacts.

If eroticism and sex were given full exposure on 1970s Spanish screens, politics came a close second. In the words of Peter Evans, 'post-dictatorship cinema in Spain succeeded in repoliticising film language' (1995: 321), and sex and politics are closely connected in the work of Bigas Luna, Vicente Aranda and Pedro Almodóvar. However, many discussions of cinema of the transition period and the first years of democracy generally concentrate on a brand of official cultural cinema espoused by the Socialist government. The serious art film, the 'quality' cinema promoted under the Miró Law of 1983, based mainly on literary or historical sources (*La colmena* / *The Beehive* (Mario Camus, 1982), *Los santos inocentes* / *The Holy Innocents* (Mario Camus, 1984), *Tiempo de silencio* / *The Time of Silence* (Vicente Aranda, 1986)), have hogged the limelight for critics and historians (see Triana-Toribio, 2003: 108–19).

The 1990s witnessed the arrival of a new generation of filmmakers, including women (Iciar Bollaín, Isabel Coixet, Chus Gutiérrez, Gracia Querejeta)[12] and young men (Alejandro Amenábar, Alex de la Iglesia, Daniel Calparsoro), as well as a new generation of actors, some of who became popular with Spanish television audiences before working in the cinema.[13] But perhaps more importantly, the 1990s witnessed a shift in audience responses to popular Spanish films, in particular young audiences (some critics would argue mainly a university-educated youth). This is perhaps evident in the box-office success of home-grown products and the revival of certain cinematic traditions related to the *españolada* in its wider sense. For instance, *Torrente, el brazo tonto de la ley* (Santiago Segura, 1997) and its sequel *Torrente 2: Misión en Marbella* (Santiago Segura, 2001) attracted Spanish audiences to the cinemas in droves, making Spanish films once again as popular as their Hollywood counterparts.[14] According to Esquirol and Fecé (2001), *Torrente* is probably the first Spanish blockbuster, and therefore it needs to be understood as a social phenomenon in the context of contemporary cultural industries. Likewise, the success and continuation in the television schedules of a celebratory programme such as *Cine de Barrio* indicates the popularity of the *españolada* with older and newer generations alike.

In his *Guide to the Cinema of Spain* (1997) D'Lugo's main purpose is to offer 'an overview of the major movements, trends, and the careers of individual artists' (1997: xii) in the different decades of Spanish cinema. And whilst there is a place in his guide for directors of popular film, his take on Spanish popular cinema seems to us highly problematic. In D'Lugo's narrative, 'popular' is associated with national culture and often with local traditions, an argument which is insightful in its analysis of early Spanish film since much of the production of the first three decades of the century relies, as we have already noted, on locally specific material – popular themes and cultural sources. Yet his narrative of the popular tendencies in Spanish film from the 1930s onwards privileges a 'serious', 'respectable' cinema over a 'banal', 'low-grade' cinema, conferring upon the former a 'critical' value and attaching to the latter a 'conservative' label. Throughout his introduction, there is a rather sweeping connection between escapism and political passivity;[15] symptomatic of this connection, for instance, are his simplistic references to the majority of films produced between 1932 and 1936 as 'escapist fare' (1997: 6) feeding off 'conservative cultural models' (1997: 7). Likewise, Spanish popular films of the 1960s, for him, 'continued earlier and easy patterns of no resistance' (1997: 18). The very same values and judgements that underlie the popular / élitist tension, which for D'Lugo has shaped the history of Spanish cinema, creep back into his own narrative. And as Sieburth has persuasively noted, 'élite culture can also serve as an escape (a concept which needs to be analysed to determine what one is escaping from and why)' (1999: 17). It seems to us that D'Lugo's narrative privileges not only a (certain) history of production but also histories of production over histories of mediation and consumption. Moreover, it passes critical judgement on a fundamental aspect of Spanish popular culture, popular film, enjoyed and consumed by a large number of Spaniards. To dismiss popular genres as 'escapist fare' reinforces those readings sanctioned by dominant culture. Our contributors think otherwise and argue for the political dimension of popular culture and its audience. They place Spanish popular films in a political and cultural context which goes beyond theoretically disabling binary oppositions – authenticity v inauthenticity, seriousness v banal entertainment – showing how audiences variously engage with the social and political discourses at stake as well as showing how audiences use and make meanings from the commodities they consume.

Popular cinema is often considered to address issues surrounding gender and identity. These areas are also crucial sites of negotiation and contestation, as audiences are offered contradictory images and representations. As Eva Woods and Peter Evans respectively argue in this volume, the folkloric musical of the 1930s and 1940s and the child-star film in the 1960s mediated the feminine ideals and fantasies of female audiences. Woods considers that female audiences were offered an alternative to accepted notions of femininity within the narratives of stardom and the films' central characters. In what he describes as the beginnings of a theorized critical biography of Marisol, Evans traces the figure of one of the most famous of all child-stars in Spain from her Francoist-constructed persona to the deconstruction of this 1960s icon. Similarly, Federico Bonaddio considers how historical and musical dramas of the early Franco period allowed ideas that were perhaps unexpected for mainstream audiences, and he shows how these popular forms offered contradictory images and representations of 'Spanishness' as well as 'foreignness'. Dreams, fantasies, self-irony and the accommodation of established cultural perceptions find their way into these films.

As has been argued, popular film, and indeed any text, can be complicit with or critical of existing norms and ideals. If Bonaddio, Evans and Woods point towards the resistant readings inscribed in different genres, Candyce Leonard, on the other hand, in her analysis of a 1998 film, *Solas* (Benito Zambrano) adroitly points out that the film endorses traditional views of the role of woman in a patriarchal society. The question of gender relations – gender and identity as crucial sites of negotiation and contestation – is of crucial relevance in popular film, in particular the representation of individual and social identities. According to Leonard, the representation of gender and sexuality in Zambrano's film reflects the conservatism of the current political system in Spain; for her, the film's form and style are designed to return women to the domestic sphere.

Another criticism of popular cinema is that it simply replicates ideology, that it is not engaged politically or socially, and remains static. Visions of popular cinema as static, whereby popular films merely project an image of some fixed national character and have 'reflected a view held by Spaniards of their own world' (D'Lugo, 1997: 15), deny audiences any investment in popular texts. Ideology is not fixed but performative. To brand popular cinema as merely reproducing ideology simplifies the cultural significance of cinema-going, its sociological dimension and the investment of the spectator, and it overlooks the complex relationship established between texts and specific audiences. Thus a consideration of the reception and consumption practices that surround popular cinema is an important area of study. In her contribution, Esther Gómez-Sierra argues for an approach to cinema that acknowledges the importance of consumption practices. She does this by focusing on the reflections of a cinema-goer from Madrid. In some ways reminiscent of the work of Jackie Stacey (1994) and following in the tradition of cultural studies writers such as David Morley (1980, 1988), Gómez-Sierra's chapter reveals how audiences' responses to films are often markedly different from the assumptions of critics. The need for Spanish popular cinema studies to address the cultural significance of cinema-going and to engage with audiences and their contexts of consumption is clear, and Gómez-Sierra offers a potential method of approaching this area.[16] It indicates the need for Spanish film studies to embrace the developments in film and television studies more generally.

Many forms of popular cinema represent history unproblematically, one only needs to think of such Hollywood epics as *El Cid* (Anthony Mann, 1961). In the case of Spanish cinema this has often coincided with 'official' versions of the past as film production closely reflected the interests of the State. In his chapter, Alberto Mira focuses on Cifesa's historical epics. He links films such as *Locura de amor* to the question of history; more particularly he examines the ways in which these epics coincided with a Francoist vision of history, not only in their content but also in the aesthetic decisions made in their production. In terms of the Cifesa epics, Mira considers in detail the relationship between cinema narrative and history. Albeit utilizing a different approach from Mira, David Archibald also delves into ideas of history and the representational process. His chapter looks at an important and diverse cinematic trend in post-1975 Spanish cinema, that of historical revision. After 1975 many Spanish film-makers have consciously reworked a specific moment in Spanish history: the Civil War and its aftermath. In his analysis of three commercially successful films of the 1990s, *¡Ay,*

Carmela! (Carlos Saura, 1990), *Libertarias* (Vicente Aranda, 1996) and *La lengua de las mariposas / Butterflies' Tongue* (José Luis Cuerda, 1999), Archibald asks how such narratives represented the Civil War for contemporary audiences.

Some of the major landmarks in the history of Spanish cinema have been attempts in one way or another to connect with Spanish popular audiences and represent their self-images on screen. Notwithstanding the different socio-political contexts in which they emerged and the specific agendas behind the different projects – the first signs of a dissident cinema that culminated in the *Conversaciones de Salamanca* (Salamanca Congress) of 1955 – cultural dissidence of this period is often represented by the voices of Juan Antonio Bardem and Luis García Berlanga. *Plácido* (1961) and *El verdugo / The Executioner* (1963), two of the less studied of Berlanga's films, the director of *¡Bienvenido, Mr. Marshall!*, are the subject of Steven Marsh's chapter. He argues that Berlanga draws on a barrage of popular forms in his work, locating it at what he calls the 'slippery juncture somewhere between popular culture and cultural populism'. The two films under analysis have the potential not only to subvert dominant ideas of society and the stability of its structures but also to interrogate the premises upon which cultural tradition, the 'popular' and the state co-exist within the boundaries of the nation.

As already outlined, the New Spanish Cinema looms large in histories of Spanish cinema; from its tentative origins in the Salamanca Congress to its supremacy in the 1960s, its rhetoric of art and quality still 'dragged on' into the 1970s and 1980s among serious critics. By referring to primary sources and focusing on the critical reception of Ibáñez Serrador's *La Residencia*, Antonio Lázaro-Reboll unpicks and exposes the implicit value judgements and aesthetic criteria underpinning the reviews of the contemporary specialist film journals. In doing so, he points towards a vast reservoir of research material that sheds light on the distribution, exhibition and consumption of popular cinema.

Whilst popular cinema is often simplistically seen as being in opposition to more auteur driven art films, many directors have, as we have been arguing, consciously chosen to work within popular forms. Their works may be considered to lie outside traditional art cinema and their engagement with popular forms makes them difficult to categorize, challenging the divisions between auteur cinemas and popular cinemas. Such a demarcation – auterism (art cinema) v the popular (formula) – needs to be re-appraised. Philip Mitchell and Chris Perriam's chapters consider, among other issues, the untenability of this demarcation through the work of two very different directors, Antonio Mercero and Alejandro Amenábar respectively. Mitchell argues that the work of Mercero is typical of the 'tercera vía' or third way of the 1970s, initially promoted by the producer José Luis Dibildós between 1973 and 1976, in its attempt to navigate a course between the popular genres of the day and the arthouse products that represented a more sophisticated image of cinema. Significantly, his study examines material that was produced for Spanish television as well as feature films. In his analysis of Amenábar's second feature film, *Abre los ojos* / *Open Your Eyes* (1997), Perriam explores the hybridity of the young director's work. For him, the film straddles popular and art cinema, moves between box-office super-status and cult status and participates in two different cultural traditions, that of Hollywood and Europe. Amenábar also features in Andrew Willis' contribution which looks at the ability of once marginalized genres to be embraced by the mainstream. This shift is nowhere more evident than in the critical and box-office success of *Los otros*, a gothic horror film not unlike the critically dismissed *La residencia*. Rather than seeing this horror film as exceptional, Willis argues that it must be seen as part of a developing cine-conscious tendency within contemporary Spanish cinema. Not all marginal genres have undergone such a re-evaluation however. Daniel Kowalsky discusses the development and popularity of one such form, the porno movie. As he reminds us, Spanish politicians, film-makers, actors and producers presided over the development of a highly unusual experiment in adult cinema in Spain during the late 1960s, the S film. The S certificate put Spain ahead of other European countries regarding the screening of soft and hardcore pornography. His contribution is a first step towards the opening up of one of the most under-researched areas of recent Spanish popular cinema.

As this collection shows, there should be no limits to the range of approaches critics are willing to draw upon. Contributors have therefore been drawn not only from researchers conducting their work in Hispanic Studies departments but also from academics working in the fields of media, film, drama, television and history, in a conscious effort to cross disciplinary boundaries. We feel this is an approach that can only assist the study and understanding of Spanish popular cinema.

Notes

1 Other contemporary classics are those of Besas (1985) and Higginbotham (1988), followed a few years later by Kinder (1993).

2 A history of the discipline in Hispanic Studies departments remains to be written. We are indebted to Peter Evans' keynote speech on the matter in the First Conference on Contemporary Spanish Cinema held in Manchester (13–15 March 2002) as part of the 8th Viva Spanish Film Festival.

3 In its contextualization of Almodóvar's films, Allinson's book seems to be influenced by more cultural studies perspectives.

4 Smith (1998), Jordan (1995), Labanyi (1997).

5 In the same way, Spanish audiences and critics would describe mainstream American and Italian films as 'americanada' and 'italianada' respectively.

6 *Esa pareja feliz / That Happy Couple* (Badem and Berlanga, 1951 (released in 1953)), the already mentioned ¡*Bienvenido, Mr. Marshall!* (Berlanga, 1952) and *Muerte de un ciclista / Death of a Cyclist* (Bardem, 1955) are given extensive treatment in studies of Spanish cinema, from Hopewell (1986) to Kinder (1993) to Stone (2002).

7 *Esperpento* is defined as 'the filmic exploitation of a long aesthetic of Spanish black humour' which was 'developed in art, literature and drama (particularly by Valle-Inclán) and promoted a view of Spain as a laughable distortion, a crude deformation of European civilisation' (Jordan, 1995: 135–6).

8 For more details on their films see Hopewell (1986) or Stone (2002).

9 For more on Eloy de la Iglesia and melodrama see Smith (1998); for more on de la Iglesia and horror see Willis (2003b, forthcoming).

10 For more see Willis (2003a).

11 See Jordan (1995) for more on the Iberian sex comedy and Lázaro Reboll (2002) for more on horror.

12 For a study of women's place and participation in cinematic institutions from a feminist perspective, see Martin-Márquez (1999).

13 Spanish film magazines and Sunday newspaper supplements devote dossiers regularly to the new voices and faces of Spanish cinema. 'Nuestro Cine. Diccionario para conocer a los jóvenes cineastas que han protagonizado el nuevo boom' in *El País* (Sunday 25 January 1998, 113, 20–50) and 'Generación catódica' in *Cinemanía* (August 2000: 67).

14 For more details on recent box-office returns, see the I. C. A. A (*Instituto del Cine y las Artes Audiovisuales*) website http://velazquez.mcu.es/cine.

15 In their seminal *Spain: Dictatorship to Democracy*, first published in
    1979, the historians Raymond Carr and Juan Pablo Fusi also associate
    mass-culture products, in particular during the dictatorship, with what
    they define as a culture of evasion 'devoid of political or intellectual
    content, and therefore innocuous' (1993: 119).
16 The importance of more audience-focused approaches has also been
    acknowledged by Labanyi who indicates moves in this direction when
    she says 'I hope myself to contribute to such research through a col-
    laborative "Oral History in Cinema-Going in 1940s and 1950s Spain",
    planned with Vicente Sánchez Biosca in Spain, and Kathleen Vernon
    and Susan Martin-Márquez in the US' (1999: 110).

Bibliography

Allinson, Mark (2001) *A Spanish Labyrinth: The Films of Pedro Almodóvar*,
    London: I.B. Tauris.
Besas, Peter (1985) *Behind the Spanish Lens*, Denver: Arden Press.
Borau, José Luis (ed.) (1998) *Diccionario del cine español*, Madrid: Acade-
    mia de las Artes y las Ciencias Cinematográficas de España, Fundación
    Autor and Alianza Editorial.
Bourdieu, Pierre (1996) *Distinction: A Social Critique of the Judgement of
    Taste*, London: Routledge.
Carr, Raymond and Juan Pablo Fusi (1993, 2nd edn) *Spain: Dictatorship
    to Democracy*, London: Routledge.
Caughie, John (ed.) (1981) *Theories of Authorship*, London: RKP/BFI.
D'Lugo, Marvin (1991) *The Films of Carlos Saura: The Practice of Seeing*,
    Princeton, NJ: Princeton University Press.
—— (1997) *Guide to the Cinema of Spain*, Westport: Greenwood Press.
Dyer, Richard and Ginette Vincendeau (1992) *Popular European Cinema*,
    London: Routledge.
Esquirol, Meritxell and Josep Lluís Fecé (2001) 'Un *freak* en el parque de
    atracciones: Torrente, el brazo tonto de la ley', *Archivos de la Filmoteca*,
    39: Octubre, 26–39.
Evans, Peter William (1995) 'Cifesa: Cinema and Authoritarian Aesthetics',
    in Helen Graham and Jo Labanyi (eds.) *Spanish Cultural Studies: An
    Introduction*, Oxford: Oxford University Press.
—— (1999) *Spanish Cinema: The Auteurist Tradition*, Oxford: Oxford
    University Press.
Graham, Helen and Jo Labanyi (eds.) (1995) *Spanish Cultural Studies: An
    Introduction*, Oxford: Oxford University Press.
Higginbotham, Virginia (1988) *Spanish Film Under Franco*, Austin: Austin
    University Press.
Hopewell, John (1986) *Out of the Past: Spanish Cinema after Franco*,

London: BFI.

Jancovich, Mark (1995) 'Screen Theory', in Joanne Hollows and Mark Jancovich (eds.) *Approaches to Popular Film*, Manchester: Manchester University Press, 123–50.

Jenkins, Henry (1992) *Textual Poachers: Television Fans and Participatory Culture*, London: Routledge.

Jordan, Barry (1995) 'Genre Cinema in Spain in the 1970s: The Case of Comedy', in *Revista Canadiense de Estudios Hispánicos* 20, 1: Autumn, 127–41.

Jordan, Barry and Rikki Morgan-Tamosunas (1998) *Contemporary Spanish Cinema*, Manchester: Manchester University Press.

—— (2000) *Contemporary Spanish Cultural Studies*, London: Arnold.

Kellner, Douglas (1997) 'Critical Theory and Cultural Studies: The Missed Articulation', in Jim McGuigan (ed.) *Cultural Methodologies*, London: Sage.

Kinder, Marsha (1993) *Blood Cinema: The Reconstruction of National Identity in Spain*, Berkeley: University of California Press.

Labanyi, Jo (1997) 'Race, Gender and Disavowal in Spanish Cinema of the Early Franco Period: The Missionary Film and the Folkloric Musical', *Screen*, 38: 3, Autumn, 215–31.

—— (1999) 'Gramsci and Spanish Cultural Studies', in *Paragraph*, 22: 1, March, 95–113.

Lázaro-Reboll, Antonio (2002) 'Exploitation in the Cinema of Klimovsky and Franco', in Shelley Godsland and Anne M. White (eds.) *Cultura Popular: Studies in Spanish and Latin American Popular Culture*, Bern: Peter Lang, 83–95.

Martin-Márquez, Susan (1999) *Feminist Discourse and Spanish Cinema: Sight Unseen*, Oxford: Oxford University Press.

Morley, David (1980) *The Nationwide Audience: Structure and Decoding*, London: BFI.

—— (1988) *Family Television: Cultural Power and Domestic Leisure*, London: Routledge.

Perkins, V. F. (1972) *Film as Film*, London: Harmondsworth.

Rolph, Wendy (1999) '*¡Bienvenido, Mr. Marshall!* (Berlanga, 1952)', in Peter William Evans (ed.) *Spanish Cinema: The Auteurist Tradition*, Oxford: Oxford University Press, 8–18.

Sieburth, Stephanie (1999) 'What Does It Mean to Study Spanish Culture?', in David T. Gies (ed.) *Modern Spanish Culture*, Cambridge: Cambridge University Press, 11–20.

Smith, Paul Julian (1994) *Desire Unlimited: The Cinema aof Pedro Almodóvar*, London: Verso.

—— (1998) 'Homosexuality, Regionalism and Mass Culture: Eloy de la Iglesia's Cinema of Transition', in Jenaro Talens and Santos Zunzunegui (eds.) *Modes of Representation in Spanish Cinema*, Minneapolis: University of Minnesota Press, 216–51.

—— (1999) 'Towards a Cultural Studies of the Spanish State', *Paragraph*, 22: 1, March, 6–13.

Stacey, Jackie (1994) *Star Gazing: Hollywood Cinema and Female Spectatorship*, London: Routledge.

Stone, Rob (2002) *Spanish Cinema*, Harlow: Longman.

Talens, Jenaro and Santos Zunzunegui (1998) 'Introduction', in Jenaro Talens and Santos Zunzunegui (eds.) *Modes of Representation in Spanish Cinema*, Minneapolis: University of Minnesota Press, 1–45.

Triana-Toribio, Núria (2003) *Spanish National Cinema*, London: Routledge.

Vernon, Kathleen M. (1999) 'Culture and Cinema to 1975', in David T. Gies (ed.) *Modern Spanish Culture*, Cambridge: Cambridge University Press, 248–66.

Vernon, Kathleen M. and Barbara Norris (eds.) (1995) *Post-Franco, Postmodern: the Films of Pedro Almodóvar*, Westport: Greenwood Press.

Williams, Raymond (1976) *Keywords: A Vocabulary of Culture and Society*, Glasgow: Fontana.

Willis, Andrew (2003a) 'Spanish Horror and the Flight from "Art" Cinema, 1967–1973', in Mark Jancovich, Antonio Lázaro-Reboll, Julian Stringer and Andrew Willis (eds.) *Cult Movies: The Cultural Politics of Oppositional Taste*, Manchester: Manchester University Press.

—— (2003b, forthcoming) '*La semana del asesino*: Spanish Horror as Subversive Text', in Steven Jay Schneider and Tony Williams (eds.) *Horror International*, Detroit: Wayne State University Press.

2

Dressing as foreigners: historical and musical dramas of the early Franco period
Federico Bonaddio

An almost complete disregard for verisimilitude in the performance of foreignness characterizes the representation of foreigners in dramas, most notably historical dramas, produced in the early Franco period by Cifesa (Compañía Industrial Film Español), the production company generally associated with the ideology of the regime (D'Lugo, 1997: 12; Evans, 1995; Monterde, 1995a: 205–6). Since no attempt is made to feign a foreign accent, the figures who appear on screen speak 'as Spaniards', whether they are Flemish courtiers in Juan de Orduña's *Locura de amor / The Madness of Love* (1948) or officers of the French army in Orduña's *Agustina de Aragón* (1950) or Luis Lucia's *Lola la piconera / Lola the Coal Girl* (1951). This works, in a peculiar way, to undermine the distinction between Spaniards and foreigners. Clearly Spaniards playing foreigners 'as Spaniards', their foreignness is signified by means other than verisimilitude of speech, such as name, costume, plot or even the possession of a dubious morality since, as we will see, foreigners often occupy (though not exclusively) the negative pole in the Manichaean discourse characteristic of these films. Ultimately, spectators, if they are to accept the foreignness of the figures on screen, are obliged to suspend their disbelief and deny the unreality of the performance. In *Agustina de Aragón*, for example, acceptance is facilitated by action sequences depicting marauding or battling French invaders. Less helpful are those instances where figures of foreignness actually speak; in other words, where the transparency of the performer's disguise is most apparent. In such cases, the dialogue struggles to maintain credibility. When Agustina (Aurora Bautista) is detained at a French army checkpoint, she is made to endure the harassment of an officer inspecting her safe-conduct. His initial 'Oh, mademoiselle', which, though betraying a Spanish accent, serves to signify his Frenchness, is followed by pronouncements in fluent, native Castilian. When Agustina informs him that she is on the way to her wedding, the officer's response is equally inconsistent as he juggles a smattering of French with synonyms in Spanish: 'Wedding? What is wedding? Ah, oui! Marriage. What sorrow! Mon Dieu! What sorrow!' ['¿Boda? ¿Qué es boda? ¡Ah, oui! Matrimonio. ¡Qué dolor! ¡Mon Dieu! ¡Qué dolor!']. By the time an infantryman, impressed by Agustina's comportment, makes the preposterous statement, 'Mon Dieu! A Spanish woman who is a match for our French women!' ['¡Mon Dieu! ¡Una española que vale por una francesa!'], the sham has been well and truly uncovered. In *Lola la piconera* our credulity is also tested as Virgilio Teixeira, who plays Gustavo, a French officer, and Manuel Luna, in the role of his commander, speak proudly in Spanish of the victories and ambitions of France. The fact that Teixeira and Luna appeared regularly in Cifesa productions also draws attention to the fictional nature of the performance. Both men are part of the star system generated by Spanish cinema at the time (D'Lugo, 1997: 12) and are recognizable, by virtue of familiarity, as actors in roles. Yet another layer of duplicity is provided by the fact that Teixeira was, ironically, Portuguese, his performance in this and other films actually dubbed into Spanish (Torres, 1996: 449–50).

Targeting foreignness

Historical dramas are thus sites of beguilement and self-revelation, moving spectators between domains of veiled and unveiled duplicity and coaxing them both into losing sight of and recognizing the unreality of their images. To lose sight of their unreality is to acknowledge the foreignness of the figures on screen and receive the full force of these films' xenophobic discourse, whether it be, to use Barthes' terminology, as a mythologist or a reader of myths (1998: 115), in other words, either with suspicion or acceptance. Of interest in the context of the Franco regime's production of myths is Vázquez Montalbán's description of how, after the Civil War, the official history of Spain taught in Spanish schools told of a nation envied by foreigners and obliged to defend its independence in the face of successive invasion attempts (1998: 42). The logic of this history of independence and invasion is essentialist and Manichaean in the way it presupposes the existence of an original, unitary, eternal and 'good' Spanishness in contrast to what it deems to be the 'evil' character of many foreigners and foreign ideas. Moreover, it allows for 'bad' Spaniards to be represented as victims of corrupting foreign influence, their behaviour as somehow inauthentic. For true Spaniards are essentially honest, devout, chaste, loyal, courageous, self-sacrificing, patriotic and, crucially in the post-Civil War period, capable of repentance and, consequently, worthy of redemption. This is the logic of the good brother / bad brother paradigm in Luis Sáenz de Heredia's infamous *Raza / Race* (1941), financed by the Spanish Council and the prototype for bellicose films of the 1940s and 1950s (D'Lugo, 1997: 92–4; Hopewell, 1986: 34–5; Pérez Perucha, 1997: 138–40; Seguin, 1999: 32–3; Torres, 1996: 393–4). Based on a script by Francisco Franco himself (under the pseudonym Jaime de Andrade), *Raza* holds foreigners responsible for the fratricide in Spain and represents the Civil War as a struggle to keep Spain Spanish. When José Churruca (Alfredo Mayo), good brother and nationalist infantry officer, is shot by firing squad (it later transpires that he miraculously survives his execution), his fall exposes graffiti scrawled on the wall behind him. The slogan reading 'Long live Russia' ['¡Viva Rusia!'] is brought sharply into focus and appears in sardonic contrast to José's patriotic last cry of 'Long live Spain!' ['¡Arriba España!']. Pedro Churruca (José Nieto), bad brother and Republican politician, though unable to prevent his brother's execution, is eventually handed the opportunity to redeem himself and save both his country and soul. A spy of the right-wing Fifth Column convinces him to surrender information about Republican troop positions. At first, he is reluctant to renounce his allegiances, though he acknowledges that they are misplaced. Yet the moment of his repentance and redemption comes as the truth of the spy's argument sinks in: 'You cannot possibly count as your own these men who have come from Moscow bent on plunging us into terrorism and barbarism' ['No es posible que tenga como suyos a los que vinieron de Moscú a sumirnos en el terrorismo y la barbarie']. Pedro cannot help but be moved by the 'truth' of this statement.

Almost inevitably, historical dramas incorporate this paradigm of repentance and redemption from foreign corruption into their narratives. What is more, they do so via some form of love interest. In *Locura de amor*, for example, Juana de Castilla (Bautista), daughter of the Catholic Kings, Isabel and Fernando, is literally driven out of her mind by the philandering of her husband, Felipe 'el Hermoso' (Fernando Rey), Archduke of Austria. In her altered state, she is too obsessed to be aware of, or even care about, the tragedy befalling her kingdom as a result of the neglectful administration of the Archduke's power-seeking Flemish advisers. Her moment of enlightenment (albeit brief) does come, as does Felipe's own. Struck down by an illness which is almost certainly a punishment from God, Felipe asks that their son, Carlos, be told only of the harm he did to Castile and not of the unjust manner in which he treated Juana. With almost his last breath, Felipe makes his final dramatic plea: 'Let him hate the King, but not his own father' ['Que odie al Rey pero que no aborrezca a su padre']. Felipe's death rescues Spain, though Juana's grief plunges her even more deeply into the madness that her jealousies and suspicions first provoked. By contrast, in *Agustina de Aragón*, Agustina, on discovering that her fiancé, Luis (Eduardo Fajardo), is sympathetic to the French cause, breaks off their engagement. She falls in love, instead, with an archetypal Spanish hero, Juan 'el Bravo' ['the Brave'] (Teixeira), a combatant in the guerrilla resistance against the French. Prompted by his rejection, Luis eventually sees the error of his ways and dies the authentic death of a Spanish martyr defending Zaragoza against its French besiegers.

Whenever lack of verisimilitude leads us to see the performance of foreignness for what it is: a *performance*, the foreignness denoted by role or plot becomes merely nominal. If, in this context, the display of 'foreignness' is perceived to be anything other than artificial, then such a perception may owe much to prejudices lying beyond the film's diegesis and in the spectators themselves. For the display is indeed artificial, as artificial as the total reconstruction characterizing the 'historical' experience of these dramas. As Hopewell has noted, though they may have 'aimed at historical lessons', historical dramas paradoxically 'denied historical accuracy' (1986: 42). In *Agustina de Aragón*, for example, an initial voice-over explains that the film is not 'an exact or detailed historical account of the heroic exploits of the siege of Saragossa but a fervent and impassioned summary of the mettle and valour of its sons and daughters, heroes and heroines' ['no pretende ser un exacto y detallado proceso histórico de la gesta inmortal de los sitios de Zaragoza sino la glosa ferviente y exaltada del temple y valor de sus hijos, de sus héroes y heroínas']. We can make sense of this disclaimer's emphasis on passion over detail in at least two ways. Firstly, it is comparable to the regime's own emphasis, so evident in *Raza*, on the historical spirit of a nation over the material conditions of its history, recent or distant. Indeed, the regime had good reason to adopt this strategy given the country's economic difficulties, exacerbated by the policy of economic autarky, and the fact that, even before the regime's ostracism by western democracies, Spain had long ceased to be a major player on either the world or European stages (Boyd, 1999: 95–9; Carr, 1980: 155–6; Carr and Fusi, 1981; Payne, 2000). Indeed, in *Agustina de Aragón*, it is only the invocation of heroic spirit that staves off the potentially humiliating and depressing reality of a country invaded and a city besieged. Secondly, it is an affirmation of the film's commitment to entertain and enrapture its audience. By no means were all historical dramas commercial successes, but those that were almost certainly owed their popularity not to a concern for historical detail or accuracy but, as D'Lugo suggests with regard to the highly successful *Locura de amor*, to their 'lavish historical reconstructions' and 'popular melodramatic style that emphasized the highly theatrical nature of particularly charged emotional moments' (1997: 69). The conflicts of history provided many such moments, as well as the opportunity to rework myths already enshrined in folklore, like that of the heroism of Agostina of Saragossa in the Peninsular Wars (see De Pauw, 1998: 137–8) or the madness of Juana de Castilla, popularly known as Juana la Loca (Joan the Mad). These conflicts also supplied a host of foreign candidates for the role of villain in the Manichaean discourse of these dramas. Importantly, foreigners could be utilized to mediate or accommodate conflictive passions that are the mainstay of melodrama yet required more tactful handling in the context of post-Civil War Spain. As Labanyi points out, Spanish audiences of the day were by no means homogeneous and divisions could only have been exacerbated by the severe repression immediately following the War (1997: 216). If the tendency of popular cinema in democratic states is to attempt to resolve contradictory ideologies (Willis, 1995: 181), in the context of dictatorship more evasive measures are required to negotiate potentially divisive issues. Targeting foreigners was a means of negotiating division and was a strategy not at odds with the duplicitous game played by a regime that cast foreign powers as anti-Spanish while seeking to secure from them economic aid (Payne, 2000: 355–9). In 1946, the year in which France closed the Pyrenean border indefinitely and the United Nations General Assembly called for the withdrawal of diplomatic recognition from the regime (though relations were, in fact, never completely severed), Franco enjoyed significant popular support (Payne, 2000: 358–9). In this period of autarky and international ostracism, there was evidently something to be gained from playing the foreign card. It is interesting how, by way of contrast, in Orduña's *La leona de Castilla / The Lioness of Castile* (1951), from which foreigners are distinctly absent, the treatment of the sixteenth-century revolt of the *Comuneros* is dominated not by outrage (despite the vociferous performance of Amparo Rivelles in the role of María de Pacheco) but by pathos.[1] The dramatic potential of this internal conflict is arguably diminished by the sense of civility that governs its depiction. As María's son lies dead outside the walls of Toledo, the safety of which he left to vent his frustrations and avenge his father's death, the imperial knight responsible for his death explains with regret: 'He killed himself. It seemed that he wanted to die' ['El mismo se ensartó. Parecía que tenía afán de morir']. Indeed, abrupt editing leaves us in doubt as to how it is the young man dies. Don Pedro Girón (Teixeira), a noble in the service of the Empire and now secretly in love with María, gives the following instruction to the party that has emerged to recover the body: 'Tell Lady María how much I would have given to be able to return him to her alive' ['Decidle a Doña María cuánto hubiese dado por devolvérselo con vida']. Overall, despite the presence of scheming politicians, a norm in post-Civil War cinema since their vilification in *Raza* by contrast to the exaltation of the military, the film lacks the bite of representations of more polarized enmities. We can only hypothesize on the reasons for the film's success. Its run of sixty-three days was bettered by only seven other Spanish films in the course of the 1950s (Monterde, 1995b: 262) and may have had something to do with Orduña's by now well-established directorial credentials in the field of melodrama (D'Lugo, 1997: 183–5; Torres, 1996: 354–5).

Evans (1995: 217) has noted how the French in *Agustina de Aragón*, because of their Republican status, may represent internal as well as external otherness, an observation which we can extend to other films that make reference to the Peninsular War, such as *Lola la piconera* or Ladislao Vadja's 1954 priest film, *Marcelino, pan y vino / Marcelino, Bread and Wine* (a Chamartín production). The condition of Spaniards playing the French 'as Spaniards' arguably enhances this duality, the images of barbaric French soldiers in

Agustina de Aragón, or drunken ones in *Lola la piconera*, cohering with the representation of uncouth militiamen in *Raza*. By contrast, in *Locura de amor*, the ambivalence which Sara Montiel's undisguised Spanishness lends to the figure of Aldara, a Moorish princess, serves to enact a fantasy of kinship with the Arab world. While plotting the Queen's downfall in order to avenge her father's defeat by the Catholic Kings, Aldara manages to conceal her true racial identity from the other characters for most of the film and even succeeds in being appointed the Queen's handmaiden. On one level, this unlikely scenario simply fits the requirements of the plot. Yet it also implies that there is no visible distinction between Spaniards and Moors. In the end, like Spaniards who fall victim to foreign corruption, Aldara has her moment of repentance and salvation. She renounces her quest for vengeance and saves Don Alvar de Estúñiga (Jorge Mistral), a captain loyal to the Queen, from certain death at the hands of Don Filiberto de Were, a scheming Flemish courtier whom she kills. If the undisguised Spanishness characterizing Montiel's performance evokes Spain's Arab past, Aldara's defence of Alvar against a European enemy and the respect each earns from the other may be understood as alluding to an alignment against the West in the context of the Franco regime's problematic relations with western democracies (see Labanyi, 1997: 223). A fantasy of kinship is also acted out in Orduña's *Alba de América / Dawn of America* (Cifesa, 1951) through Antonio Vilar's performance as Christopher Columbus. Here the transparency of the disguise allows Spain to claim the Old World Italian as her own. Once again a Frenchman is cast as the villain of the piece with Fajardo in the role of an ambassador of the French court scheming to lure Columbus into the service of France.

Breaking the paradigms

Although sympathizers of the Franco regime in the 1940s regarded historical dramas as an opportunity to promote Spain's 'glorious' and 'magnificent' history to audiences within and beyond her national borders (Monterde, 1995a: 234), the official system of awards and rebates that was in place in the period suggests that ideological conviction was not necessarily the motivation for the production of such films. With the establishment of a sliding scale of classifications in 1941, licences to import and dub foreign films

(extremely popular with Spanish audiences) and rebates for production costs were awarded to producers whose films obtained classification in the top categories. Films in the lowest category received
nothing at all (Higginbotham, 1988: 7–17; Monterde, 1995a:
189–203). This official system of remuneration, represented as a
protectionist measure, served, along with censorship, to ensure that
Spanish films conformed with the ideology of the regime (D'Lugo,
1997: 10; Higginbotham, 1988: 8; Labanyi, 1995: 210–11; Monterde, 1995a: 195). In 1944, a new top category of 'National Interest' was introduced to encourage not just conformity but a more
active representation of Spanish themes and the exaltation of Spain's
'racial values' and 'moral and political principles' (Monterde,
1995a: 198–9). The apparent suitability of the subject matter of historical dramas in the eyes of officialdom, combined with the high
production costs they entailed, meant that they were attractive to
producers as financial propositions: for, despite the usual risks of
failure at the box office, they at least seemed strong candidates for
the award of import licences and rebates: up to 50 per cent for classification in the highest category (Higginbotham, 1988: 10; Torres,
1996: 26). These circumstances arouse the suspicion that the ideological stance adopted by many historical dramas may itself have
been nothing more than a sham: one forced upon producers in their
quest for financial viability and success (Monterde, 1995a: 196). It
is interesting, therefore, that a critical awareness of the formulaic
representations of foreignness should have found its way into two
Cifesa productions that seem, on the surface, to exploit the very
same formula. These are Orduña's *La Lola se va a los puertos* / *Lola
Goes off to Sea* and Lucia's *Lola la piconera*, films whose release
dates (1947 and 1951 respectively) coincide with the beginning and
end of the historical drama's period of peak production. Both films
contain a historical and musical element (the singing is provided in
both cases by Juanita Reina in the respective roles of Lola); but
whereas *La Lola se va a los puertos* is strictly speaking a folkloric
musical set in the past (its historical dimension is provided by its
transposition to 1860 of the events of the Machado brothers' play
from which it is adapted), *Lola la piconera* is more properly a
hybrid: a convergence of the historical drama and folkloric musical.
These films' musical aspect is significant because the stagy quality of
musicals, even more than the theatricality of melodrama, lends itself,
as Babington and Evans point out (quoted in Labanyi, 1997: 229),

to self-reflexivity, thereby promoting an awareness of the artifical nature of the events on screen. Moreover, as Vernon explains (1999: 251), though it is not precisely the case that folkloric musicals 'offered settings and stories outside history and politics', it could be argued that they 'existed on the margins of official Francoist culture', particularly since very few were favoured by the official system of awards.

If in some dramas of the period the siege mentality characteristic of a country at odds with its neighbours is acted out through the actual reconstruction of historical sieges, in *La Lola se va a los puertos* it finds its expression in the fervent cries of 'Spain is different' and 'Spain is best' which may be interpreted as a sign of defensiveness in relation to the influence of foreign cultures, though they may well explain why the film was awarded, as Vernon points out (1999: 251), the category of 'National Interest'. Although no foreigners are actually represented, the paradigm of foreign corruption, repentance and redemption which we noted in historical dramas still applies. The film tells the story of how an enchanting flamenco singer, Lola, comes unwittingly between a wealthy landowner, Don Diego (Jesús Tordesillas), and his son, José Luis (Ricardo Acero), and in the process threatens the latter's engagement to Rosario (Nani Fernández). In a deviation from the play, Rosario and her uncle, Tío Willy (Nicolás Díaz Perchicot), have returned to Andalusia after completing a grand tour of London and Paris. Each has become Frenchified, preferring the 'sophisticated' mores of Paris salon life and the opera to the 'down-to-earth' values of Andalusia and flamenco. As a result, José Luis falls out of love with Rosario and into love with Lola who is presented as the embodiment of all things Spanish: 'To no one does Lola deny', sings the flamenco artist, 'that the blood in her veins is Spanish' ['A nadie niega la Lola / que lleva sangre española']. Both Tío Willy and Rosario are eventually brought back into the fold: the former, no sooner than he has seen and heard Lola perform; the latter, when she realizes that she has all but lost José Luis by not being true to her own 'innate' Spanishness. The influence of foreignness is shrugged off as easily as someone might take off a costume. Like so many real actors in historical dramas, the characters Tío Willy and Rosario were themselves, it seems, only ever pretending.

That the French should provide the counterpoint to Spain's 'greatness' in *La Lola se va a los puertos*, as in other films of the period, is explicable in the context of the two countries' historical rivalries, their mutual border, then constituting, in effect, the frontier between Spain and western European democracies (together with the fact that France closed the frontier and, for a time after 1944, the southwest of France provided a degree of sanctuary to communist insurgents) (Payne, 2000: 344–5, 357, 376). Interestingly, *La Lola se va a los puertos* is set at a time when Spain's programme of economic expansion relied heavily on investment from its influential neighbour and French culture was highly favoured by the Spanish ruling classes (Carr, 1982: 271, 284). The film does acknowledge France's cultural influence in its depictions of the opera house which, whilst serving as a pretentious counterpoint to Lola's homespun popular folk songs, also remind us that Spain's cultural borders are by no means impermeable. The film's references to Alexandre Dumas' *La Dame aux camélias* act in the same way. The similarities with the novel already present in the play – a tale of interclass love and attraction – are emphasized not only by the film's nineteenth-century setting or scenes depicting the performance of Giuseppe Verdi's adaptation, *La Traviata*, but by actually incorporating the novel as a prop within the film's *mise-en-scène*. In one scene, we find Lola reading in the house to which she and José Luis have stolen away. The camera zooms in to a close–up of the book's cover behind which Lola's face is concealed as she reads. The title, *La Dama de las camelias*, is brought to our attention in an instant, as are the points of contact between Lola and Marguerite Gautier, the ill-fated courtesan of Dumas' novel. Ultimately, the connection between the two that is most exploited is the capacity of each for self-sacrifice. Lola's decision to give up José Luis (just as Marguerite gives up her own aristocratic lover, Armand Duval) coheres with the predominantly conservative tenor of the film's discourse which subordinates individual desire to principles of religiosity and familial harmony. The flamenco singer denies herself her own happiness in order to keep a promise she makes to the Virgin of the Sorrows in return for the life of the young man who has been wounded defending her honour. In turn, this display of religious devotion brings with it the possibility of an end to the conflict between José Luis and his father, divided as they have been by their competing desires for Lola, as well as José Luis's reconciliation with his fiancée Rosario who, by now, has been well and truly cured of her Francophilia. Yet, however conventional the ending may seem in the context of the regime's emphasis on the value of patriotism, religion and family, the parallel drawn between the stories of Lola and Marguerite allows for alternative readings. For the circumstances of Marguerite's sacrifice foreground questions of class and decency; while the fact that Lola, the very embodiment of Spanishness, should ever be compared to a foreigner or even be engrossed in the drama of a foreign novel is no less than telling. Like a Trojan Horse, the novel, at the level of plot and prop, has trespassed into the domain of the film's pro-Spanish and anti-Gallic discourse. What it signals, albeit by stealth, is the futility of cultural autarky in face of both the commonality of experience expressed through art and the common appeal of dramatic scenarios that surpasses national boundaries (a fact to which the very popularity of foreign films in Spain attested).

The impermeability of national boundaries is also tested in *Lola la piconera* which, against the background of the French siege of Cádiz, centres on the love affair between Lola, patriotic Spanish folk singer, and Gustavo, officer of Napoleon's army. Despite the initial images of drunken revelry in the French encampment, the film depicts the officers of both armies with a similar respect, contrasting military honour with the scheming of politicians, this time in the shape of Juan de Acuña, a Spanish traitor who seeks to aid the French in their attempt to seize Cádiz. Nationality does not guarantee its subjects either a heroic or villainous status; nor does it give any assurances in matters of love, Lola choosing Gustavo over Rafael, an equally honourable officer and in the Spanish army to boot. Moreover, despite the divisive nature of war, the film offers a number of reconciliatory moments and examples of commonality. Gustavo, we learn, spent part of his youth in Cádiz and retains an affection and admiration for the city. It was in those early years that he first fell in love with Lola and gifted her a crucifix. Despite her fervent expressions of patriotism and anti-Gallic feeling, Lola still chooses to wear the cross and justifies her choice by pointing to the irrelevance of nationality in the eyes of God: 'The Lord is nobody's enemy' ['El Señor no es enemigo de nadie']. After Gustavo is wounded on the way to a rendezvous with Acuña within the city walls, Lola's decision to give the Frenchman sanctuary and Rafael's decision to accompany him out of the city and to safety testify to bonds and feelings that conflict with the dictates of patriotic duty. When Lola does act on her patriotism by volunteering to take a message to Spanish troops positioned beyond French lines, she becomes, ironically, a victim of Acuña's scheming. The message which she delivers is blank and she is captured by the French and executed. The scene in which Gustavo returns Lola's body to Rafael and the people of Cádiz is governed by a sense of shared grief which is reminiscent of *La leona de Castilla*. Above all, it is Lola's and Gustavo's mutual love that emphasizes commonality and renders nationality in the context of war a tragic obstacle. When Lola and Gustavo come across a caravan of gypsies (many of whom will have been Spaniards in the role of gypsies), the officer remarks enviously: 'Their country is where they set up camp. They are neither French nor Spanish' ['Su patria es donde acampan cada noche. No son ni franceses ni españoles']. Together Gustavo and Lola exchange their dreams of 'a world without hate, without wars, without frontiers' ['un mundo sin odios, sin guerras, sin fronteras'] and agree to live the day as gypsies without a country, albeit in the knowledge that the following morning they will wake up a Frenchman and Spanish woman once again.

The clichéd representation of gypsies as free and passionate spirits is compounded by a number of song and dance numbers set amidst the ruins of a monastery where the travellers have set up camp for the night. Yet even this scene of gypsies dancing around a camp fire is too real for our lovers. 'Let us dream that these dancing gypsies are creatures from a world of fantasy and joy' ['Soñemos que estos gitanos que bailan son seres de un mundo de fantasía y felicidad'], asks Gustavo, eager to escape reality. These words set in motion a dream sequence in which the stereotypical gypsy camp gives way to a more overtly artificial and theatrical world of tinsel, paper flowers, illuminated tambours and lily ponds. The choreography, like the music, set and costumes, is a hybrid of flamenco and classical styles. The dancers act out a tale of love and liberation in a sequence whose glitz and staginess are highly reminiscent of the production numbers of Hollywood musicals and can be read as a self-conscious statement about the Spanish historical drama. For, in a film which moves between historical and musical genres, this fantasy sequence represents a moment of refuge not only from the pressures of patriotic duty bearing down upon Gustavo and Lola in the 'real' world, but also from the formulaic conventions of the historical drama which pit Spaniards against foreigners. In this sense, the couple's desire to live as gypsies without a country may be read as an indirect call for scenarios that break with the paradigms of international conflict reproduced in films of the early Franco period. It also alludes, intentionally or otherwise, to the gypsy roles into which Spaniards stepped in so many folkloric musicals (Labanyi, 1997: 224–9; Vernon, 1999: 252-4). It is, at the very least, a sign of a change in mood and emphasis, of an ever-increasing desire for escapism, the tension between the historical and musical genres in *Lola la piconera* being indicative of the conflictive agendas of politicizing and depoliticizing tendencies within Spanish cinema. As Monterde points out, after 1951, the year in which *Lola la piconera*, *La leona de Castilla* and *Alba de América* were all released, there was a sharp decline in the production of historical dramas. What is more, from 1952 the name Cifesa disappeared from screens, the company choosing to involve itself in distribution rather than production, no doubt because, as Monterde suggests, the criteria governing its productions no longer met the demands of audiences (1995b: 265–7).

In 1954, Lucia enjoyed some success with his folkloric musical, *Un caballero andaluz / An Andalusian Gentleman*. A Perojo-CEA production, it was declared to be of 'National Interest' and shares twelfth place in the list of longest running Spanish films released between 1951 and 1961 (Monterde, 1995b: 262). In this period, rapidly improving relations between Spain and western democracies, aided by the advent of the Cold War and the Franco regime's fiercely anti-Communist stance (Payne, 2000: 383), meant increasingly that the vilification of foreigners was no longer relevant as a means of negotiating internal anxieties. What is more, in 1952, the Uninci production, *¡Bienvenido, Mr. Marshall! / Welcome, Mr. Marshall!*, directed by Luis García Berlanga, served to expose the hypocrisy of a regime that encouraged its cinema to extol the virtues of a glorious or exotic Spain at the expense of foreigners and foreignness whilst seeking to attract inward investment from those it cast as its enemies and inferiors (Hopewell, 1986: 48–50; Kinder, 1993: 20, 22). What is interesting about Lucia's post-*Bienvenido* musical is the way in which it responds to foreignness in this climate of increasing openness and self-awareness. It is a tale of interracial and interclass love as Carmen Sevilla, in the role of a blind gypsy, Colorín, falls in love with and eventually marries Don Manuel, a wealthy landowner played by Mistral. In the course of events, it presents two sets of circumstances which bring into play the question of Spain's relationship with the foreign. On the one hand, Don Manuel's son is enrolled in an English boarding school; on the other, Colorín's sight is restored by an eye specialist in the United States.

Both sets of circumstances receive qualification. Firstly, the boarding school, Don Manuel tells us, is run by Jesuits and José Luis is its equestrian champion. In an early scene, set at the school's show-jumping event, an English gentleman (or rather a Spaniard playing a gentleman whose Englishness is signified by his tailcoat and monocle) suggests to a Spanish military officer among the spectators that his compatriot's victory is all the more of an achievement given England's great equestrian tradition. This opinion stirs the patriotism of the officer who pays tribute to the horse-riding skills of José Luis's father, his commentary running, via an overlap sound cut, into a close-up of the elegant stepping of an Andalusian horse ridden by Don Manuel. Secondly, Don Manuel makes it clear, before the trip to the United States, that the renowned specialist who will treat Colorín is, in fact, Spanish. Both sets of circumstances might have undermined the notion that 'Spain is best' had it not been for these important qualifications. Yet ambivalence still characterizes the attitude towards foreignness contained in each. Each articulates the requirement to reassert Spain's own 'superior' value and achievements, but also acknowledges Spain's contact with the world beyond her borders, as well as the merits and advantages of that world. In the final scene in the eye specialist's surgery, Don Manuel, the Andalusian gentleman, has swapped his more traditional and formal attire for a short-sleeved, American-style print shirt, while one of the many little gypsy boys adopted by the maternal Colorín appears wearing a cowboy outfit. Here we have two Spanish figures dressed as foreigners in a film that, despite its manifestations of national pride, seeks to entertain in the manner of a Hollywood musical. Indeed, it contains many of the ingredients, described by Ethan Mordden as:

> seventy-five to one hundred minutes of love plot crossed with some instance of personal and communal achievement, using four or five songs and possibly a dance or two, keeping the whole as often as possible in a modern and comic frame; the music is easy to pick up, the lyrics are simple, and the lead personalities are essentially innocent and giving, even valiant, though such minor flaws as sloth or cowardice are okay if they are redeemed by some life-changing act in the final reel. (1981: 140)

Un caballero andaluz, however Spanish it may appear on the inside, 'dresses American'. It is fitting, therefore, that when the little gypsy boy finally holds up a sign reading 'The End' ['Fin'], this self-reflexive act should bring the film to a close not in Spain but in America.

Note

1   According to Elliott (1970: 152), this essentially urban revolt, which began May 1520 and ended with the defeat of the *Comuneros* at Villalar on 23 April 1521, was 'a movement of angry reaction to a long period in which royal government . . . had eroded away many of the traditional powers and prerogatives of the Castilian towns'. Among the demands of the *Comuneros*, therefore, was 'the request that the towns should have the right to assemble Cortes on their own initiative every three years'. Yet, as Elliott (pp. 152–3) also notes, perhaps more than the constitutional grievances of the municipalities, it was 'a burning hatred of foreigners and of foreign rule' (in the shape of Charles V's advisers) that spurred the Castilian populace to revolution. Foreignness, however, is not an aspect emphasized in Orduña's film which focuses instead on the 'internal' tensions between old Castile and its Imperial destiny.

Bibliography

Barthes, Roland (1998) 'Myth Today', in John Storey (ed.) *Cultural Theory and Popular Culture: A Reader*, Harlow, England: Longman, 1998: 109–18.

Boyd, Carolyn P. (1999) 'History, Politics, and Culture, 1936–1975', in David T. Gies (ed.) *Cambridge Companion to Modern Spanish Culture*, Cambridge: Cambridge University Press, 86–103.

Carr, Raymond (1980) *Modern Spain*, Oxford: Oxford University Press.

—— (1982) *Spain 1808–1975*, 2nd edn, Oxford: Clarendon Press.

Carr, Raymond and Juan Pablo Fusi (1981) *Spain: Dictatorship to Democracy*, 2nd edn, London: George Allen & Unwin.

De Pauw, Linda Grant (1998) *Battle Cries and Lullabies: Women in War from Prehistory to the Present*, Norman: University of Oklahoma.

D'Lugo, Marvin (1997) *Guide to the Cinema of Spain*, Westport, Connecticut: Greenwood.

Dumas, Alexandre, fils. (1974) *La dame aux camélias*, Paris: Éditions Gallimard.

Elliott, J. H. (1970) *Imperial Spain 1469–1716*, Harmondsworth: Penguin Books.

Evans, Peter (1995) 'Cifesa: Cinema and Authoritarian Aesthetics', in Helen Graham and Jo Labanyi (eds.) *Spanish Cultural Studies: An Introduction*, Oxford: Oxford University Press, 215–22.

Higginbotham, Virginia (1988) *Spanish Film Under Franco*, Austin: University of Texas Press.

Hopewell, John (1986) *Out of the Past: Spanish Cinema after Franco*, London: BFI.

Kinder, Marsha (1993) *Blood Cinema: The Reconstruction of National Identity*, Berkeley: University of California Press.

Labanyi, Jo (1995) 'Censorship and the Fear of Mass Culture', in Helen Graham and Jo Labanyi (eds.) *Spanish Cultural Studies: An Introduction*, Oxford: Oxford University Press, 207–14.

—— (1997) 'Race, Gender and Disavowal in Spanish Cinema of the Early Franco Period: The Missionary Film and the Folkloric Musical', *Screen* 38: 3, Autumn, 215–31.

Machado, Antonio and Manuel Machado (1951) *La Lola se va a los puertos*, Buenos Aires: Espasa-Calpe.

Monterde, José Enrique (1995a) 'El cine de la autarquía (1939–1950)', in Román Gubern et al. (eds.) *Historia del cine español*, Madrid: Cátedra, 1995: 181–238.

—— (1995b) 'Continuismo y disidencia (1951–1962)', in Román Gubern et al. (eds.) *Historia del cine español*, Madrid: Cátedra, 1995: 239–293.

Mordden, Ethan (1981) *The Hollywood Musical*, New York: St. Martin's Press.

Payne, Stanley G. (2000) *The Franco Regime 1936–1975*, London: Phoenix.

Pérez Perucha, Julio (ed.) (1997) *Antología crítica del cine español 1906–1995. Flor en la sombra*, Madrid: Cátedra.

Seguin, Jean-Claude (1999) *Historia del cine español*, 4th edn, Madrid: Acento.

Torres, Augusto M. (1996) *Diccionario del cine español*, 2nd edn, Madrid: Espasa Calpe.

Vázquez Montalbán, Manuel (1998) *Crónica sentimental de España*, Barcelona: Grijalbo.

Vernon, Kathleen M. (1999) 'Culture and Cinema to 1975', in David T. Gies (ed.) *Cambridge Companion to Modern Spanish Culture*, Cambridge: Cambridge University Press, 248–66.

Willis, Andy (1995) 'Cultural Studies and Popular Film', in Joanne Hollows and Mark Jancovich (eds.) *Approaches to Popular Film*, Manchester: Manchester University Press.

3

From rags to riches: the ideology of stardom in folkloric musical comedy films of the late 1930s and 1940s

Eva Woods

> When I was four years old I already knew that I wanted to sing and be what I am today. I didn't think about getting married to a rich husband who would give me a lot of money. I thought about my own career, about how I was going to become a really famous star and get out of that poverty. (Montiel 2000: 46)

> People at that time thought that we entertainers were all sluts. (2000: 56).[1]

Recent critical assessments of the pejoratively termed *españolada* film concur in their assumption of an incomplete hegemony of the Francoist state: the surveillance of its citizens – through the education system or the media – is never unproblematically coherent.[2] I would go even further to say that these films were ostensibly *unconcerned* with Francoist discourse unless they were parodying it. While the regime focused its energies upon the historical epics and military films, folkloric musical comedies were left to their wiles, with the exception of hysterical condemnations from the Church. Not only were official discourses permeable and censorship vulnerable, but inherent instabilities and excess undermine interpretations of these films as simple reflections of fascist or National Catholic rhetoric.[3] In the following analysis I aim to contribute to and build upon these claims by exploring the dense ideological constellation of stardom in such films and its various manifestations as narrative device, lived reality, audience fantasy, and complex multi-layered star persona. My intention is to show that folkloric musical comedy films such as *Suspiros de España* / *Longings for Spain* (Benito Perojo, 1938), *Mariquilla Terremoto* (Perojo, 1939), *Torbellino* (Luis Marquina, 1941) and *Filigrana* (Marquina, 1949) flaunt myriad contradictory

and ambiguous representations of womanhood through the performance of the female protagonist and *folklórica*.[4] Such ambivalent
gender constructions, I will argue, are the product of the juxtaposi-
tion of the ideological discourses of stardom with those that prescribed a static model of femininity based on traditional gendered
discourses of domesticity and Catholicism. The catalyst for this
discursive collision were the narratives of stardom, or the plots
recounting the story of the *folklórica* / protagonist's rise from
humble origins to professional success, wealth and, in some cases,
international recognition.

The *folklórica* protagonist, materially and professionally ambitious and unconcerned with childbearing directs her energies
towards furthering her career, with or without a husband. Both the
depiction of the shift from the space of the working class to that of
cosmopolitan glamour, and the vindication of her sullied honour by
an upper-class *señorito* (wealthy playboy), champion the cause of an
emergent class and the individual in the process of becoming, and
thus enacting, a profound transformation in the realm of the personal. Although the *folklórica* icon was not a model of revolutionary resistance but rather one of negotiated class interests, the
potential for imagined and vicarious solidarity for Spanish spectators was certainly possible. Commenting on the phenomenon of the
female performer Rachel in Cuba in the 1920s, Michael Aronna
notes that '[n]o matter how few and illusory such cases may have in
fact been, this story line nevertheless became a source of vicarious
solidarity and luxurious hope for the female consumers of film, the
tabloid press and sundry film magazines' (25).

In order to understand the conditions that allowed for the development of such an over-determined figure, I want to outline the historical and ideological underpinnings of '*folklórica* stardom' and its
peculiar manifestation in Andalusian musical comedies. Over-determination refers to a situation in which overlapping forces come into
interaction or, hermeneutically speaking, where a specific image,
word or phrase can have its origin in many sources, thus constituting a site of excess. Because the *folklórica* sign is a collective config-
uration of different ideological formations of the media, the
audience and the historical living and breathing individual, we can
say that this *folklórica* icon functions as a metaphor of how ideological over-determination plays itself out in society. It is also useful
to conceive of the ideology of stardom as existing within structural

causality in which 'the function of every element [of the structural totality] is simultaneously a condition for the function of every other' (Dowling, 1984: 68). This model asserts that things such as the media or film stardom are not just reflections of the economy but functions of it. Thereby individuals do not just labour but also think, believe and perform and their agency has some effect on the economic structure in which they fantasize and perform (1984: 69–70). It follows that structures like the media are relatively autonomous from other structures such as religion, politics and the economy, as they simultaneously function as a part of these other structures and continue to reciprocally influence one another. We come closer to understanding how stardom was informed by other structures and ideological discourses, how it informed these same structures (reciprocity) and finally how it gave the illusion of being autonomous even when it was only *relatively* autonomous with respect to these other structures. Thinking of stardom, filmic discourse and forms of public subjectivity as *relatively* autonomous allows us to interpret the *folklórica* icon as not only a site upon which disparate social contentions (such as class, sexuality, race) were inscribed and produced, but also a space where women in the 1930s and 1940s could imagine alternative subjectivities and formulations of sex, work and class, even if they could not live them.

Because *folklórica* stardom functioned as a relatively autonomous structure vis-à-vis the dominant political and religious institutions, we can see how its cinematic and extra-cinematic representations at different historical points retained residues of its earlier and more sexually provocative phases, even during the most oppressive years of the dictatorship. In the following I signal the repetition of certain patterns in stardom narratives, star texts and contexts of stardom between the 1920s and the late 1940s in order to show how these paradigms constituted ambiguous and slippery ground for early fascist and Catholic discourses attempting to secure definitions of womanhood.

From Sicalipsis to acceptably sexy

Between 1900 and 1936 Spain's urban centres experienced a rise in the production and consumption of erotic novels, images, and songs. According to Timothy Mitchell, this phenomenon, funded by a '[p]olitico-erotico-literary-business project' engaged in countering authoritarian sexuality, paralleled the struggle of leftist modernizing urban middle classes against the politics of the more affluent classes (1998: 63). Drawing upon Mitchell's argument, I contend that during this period an unwitting, affective and ideological consensus between entertainment performed by women and anticlerical social reform movements found expression in the construction of 'female' on stage and later on screen. This outpouring of erotic discourse, along with the economic growth experienced in several sectors in the first third of the century, provided the conditions for sexually titillating popular music and theatre traditions to flourish. The construction of the female cinema star in the 1920s, and the later *folklórica* star system of the 1930s and 1940s, was predicated on the model of the female entertainer / *cupletista* (singer of *cuplés*, short narrative songs with suggestive and sometimes politically subversive lyrics) that dominated the genres of the variety shows and the *género ínfimo*. An erotic spectacle performed in cafés and concert halls catering to all-male audiences, the *género ínfimo* provided fuel for the genre's characterization in the middle-class mind as a pretext for upmarket, call-girl types of prostitution (Barreiro, 1994: 27). The indispensable ingredient that defined and assured the survival of these genres was *sicalipsis*, or sexual suggestiveness.[5] The thriving business of music halls and *varietés* between 1900 and 1936 incited thousands of women to seek work as singers, and the small spaces of the locales allowed for more intimate interaction between the singer and audience that not only encouraged fantasy but also led to a demand for more singers to work in these ever-proliferating establishments. During the Civil War, as more established stars fled to Latin America, an eager new generation of singers filled the resulting gap, profiting from the success of the genre, higher wages and increased control of their shows. In the first advances of cinema into the theatre space, live female performances predominated over the simultaneous projection of short films. As the new art began its hegemonic claim over the theatre, *artistas* desiring to take advantage of this new opportunity re-modified their 'look', becoming more 'decent' even while clinging to the memory of their earlier daring days.

The career trajectory of Raquel Meller, perhaps the first star of the Spanish cinema star system, exemplifies these trends. Meller made her debut in 1907 in the *género ínfimo* (Barreiro, 1994: 85), but as her notoriety spread she moved into genres more adequate for general consumption, eventually became successful in the cinema and boosted her reputation to the status of international film idol. Meller's flexibility in roles as innocent young women or fame-weary circus performers constituted a hybridization of the femme fatale and the girl next-door. By 'femme fatale' I mean an independent female protagonist capable of undermining male identity and authority by manipulation and seductive prowess, both qualities that are antagonistic to male patriarchal values. As sex object and per-former-spectacle, Meller embodied modern societal values calling for new definitions of female sexuality that would promote erotic and commodified culture.

The dynamic of ambiguity evident in Meller would later appear in the *folklórica* stars of the late 1930s and 1940s, albeit in a different form. Although the inchoate stardom films of the 1920s up until the Spanish Civil War more openly contested gender and sexuality (we see obvious pornographic discourse in films such as *Carne de fieras* / *Savage Flesh* (Armand Guerra, 1936)), we can nevertheless detect repeated patterns and residual effects in the films of the late 1930s and 1940s. It must be recalled that in the early 1940s approximately 1,100 bordellos were legally functioning under the politics of *la doble moralidad* (double standard) and continued to do so until the mid-1950s. In contradictory fashion, female sexuality was instru-mental in the maintenance of the National Catholic myth of the self. If Andalusian musical comedy films presented these contestatory models of womanhood in a positive light – models unable to shed their former erotic and sexual trappings (collective memory tran-scends pre- and post-war divisions) – then something was definitely and uncontrollably slipping by the censors. The focus on perfor-mance artists, models of 'becoming', rather than on static figures of Isabel II or Teresa de Jesús, was not a revolutionary gesture, so to speak. But in an atmosphere of *abulia*, residues of sexuality that harkened back to former times of liberation cast an ironic shadow over the characters of nuns or chaste peasant girls that Imperio Argentina and others moulded into 'acceptable' icons of sexiness.

The rise to stardom plot

The institutionalization of the star system 'à la Hollywood' was real-ized at the production company Cifesa in the mid-1930s (Fanés, 1982: 28). Cifesa's efforts to approximate the Hollywood model were evident from its serial production and the star privileges (exclusive contracting whether they were filming or not, high salaries and publicity paid for by the company) granted to actresses such as Amparo Rivelles, Imperio Argentina, Ana María Custodia, and Antoñita Colomé (Freixas, 1983: 20; Rotellar, 1989: 23). *Folklóricas*, or *cupletistas* (a reference to their previous stage and radio careers), were the lead singers / actresses and 'star' characters upon which these films pivoted. Well-known singers such as Concha Piquer, Estrellita Castro or Imperio Argentina problematically starred as light-skinned 'gypsies' and aspiring singers of popularized flamenco.[6]

The theme of stardom appeared much earlier in Spain in the form of both the *zarzuelas* and silent films and thus already comprised part of the spectator's horizon of expectation.[7] A year before the release of Alan Crosland's *The Jazz Singer* (1927), often considered the film that consolidated the rise to stardom plot, Benito Perojo directed *El negro que tenía el alma blanca*. This film prefigures the future hegemony of white female stardom over male racialized stardom and the obsession with narratives of becoming, exemplified through the discovery and subsequent fame of the female protagonist. The Hollywood melodrama *A Star is Born* (1937) constitutes a further entrenchment of the stardom plot in the collective film imaginary. Not only did MGM release a *A Star is Born* in Spanish theatres but it also launched an enormous publicity campaign in connection with local theatres and newspapers which bonded citizens of these towns and cities even more closely to this culturally re-inscribed myth, unsurprisingly popular during the war and the 'years of hunger'.

Jackie Stacey refers to the 'semi-magical transformation of screen identification' in which the female spectator's image of self feels partly transformed by a star image into a more pleasurable form of femininity (1994). The cinema-centred contest, mainly focusing on the 'concurso de parecidos' (look-alike contest), was very popular in 1930s Spain and fundamental in building fan support and creating star images that encouraged forms of gratification and fulfilment. Contests provided a 'practised space' in which female spectators could manipulate their fantasies within a controlled environment that fused their potential selves with their real self. Beauty contests, promoted by risqué magazines such as *Vida Galante* and *Pentalfa*, had already arrived in 1929, setting a precedent for the channelling of erotic desire and ambition through the framework of the contest. In Zaragoza, the screening of *Grand Hotel* (Edmund Goulding,

1932) had an incredible pre-publicity build-up. The campaign included the opening of an actual Grand Hotel, elaborate trailers, the publishing of the plot in the *Heraldo de Aragón* and finally a Joan Crawford and Greta Garbo look-alike contest. The winners of the 'Concurso Internacional de Parecidos' won a 21-day trip around France, Spain and Belgium where they would be lodged in the best hotels and treated, in effect, as movie stars (Sánchez Vidal, 1996: 193). Thanks to the look-alike contest, MGM established an intimate connection between the spectators and the characters played by their top stars (1996: 198). In *Suspiros de España* Sole wins a beauty contest sponsored by a Cuban *empresario*, while in *Torbellino*, Carmen makes herself known through a contest between various radio stations. Reflexive film commentary on contests coupled with the fact that so many real-life stars initiated their careers through contests (and still do) served to legitimize the ideologies of 'becoming' and ambition that were such an anathema to fascist and Francoist dogma. Vanity and frivolity were the symptoms of 'bourgeois decadence from which the virtuous woman must be protected' (Grothe, 1999: 519).

In the 1930s in Spain, women were entering show business in droves and folkloric musical comedy films reflected this, thus reinforcing reflexive accounts of the stardom narrative. *Torbellino* relates the process by which Carmen's 'spontaneous' and 'natural' outbursts of song lead up to her performance for the radio programme which will make her a star. Like Hollywood backstage musicals, *Torbellino* is concerned with chronicling 'the neophyte entertainer in the process of becoming professional, a star in the process of being born' (Feuer, 1993: 15). The sequence that introduces Carmen is an instance of the projection of the dream for stardom through spontaneous performance. It begins with the camera panning from a 'hand-made' microphone to Carmen's face, while the spectator hears the out-of-frame voice of her aunt pretending to be a master of ceremonies. The aunt-as-MC introduces Carmen as a star to a make-believe, or extra-filmic, audience, thus initiating a reflexive commentary on the dynamics of the relationship between the fan and the star. This scene deftly exploits identification with extra-cinematic audience members who have had star fantasies, or who have 'practised' at home in front of their mirrors, by suturing this fantasy to Castro's real star status and thereby securing a more complex meaning. The rehearsal of becoming a star constitutes a humorous anecdote to the conduct manuals written by Catholic mouthpieces such as Graciano Martínez (*La mujer española*, 1921) and María Pilar Morales (*Orientación femenina*, 1944) who hysterically condemned the excess of independence and liberty that women were experiencing due to the ruffling of tradition by new currents of modernity (Grothe, 1999: 528).

The meta-cinematic narratives of these films celebrated the model of becoming through the fusion of the cosmopolitan off-screen life of the *folklórica* with the unobjectionable on-screen character. The reiteration of the autobiographical rise to stardom that enriches the meanings of the film is illustrated in *Filigrana*, which stars Concha Piquer, the internationally famous *cupletista*. Piquer, the daughter of a bricklayer and a seamstress, was a product of the working class and has recalled that her childhood was a tramautic period filled with struggle and poverty (Moix, 1993). She debuted at eleven years of age, and at sixteen, still illiterate and only speaking Valencian, the *zarzuela* composer Penella took charge of her career, an eyebrow-raising situation for the time. *Filigrana* begins in *media res*, that is, in 1927 when Filigrana has returned from her successful years of living abroad, the same date as the return of Piquer to Spain after several years of working in the Americas. At that point, Filigrana recounts her life story. Beginning as a poor 'gypsy' street vendor, she is seduced and dishonored by the Count of Montepalma who rejects her for a woman of his same class. She then pursues a singing career, travels to the Americas where she becomes a star and returns so much wealthier than the count that she is able to buy his mansion and property in revenge for his earlier conduct. During the film she sings the famous *cuplé*, 'Ojos verdes', a song well known by audiences for its story of a prostitute who laments her lost love as well as for Piquer's erotic rendition of it. Although songwriters for the film altered the lyrics, the conflation of the prostitute of the original song with the character of Filigrana, and the added bitterness and raw emotion of Piquer's performance of the song, surely triggered memories of resistance and the kind of oppositional popular culture that the *cuplé* constituted. Silvia Bermúdez signals Piquer's performances of the *cuplés* as the battleground for the 'confrontation between those who sought to impose a single, monolithic cultural model and those who struggled to keep a space for cultural difference in the Spain of the 1940s' (1997: 33).

Sara Montiel's recently published memoirs of her rise to success against all odds interfaces with the fictionalized stardom plots and real testimonies of earlier stars through the narration of a 'discourse of female survival'. Montiel defiantly remembers her will to live as she chose (marrying outside the Church and maintaining several lovers) and the ostracism she experienced as a result of her threateningly rebellious sexuality and unbridled ambition. Montiel recalls watching these Andalusian musical comedy films of the 1930s and 1940s as a teenager and then returning to Spain from a seven-year period in Mexico – during which her career took off – to star in the quintessential biopic of Raquel Meller's life, *El último cuplé* (1957). She reminisces, 'I discovered myself through these films . . . I collected magazine photos and copied them because I wanted to be like those stars' (2000: 75). Montiel's admiration for these stars, her exposure to them at an impressionable age and her resulting ambition reaffirmed values contrary to conventional definitions of womanhood in 1940s Spain and signals how other women must have felt even though their voices went unheard.

Regarding another aspect of stardom narratives, the mimicry of the stardom industry through the dynamics of the family was a key meta-cinematic mechanism in the normalization of the ideology of stardom and reinforced the notion of the industry as an institution accessible to the common Spaniard. In *El negro que tenía el alma blanca* the father of the budding star, Emma, manages her career while in *La venenosa* (Roger Lion, 1928 with Raquel Meller) and *La patria chica* (Fernando Delgado, 1943 with Estrellita Castro) success is due to a surrogate father figure. This mimicry extends to the portrayal of the star system not as a capitalist venture but as the outcome of personal relationships between the female protagonist, her parents and individual agents. In *María de la O* (Francisco Elías, 1936) María's surrogate mother, tellingly played by Pastora Imperio, herself a product of such a system, manages the careers of both of her daughters. In *Suspiros de España*, much of the film is about the struggle between Solé's uncle and her suitor to manage her career. Filigrana's parental figures use her as bait to attract wealthy customers, while María de la O is trained by a surrogate mother to dance *and* attract wealthy patrons. However, a darker side to the story emerges through tabloid press stories such as that of La Bella Chelito, a real-life singer of the teens and twenties, whose mother prostituted her into show business. Interpersonal relationships of family therefore indexed relationships of exploitation rampant in patriarchal society – surrogate parents and star children – and reinforced the intertexts of extra-cinematic gossip. Later *folklóricas* and fictional stardom plots would carry residues of these well-known stories of exploitative 'parents'. In virtually all Andalusian musical comedy films the female protagonist is an orphan and the biological mother and father are absent, replaced by surrogates. Such a lack was perfectly consistent with a war and post-war society of orphans, missing fathers and absent mothers, and radically departs from any Catholic authoritarian notion of unified families and patriarchal hierarchy; rather it symbolically dismantles patriarchy through the parody of family as dysfunctional.

Undermining Spanish masculinity, another popular trend in these films, was achieved through the subordination of the male supporting actor to the artistic abilities and moral qualities of the female lead. This may be seen as an indirect quotation of Hollywood's *A Star is Born* in which Vicky Lester gradually outshines the pathetic and tragic Norman Maine. Whereas the *folkórica* is talented and good-natured, the male protagonist is often dependent on alcohol, a philanderer or unable to successfully launch a career. In *Suspiros de España* the uncle of the female protagonist is a *golfo* and is beaten up by his wife. In *Mariquilla Terremoto*, Quique, the *señorito* with whom the protagonist is in love, is a Don Juan and alcoholic while her surrogate father is an unrealized and apparently unsuccessful former bullfighter, a parody of the stereotype of the aggressive 'masculine' image of the Andalusian male. In *Filigrana*, the count, a playboy and incompetent businessman, loses his estate to Filigrana who, having become rich, buys the mansion along with the furniture and his noble title. And in *Embrujo* (Carlos Serrano de Osma, 1947), Manolo drinks himself to death out of jealousy and despair for the rich and successful female protagonist (Lola Flores). Clearly, these films not only parody gender hierarchies, but they also refute claims that they provide only sterile models of *españolidad*.

Glamour and consumption

As industrialization, consumerism and urbanization worked their way into the fabric of Spanish culture, dramatic changes were seen in the realm of gender which challenged restrictive norms that relegated women to the private sphere (Salaün, 1990). For women, consumerism paradoxically fostered access to the public sphere at the same time that it promoted the spectacularization of the female body. Practices of consumption such as window-shopping and department store browsing bridged the connection between the display of commodities and spectacle, in short, the way people were looking at bodies and objects. Jonathan Stratton has pointed out that the 'exhibition of the female body [was] one of the building blocks of consumer culture' (1996: 39). Women were both looking and being looked at. As consumers, they were participating more in the regulation of their bodies and identities, and as female entertainers they were allowing the paying spectator to gaze upon their fetishized bodies. The increased circulation of images of women in mass media venues such as newspapers, magazines, gazettes, popular biographies, gossip magazines and expositions opened up new spaces for the creation of female identities, especially positive sexual ones, previously confined to the models of motherhood, sainthood, or that of the 'Bad Woman'. The mass-produced images of *cupletistas* and female entertainers that were circulated on the covers of many magazines, calendars, match boxes, chromolithographs, labels for bottles of anise and postcards invaded daily life and reinforced the marriage of the spectacle with commodity capitalism. Popular magazines and interviews incessantly described Meller's fame, wealth and decadence, while perfume, fans, hats, beauty products and cigarette papers all carried Meller's name (Barreiro, 1996: 85).

Folklóricas bridged the public and the private sphere but were not destined to exist at the margins of society as they had been prior to the opening up of the space of leisure and consumerism to women. Granted, they were not held up as models for the conservative sectors of society, but they were given a place to thrive among the new discourses and practices of capitalist-consumer culture. Networks of kinship in small towns and rural societies and the construction of social and moral norms through religion and public ritual constituted a traditional means of regulating behaviour. In large urban settings, where society was more dispersed, mobile and unknowable, new ways of communicating emerged and technology such as the mass media could be used as a contemporary communicator of moral fables. In the same way that the rise of consumer culture provoked a struggle to impose definitions over womanhood in order to secure a system of values, the representation of *folklórica* stardom in these films functioned as a site for 'talk' about the role of women in society. But upon this site circulated new definitions of women as public individuals that constituted rebellious replies to the reactionary ideal of women as sheltered and homebound.

In the musical comedies, during and after the war, that starred Estrellita Castro (*Suspiros*, *Mariquilla*), the image of *folklórica* stardom retains its ties to consumerist discourse even though we do not see explicit scenes of *folklóricas* gazing through shop windows. Stars were leaders in fashion and the sequences in which the *folklórica* returns from touring (*Mariquilla*, *Filigrana*) spectacularized their furs and jewels. Moreover, memory of her lower-class origins encourages a more fulfilling consumption of glamour, increasing the spectator's enjoyment of this new wealth. In *Mariquilla Terremoto*, the glamorous arrival of Mariquilla to her hometown after becoming an international star underscores the contrast with Quique, the now drunk and begging *señorito* that dishonoured her. Formerly cast out because of her scandalous relationship with Quique, her hometown now applauds her as a heroine, celebrating her arrival with great fanfare. Entering a large new car with chauffeur, Mariquilla wears the emblems of modernization in her elegant clothing and diamonds. A heroine who has managed to escape the petty politics and gossip, Mariquilla has risen above her small-minded existence, seen the world and made a fortune. The town, the mirror of the extra-diegetic audience, is now literally consuming her, *instead* of Quique who formerly cruised the town in his flashy convertible. The replacement of Quique by Mariquilla evokes the shift from stars as 'heroes' – aristocrats, businessmen, bankers and *futbolistas* (Gubern, 1989: 24) – to stars as heroines of consumption and 'organized leisure time' (Dyer, 1993: 45), a reflection not only of how the tastes of audiences have changed but also of how the star system has marketed lower-class female stars as the most interesting figures to consume.

Consumption involves not only material goods but also the fetishized image of the *folklórica* icon. In *Torbellino*, Carmen imagines that she is performing before an audience in the recording studio of Radio Mundial. Through trick cinematography an entire orchestra appears, suggesting the power of fantasy to turn her into a star of the *canción andaluza*. Significantly, she watches herself in the recording booth consuming her own star image at the same time that she projects it. The scene, then, visually portrays the idea of escaping into one's own fantasies. The external spectator's previous knowledge that Castro has achieved stardom in her 'real' life makes this fantasy not imaginary but a foreshadowing of the inevitable and a complex metaphor of star ontology. Indeed, this scene doubly reinforces the spectators' consumption of the star image, ambiguously displaying both a contestatory moment in the narrative and the problematic pressures of modernization associated with consumption.

Working girls: consensus and conflict

As a semi-independent working woman, the *folklórica* protagonist represented polemical issues of female public visibility. In 1938, the nationalists were already attempting to shape attitudes towards working women so as to force them into the role of a crutch for the rebuilding of the nation by forming them into the ideal Catholic mothers, wives or nuns. The 1938 *Fuero de Trabajo* (labour charter) was initially motivated by the fear of an independent organized working class, but it also prohibited night work by women, regulated work at home and 'liberated' the woman from the factory and workplace. Traditionally, women were denied identity as workers and their labour was devalued: 'the cultural identity of women was not formulated through paid work but through the assumption of services inherent to the figure of a wife and mother' (Nash, 1991: 28). Catholic conduct manuals prescribed roles for women as humble, self-effacing and motivated only by their emotions. Accordingly, a woman should dedicate herself to serious and useful things, exercising her faculties so as to benefit communal social work. However, only to the extent that this work will grant her experience to better carry out her future role as wife and mother, the goal to which she should ever aspire (Grothe 1999: 531).

The ideology of stardom in these films therefore offered spaces where alternative forms of identity could be imagined and in this sense they challenged prevailing hegemonic norms. Their models of public visibility, ambitious working women, plots of social mobility and attacks on the decadent upper classes posited modes of becoming and utopian feelings of change. Nevertheless, the *folklórica* protagonist was not a metaphor for proletarian revolution; rather she was a symbol of the consensual relations that developed between the working class and the upper classes through the presence of a new entrepreneurial class that was prospering from mass entertainment and its violation of Catholic norms. Finally, *folklóricas* such as

Imperio and Juanita Reina (and earlier on, Raquel Meller) were and are famously reactionary when confronted in interviews, despite the fact that they have enjoyed privileges and liberties of which most women could only dream.

However, just as these so-called escapist films are prone to instabilities that betray their apparent conservatism, the slippages themselves are also prone to the tentacles of capitalist ideological discourses. Before and during Francoism these films were not aligned explicitly with either the left or the right but rather with capitalism and its self-reflexive promotional nature. Its main enemies were the agents and institutions that tried (unsuccessfully) to annihilate or control sexual, frivolous performances whether they were films, live shows or written texts. This meant, in particular, the control of women's activities, for female performers were the centrepiece and the economic cornerstone of all of these forms of cultural production. The filmic narratives of this cinematic genre, like entertainment in general, thus 'imply wants that capitalism itself promises to fulfil' (Dyer, 1993: 278). So working performance artists, ambition, success, and childless heterosexual partnerships counter Catholic norms at the same time as they support the necessary conditions for continued entertainment enterprises and, by extension, enrichment of the entrepreneurial classes.

In several films the *folklórica* protagonist works in the public sphere as a washerwoman (*Suspiros* and *Mariquilla*) or hawking merchandise (*Filigrana*) before she initiates her singing career. The establishing shot of *Mariquilla Terremoto* portrays Mariquilla engaged in labour: washing a white dog while, of course, singing as the camera pans over to linger on townspeople engaged in their respective trades. This immediate identification with labour connects the *folklórica* with the working-class sectors of society, whereas her later life as a star, instead of distancing her from the lower class, consolidated the capitalist myth of success that suggests that anyone can 'make it' and that success, and particularly money, are worth having because they compensate and reward the star for her hard work. Again, this equation functions in the service of capitalist entertainment ideology by garnering support for the needs of entertainment.

Although the star as a symbol of success contributed to the capitalist system, and though she sometimes partially controlled her performances, she did not own the theatres or generate any profits, but rather manipulated the system from within when possible. This important distinction justifies the *folklórica* / protagonist as a popular working-class subject, in alignment with the lower classes who must enter into consensual relations with the accommodated middle classes that control the media (radio, film and the press). The portrayal of *folklórica* protagonists as amateur singers and dancers eliminates the context of exploitation of the spectator / consumer that occurs with professionalism and stresses a paradox that is the crux of the ideology of stardom: while stars are special because they live luxurious lives, they are also made to appear as ordinary: stars are just like us. Capitalist ideology benefits from the idea that 'anyone can make it' even though specialness is a factor in the *folklórica*'s success. These films precisely make clear that only those subjects appropriate to symbolize Spanish modernity can or should 'make it'.

The myth of success is also intimately linked to the idea that social mobility is possible through work. In a melodramatic microcosm of the political, Mariquilla participates in a rhetoric of revenge through which she will not only transcend her economic and social status but also usurp such status from the man that had dishonoured her. Mariquilla, an aspiring singer in an oppressively small village outside Seville, is a failure as a performer. Searching for consolation she encounters the *señorito* Quique, a spoiled playboy and Don Juan, who seduces her, ruining her reputation in the town and forcing her to run away. However, Mariquilla befriends artists and bohemians (symbols of an oppositional class) who will help her launch a successful career that culminates in international stardom. Meanwhile, Quique rots away, addicted to gambling, drinking and women, an obvious critique of the endemic social problem of the parasitical *señorito*. Upon Mariquilla's triumphant return, instead of dominating and overpowering the frame, Quique now kneels at Mariquilla's feet as the object of her scorn and amusement. Quique begs Mariquilla to take him back, promising to work for her while she tours America. Knowing that outside Spain no one will treat him with the respect that he commands by means of his birth, Quique is terrified, for in America he would have to work like a 'negro' and therefore could never survive. But despite Quique's reticence and his subsequent refusal to leave, he recognizes that the world is now against him, 'El mundo entero contra mí, el mundo entero a humillarme' (the whole world against me, the whole world humiliating me) and that the previous order is being turned on its head. As

Mariquilla prepares for her departure to America she exclaims, 'Tira para el otro mundo, éste ya se ha quedado chico' (off to another world, this one is already too small), implying that hope remains for a new life and a new order. Rather than a thematic of blood and honour, as critics have implied these films to contain, we have a discourse of social mobility pertaining to a capitalist and melodramatic mode of thought.

In the same vein, Orduña's brilliantly ambiguous 1947 film version of the Machado brothers' play, *La Lola se va a los puertos*, shakes the social hierarchy through the affective structure of romance. *La Lola* recounts the story of the *cantaora* Lola (played by the *folklórica* Juanita Reina) who falls madly in love with the son of don Diego, a powerful Andalusian landowner. In the earlier play, Lola is consistently civil and polite to the father, mostly acknowledging his social position and his condescending generosity. Lola, however, cannot hide her aversion to the *señorito*, poorly concealing her disdain. Both the mocking and derisive tone that Lola uses with don Diego and the budding romance between her and the son, José Luis, is an insult to don Diego's position as patriarch and aristocrat. Coming from a *cantaora andaluza*, the affront bears even more weight.

In *Torbellino*, the film's portrayal of the female protagonist's rise to stardom symbolizes an emergent entrepreneurial class that competes with and threatens the dominant classes and their cultural tastes. *Torbellino* incorporates cultural and spatial hierarchies of high and low into its ideological discourse of stardom: Andalusian folklore entertainment, the radio and the cinema as compared to classical music; and the glorification of the South (embodied in Carmen) over the traditional North (symbolized by don Segundo, Basque radio station owner, and manifestation of bourgeois resentment of the encroachment of low culture upon high). During the 1920s and 1930s, cultural domination of Spain depended upon who dominated the transmission and diffusion of song (Salaün, 1990: 155). Ultimately, by celebrating the triumph of mass-market folk culture over high art and the subsequent flamencoization and homogenization of the different regions of Spain, an 'inferior' sphere of culture surfaces as culturally dominant. The historical privileging of the South was *not* a central concern per se of militant Francoism, monarchical or neo-feudalist ideological matrices but of capitalism that was concerned with what would sell and, indeed,

Andalusian mass culture sold well. The representation of class through *folklórica* stardom in these films champions a lower class that will support a new middle class that will protagonize Spain's capitalist project of modernity.

Happy endings

Despite shades of unification discourse, the majority of the film has concentrated on Carmen's untraditional pursuit of her career and the celebration of stardom, technology and mass culture. Similarly, some films depict the protagonist-*folklórica* leaving for the Americas either half way through the film (*Suspiros de España*, *Filigrana*, *Patria chica*) or at the end of the film (*Mariquilla Terremoto*, *La Lola se va a los puertos*). Surely, we cannot deny the existence of an over-arching *attempt* by the Spanish nationalist cinema to colonize Latin American cinemas or the minds of all of its spectators. I am merely underscoring both its possible failure and the idea that 'going to America' in many of these films also meant leaving behind the old, embracing the new, and accepting risks and adventure. That *folklóricas* both in real life and on screen were travelling and going to 'America' to further their career implied that these women were realizing their own dreams and desires to be successful and rich. Such identification with movie stars was surely not what Catholic censors had in mind. In addition to formulaic endings, spectators perhaps remembered Castro's star persona and her fictional display of success and freedom when they reflected upon the film rather the orthodox part of the plot ending. This acknowledgement of potential, even if not palpable, change echoes Molly Haskell's observation that, when everything is said and done, we remember the transgressive qualities of the leading female roles, not the fact that they succumbed to a conventional ending (1974: 3).

These films' ambivalent relationship with ideological discourses of nationalism, fascism and Catholicism that were present already before Franco took power is the effect of over-determination by both ideologies that conform to these conservative values and by those that distort and caricaturize such models. Upon analysing the syntax of the ideology of stardom in connection to the prescriptive nationalism of the right, scenes that might initially be interpreted as reinforcing the resuscitated imperial discourse of nationalist propaganda prove instead to be contortions and displacements of such ideological discourse. The *folklórica* protagonist and the representation of her stardom embodied multiple social contentions, demonstrating an alternative way in which femininity in the first half of the twentieth century was actually manifest and lived. The *folklórica* protagonist exemplified the working girl whose broad range of meanings oscillated between the racy and the respectable, addressing both working-class and middle-class audiences, affirming notions of national, racial and heterosexual identity, while she simultaneously disavowed those of rigid class and gender hierarchies, and religious ideology. This alternative route was not problem-free in that the *folklórica* was doubly marginalized, rejected by both the left and the right. Although early feminists did not embrace her difference, considering her an unacceptable example of the 'New Woman', neither was the *folklórica* as threatening to the religious right as the vamp, the flapper or the suffragist. Occupying a liminal space, this figure more closely resembled a fragmentary emergent class and a reflection of the tumultuous social forces in motion during the first half of the twentieth century.

Notes

1 My translations.
2 This study follows the arguments of Vernon, Labanyi, Martin-Márquez and Marsh, who have underscored the emergence of a subversive discourse through the performances of characters in *españoladas* of the Francoist years.
3 The dominant characteristics that have served to characterize the cousin of the *españolada*, the Andalusian or folkloric musical comedy film, are a narrative punctuated by song and dance performances, a wide array of stereotypical images of Andalusia, Spanishness and 'Gypsiness', and a rhetoric that tends to avoid political and historical topics.
4 The term *folklórico* originally referred to both female, male and sometimes transvestite artists whose repertory included traditional regional songs or dances with hints of regional flourishes, regardless of the artist's own regional identity. The reduction of the term to mean only women who performed Andalusian folklore produced a negative connotation, partly because of the abuse and repetition of the term and partly because the term indiscriminately referred to any artist that dedicated themselves to any kind of remotely Andalusian spectacle. The term deserves problematization given its instrumental links to the shaping of a notion of female Spanishness.

5   'A neologism first seen on a theatrical bill in Barcelona that had clum-
    sily misspelled *apocalipsis* in an effort to sell tickets. The word [. . .]
    spread quickly through the world of Spanish show business and jour-
    nalism and came to mean anything naughty, erotic or pornographic in
    connection with any size musical production or publication' (Mitchell,
    1998: 69).
6   Elsewhere I deal with the crucial issues of race in these films.
7   Early films dealing with stardom include: *La gitana blanca* (Ricardo de
    Baños, 1919, 1923), *La sin ventura* (Benito Perojo, 1923), *La venenosa*
    (Roger Lion, 1928), *El misterio de la Puerta del Sol* (Francisco Elías,
    1929), *La malcasada* (Francisco Gómez Hidalgo, 1926), *Rosario la cor-
    tijera* (José Buchs, 1923), *El negro que tenía el alma blanca* (Benito
    Perojo) and *La terrible lección* (Fernando Delgado, 1927).

Bibliography

Althusser, Louis (1969) *For Marx*, London: New Left Books.
Aronna, Michael 'Testimonial Intent and Narrative Dissonance: The Mar-
    ginal Heroes of *Biografía de un cimarrón* and *Canción de Rachel* by
    Miguel Barnet', unpublished paper.
Barreiro, Javier *Cupletistas aragonesas*, Zaragoza: Caja de Ahorros y Monte
    de Piedad.
—— (1996) 'Las artistas de varietés y su mundo', in María Luz González
    Peña, Javier Suárez-Pajares and Julio Arce Bueno (eds.) *Mujeres en la
    escena. 1900–1940*, Madrid: Sociedad General de Autores y Editores.
Bermúdez, Silvia (1997) '"Music to My Ears": Cuples, Conchita Piquer and
    the (Un)Making of Cultural Nationalism', *Siglo XX / 20th Century*, 15:
    1–2, 33–54.
Dowling, William C. (1984) *Jameson, Althusser, Marx: An Introduction to
    the Political Unconscious*, Cornell: Ithaca.
Dyer, Richard (1979) *Stars*, London: BFI.
—— (1993) 'Entertainment and Utopia', in Simon During (ed.) *The Cul-
    tural Studies Reader*, London: Routledge, 271–83.
Fanés, Felix (1982) *Cifesa, la antorcha de los éxitos*, Valencia: Institución
    Alfonso El Magnánimo.
Feuer, Jane (1993) *The Hollywood Musical*, Bloomington: Indiana Univer-
    sity Press.
Freixas, Ramón (1983) 'Cifesa: Un gigante con pies de barro'. In *Dirigido
    por*, 104, 16–27.
Grothe, Meriwynn (1999) 'Franco's Angels: Recycling the Ideology of
    Domesticity', *Revista de Estudios Hispánicos*, 33, 513–37.
Gubern, Román (1989) 'La decadencia de Cifesa', *Archivos de la Filmoteca*,
    1: 4, 58–65.

Haskell, Molly (1974) *From Reverence to Rape: The Treatment of Women in the Movies*, Penguin: Harmondsworth.

Labanyi, Jo (1999) 'Raza, género y genegación en el cine español del primer franquismo', *Archivos de la Filmoteca*, 32, 23–42.

Marsh, Steven (1999) 'Enemies of the *Patria*: Fools, Cranks and Tricksters in the Film Comedies of Jerónimo Mihura', *Journal of Iberian and Latin American Studies*, 5: 1, 65–75.

Martin-Márquez, Susan (1999) *Feminist Discourse and Spanish Cinema: Sight Unseen*, Oxford: Oxford University Press.

Mitchell, Timothy (1998) *Betrayal of the Innocents: Desire, Power, and the Catholic Church in Spain*, Philadelphia: University of Pennsylvania Press.

Moix, Terenci (1993) *Suspiros de España: La copla y el cine de nuestro recuerdo*, Barcelona: Plaza y Janés.

Montiel, Sara and Pedro Manuel Víllora (2000) *Memorias: Vivir es un placer*, Barcelona: Plaza y Janés.

Nash, Mary (1991) 'Protonatalism and Motherhood in Franco's Spain', in Gisela Bock and Pat Thane (eds.) *Maternity and Gender Policies: Women and the Rise of the European Welfare State, 1880–1950s*, London: Routledge.

—— (1999) 'Un/Contested Identities: Motherhood, Sex Reform and the Modernization of Gender Identity in Early Twentieth-Century Spain', in Victoria Lorée Enders and Pamela Beth Radcliff (eds.) *Constructing Spanish Womanhood: Female Identity in Modern Spain*, Albany: SUNY Press, 25–50.

Rotellar, Manuel (1989) 'Cifesa y su cine de los años 30', *Archivos de la Filmoteca*, 4, 16–25.

Salaün, Serge (1990) *El cuplé*, Madrid: Espasa Calpe.

—— (1996) 'La mujer en las tablas: grandeza y servidumbre de la condición femenina', in María Luz González Peña, Javier Suárez-Pajares and Julio Arce Bueno (eds.) *Mujeres de la escena 1900–1940*, Madrid: Sociedad General de Autores y Editores.

Sánchez Vidal, Agustín (1996) *El siglo de la luz: aproximaciones a una cartelera*, Zaragoza: Caja de Ahorros de la Inmaculada Aragón.

Stacey, Jackie (1994) *Star-Gazing: Hollywood Cinema and Female Spectatorship*, London: Routledge.

Stratton, Jonathan (1996) *The Desirable Body: Cultural Fetishism and the Erotics of Consumption*, Manchester: Manchester University Press.

Vernon, Kathleen (1999) 'Culture and Cinema to 1975', in David T. Gies (ed.) *The Cambridge Companion to Modern Spanish Culture*, Cambridge: Cambridge University Press, 248–66.

4

Spectacular metaphors: the rhetoric of historical representation in Cifesa epics

Alberto Mira

The Cifesa historical epics

In 1948, *Locura de amor* quickly became the biggest box-office hit in post-Civil War Spain and started a short-lived series of historical epics culminating in 1951 with the relative failure of *Alba de América*. These featured big, expensive melodramatic plots often starring women (*La princesa de los Ursinos* (1947), *La duquesa de Benamejí* (1949), *Pequeñeces* (1950), *Agustina de Aragón* (1950), *La leona de Castilla* (1951), *Lola la piconera* (1951)), all of them produced by Valencian studios Cifesa, the most successful Spanish film company of the period, now recovered from the 1945 crisis. Cifesa was in 1932. Soon after the Casanovas, a family of Valencian oil manufacturers, bought the majority of the shares. It started as a film distribution company, but by 1934 it had already developed into production. Cifesa was the first film company in Spain to adopt an 'American' system: star policies, studios, permanent technical teams. Under the leadership of Vicente Casanova, Cifesa ('The Torch of Hits') would be the centre of the Spanish film industry during the early 1930s. The Civil War brought about a crisis, but good contacts with the Francoist government guaranteed its success in the early post-war period. Excess of production and the end of World War II were the causes of a second crisis around 1945. In an attempt to get out of the crisis, Casanova tried a new formula: a series of expensive, star-studded historical epics that became their most distinctive product. These films would meet popular and critical success, but not for very long. By 1951 lack of official support together with the difficulties inherent in the model would lead to yet another, final, crisis for the company. Félix Fanés, in his study of the company (Fanés, 1989), has outlined the features shared by this group of films. All of them had high production values and a number of contracted stars appeared recurrently. (Aurora Bautista, Amparo Rivelles, Ana Mariscal and Juanita Reina were among the highest grossing stars of their time.) In each of these films, strands containing a 'political' and a 'romantic' plot are developed simultaneously, although their relative importance varies. Whereas *Alba de América* and *Agustina de Aragón* emphasized the politics and carefully attempted to reproduce the 'historical truth', *Locura de Amor* became an intense melodrama set in a historically charged period. The way in which historical fiction as featured in these films related to history, and to Francoist historiography in particular, was another defining characteristic in the group. There had been films set in the past both before the Cifesa cycle (e.g. *Inés de Castro*, 1944) and after (e.g. the series of hugely popular musicals starring Sara Montiel). But in these cases history was or would become merely the excuse for spectacle or for empty nostalgia. *Inés de Castro* tells a story set in the past, but there is no attempt to use history for contemporary political comment. Indeed, some of the most successful Spanish films with a historical topic were made after the demise of Cifesa in 1956. But now we see a reluctance to give a version of the past that is relevant to the present: in the Sara Montiel films (for instance, *El último cuplé*, 1957; *La violetera*, 1958) it is easy to see how the historical setting of the film silences anything politically complex happening in the period that could even bring to mind more recent events. Even a film like the box-office hit *¿Dónde vas Alfonso XII?* (1958), ostensibly about a head of state, is remarkably free from historical consciousness, actively refusing to place its protagonist at a historical point where so much was at stake. In the new formula adopted from the mid-fifties, closely following Hollywood patterns and popular European historical films such as the *Sissi* series, the past is the stage for escapism, not an area to explore (or construct) a version of how the Spanish had become what they were. The teleological or 'mechanical' version of the past is rejected, and what characterizes the past in these films is not its connection to the present, but its visual spectacularity. The causes of this shift in the relationship between 'history' and 'historical fictions' are complex: they have to do with a corresponding shift in the propaganda strategies of successive Francoist governments, but also to do with what audiences were now expecting from popular culture. In an increasingly prosperous country that had left behind the direct consequences of the war, the explicit propaganda element in popular art was being replaced by simple entertainment. In the end it is the very idea of historical continuity, of process, that is disavowed. These are historical films without a theory of history: as if suddenly, when the end to autarky was in sight and consumerism and international relations were on the political agenda, the Spanish government had become uninterested in justifying itself through history.

What is distinctive about the Cifesa model is the way it responds to the Francoist version of Spanish history. Leaving aside the series of films concerned with the Civil War (which could be considered historical epics but in which the ideological meanings are directly, rather than indirectly, represented), this version had also featured in a handful of films of the mid-1940s (for instance *Los últimos de Filipinas* and *Fuenteovejuna*). But the attempt at appropriation of history only becomes systematized in the Cifesa series: this shift from individual instances to a series of narratives produced under a common set of circumstances and following similar rules encourage discussion of this group in terms of a 'cycle'. The compactness we have been referring to can be described in terms of a short-lived 'chronotopic model', a sub-genre created by historical circumstances and commenting on those circumstances. The model would have its centre in the Cifesa films and its margins in other films reflecting Francoist ideologies of history.

The defining characteristic of the model is their acceptance of what Hayden White (1978) has called 'the burden of history': historical processes and their consequences matter in the present. As Carlos F. Heredero points out in *Las huellas del tiempo* (1993), the success of the model among the authorities (early Cifesa epics successfully attracted government funding) can be linked to the socio-political circumstances. In the late 1940s there is still a perceived need to build a national identity based on history, following the change in attitude towards the past brought upon by the end of the Civil War. Fanés has collected public statements from the head of Cifesa, Vicente Casanova, insisting on the political importance of history and ideological relevance of this series of films. As indoctrination became less of a priority, the model starts losing some of its appeal to political authorities. Heredero's account is convincing and several elements within the films themselves would bear it out. For instance, the periods the Cifesa films are set in are clearly what reactionaries would consider 'heroic' or 'glorious' moments in Spanish history: key moments of triumph for traditionalist versions of Spanish history (the late fifteenth century under the Catholic Monarchs, the early nineteenth century after the defeat of Napoleon and the return of Ferdinand VII). They are moments in which Spain is in danger, under the attack of foreign forces, about to be annihilated by war or politics and then it is almost miraculously saved. Of course this narrative frame was bound to remind audiences of more recent events: salvation from annihilation under the weight of 'foreign' ideas (such as Communism) was the way in which the Civil War (the 'Holy Crusade') had been systematically represented to the Spanish. The heroes and heroines in the films could become models to be followed by the Spanish. Whatever else these films were about, the idea of a national identity was prominent. Characters are defined in terms of their essential 'Spanishness' and the idea of 'the eternal Spain' is a central myth in the plots.

History as fiction

In the rest of this chapter I will discuss the specificity in the films of the Cifesa cycle in terms of their use of history for ideological purposes with an emphasis on how a theory of history determined particular aesthetic choices. In particular I am interested in the ways in which history can be read into the films, and in the way historiographic ideology becomes narrative rhetoric, following White's work on the subject. I will be studying the articulation of the historical metaphor constructed by the Falange and Francoism (the myth of the golden age, the salvaging of decadence by divinely inspired leaders, the essence of national identity) in terms of film narrative and the ideological uses this could be put to.

By reading the work of historians (and metahistorians, a term he uses to emphasize that reflection on the method and aims of historiography entails a reflection on historical process and an emphasis on the rhetoric of representation) as necessarily expressed in terms of literature, White is bringing fiction and historiography closer together. In other words, if one cannot approach historical writing without taking into account its literary qualities (in terms of construction and use of literary tropes), then it follows that the distinction between historical essay and historical fiction is less deep than we can assume. Naturally both types of discourse have different aims, but they also share strategies and formal structures. He develops some of Foucault's ideas on reality and textuality to conclude that historical

truth is an effect of a certain way of writing and that without reliance
on tropes and textual strategies historiography wouldn't make sense
culturally. Historical writing, both 'real' and fictive, makes use of
both 'iconic' and 'symbolic' elements. The latter are responsible for
the meaning of the narrative:

> historical narratives are not only models of past events and processes,
> but also metaphorical statements which suggest a relation of simili-
> tude between such events and processes and the story types that we
> conventionally use to endow the events of our lives with culturally
> sanctioned meanings. Viewed in a purely formal way, a historical
> narrative is not only a *reproduction* of the events reported in it, but
> also a *complex of symbols* which gives us directions for finding an
> *icon* of the structure of those events in our literary tradition. (White,
> 1978: 88)

Then he moves on to identify some of the tropes and 'story types'
that articulate the relationship between history and reality (for White
perfectly different notions) in historical writing. By justifying the use
of a set of literary categories to read history, he effectively blurs the
limits between historiography and historically motivated narratives,
such as the ones that concern us here. It is through these structures
that Falangist historiography finds its way into narrative films which
are ostensibly about romance, costumes and action, just as in latter
films, the fact that such tropes and plot types do not concern historical process will make them less relevant in historical terms. This idea
can help us to develop the way in which historical discourse is articulated in particular texts. Every film will contain some iconic elements, and the Cifesa series was careful in recruiting a number of
experts in the period to guarantee historical accuracy.[1] But it will also
use the modes of symbolical 'emplotment' dictated by Falangist narrative. To give an example, history is not at the centre of a film such
as *Locura de amor* (it is probably the Cifesa historical epic in which
emotional motives are most prominent in terms of narrative), and
yet the film is historically relevant in two different ways. First,
because it is constructing a version of Spanish history that often
reflects the version proposed by Falangist historians and Francoist
propagandists. In this particular instance, this is done on the margins: for instance the death of Queen Isabella appears in the film as
a moment of cosmic chaos, a Shakespearean storm marks the passing of Romance (as defined by White, 1978: 66) and gives way to the

age of Machiavellian politics (personified by de Were and the Dutch noblemen). Second, because the film itself opened at a historical moment in which that version of history and the film as a whole have a historical meaning: plot motives reproduced myths carefully represented in Francoist propaganda, such as certain images of the 'eternal Spain' and the perniciousness of external interference. Through its fiction elements and 'artistic' devices (sets, participation of stars, mannered performances, melodrama), the film asserts its difference towards actual historical events: director Juan de Orduña's pictorialism continually reminds us of the spectacular aspects of the fiction. At the same time, the explicit use of history gestures towards those events and claims to reflect them 'iconically' in some ways. As Hayden White reminds us, the rhetorical figure that asserts similarity of different elements is called metaphor (1978: 72) and, by activating historical relevance, this is exactly the way the film works. It is through a metaphorical strategy that the film is connected, first, to the 'truthful' historiographical account of the facts and, second, through the actual historical moment of the late 1940s.

Let us concentrate on the two aspects that define the relationships between Francoist historiography and narrative films suggested above. As Heredero (1993: 71) points out, the cycle's specificity is indebted to the peculiarity of the historical moment we are discussing: its discourse was never articulated before in film (Fanés points out a few exceptions) and it would not make political sense afterwards. This is probably the peak of national-Catholicism as an ideology. Between the Civil War and before the arrival of 'tecnócratas' in the late 1950s Francoism strongly identified with the ideas of its ideological arm, the Falange; whereas, it has been argued, Franco never trusted (even less identified with) any set political ideology (not even fascism), his only interest being to remain in power (and in order to do this he had to seek the support of reactionaries, bourgeois classes and Catholics). The Falange on the other hand was a political movement with a clearer ideological content. Whereas for Franco ideology could be negotiated, for the Falange ideology was part of its essence and compromising this would mean compromising the very existence of the group. This would eventually happen when economic reform in the early 1960s forced a release of ideological pressure: the Falange became quickly obsolete as a strong force in the running of the country. For Francoist historians, whether Falangist or not, the construction of a past that justified the present situation was a need. Furthermore, the account of the past was to be constructed so as to become the cause for the present situation.[2]

This is an instance of the process White calls 'emplotment', according to which events are organized according to one of four possible 'modes of explanation': mechanicist, organicist, ideographic and contextualist, roughly corresponding to the four basic types of plot (Tragedy, Comedy, Romance and Satire). More than mere justification, the mechanicist emplotment encouraged by early Francoism declared the inescapable necessity of the Francoist regime, its fatefulness. Franco is what Spanish history was leading to, its summit. Reflection of this approach to history in narrative is an affirmation *within* the narrative of this necessity.

Let us look more closely into this form of emplotment. The Falange partook of one specific version of Spanish history that had been coming together since 1898 and reached fruition in the late 1920s. Historical fact was then arranged rhetorically in terms of particular 'narrative fictions'.[3] The 1898 'disaster' gave rise to views in which Spanish decadence was emphasized. There was a need for a new Spain, and this could only be the consequence of an interpretation of Spanish history. The key metaphor future historiography was to build on was that of 'decadence'. It was clear that the final blow of losing the last colonies in the Caribbean and in the Pacific meant the time had come to re-think the meaning of Spanish history. For some, this gave rise to a new belief in the progress of Spain that could finally take its place in European history. But a very influential group of historians following the lead of Menéndez Pidal came to a reactionary, essentialist vision of Spanish history, centred on the 'Castilian dream' of unity which had vanished through petty interests of the peripheral nationalists but could be resuscitated. Rather than moving forward, they claimed, we had to retrieve that glorious past. For the such historians, the Spanish Golden Age was the period of the Catholic Monarchs: Spain had then a strong sense of identity, there was a strong government that stifled dissidence, a clear idea of what was *essentially* Spanish and what wasn't, a rejection of 'foreign' cultures, emphasis on empire and Catholicism as identity-building ideologies. Spain had become a failure because these principles had been forgotten. This was ostensibly the view of history held by the winners of the Civil War. Even Ortega y Gasset in such an influential work as *España invertebrada*, claimed that the problem of Spanish culture is the lack of a central core shared by all of the Spanish people and the weakening of the 'Castilian dream' had provoked insurrection in the peripheral nationalities. This would become one of the key texts for Falange historiography.

Historical truth as film rhetoric

As we can see, Falangist historiography satisfies Levi-Strauss' dictum that history is not just history *of* but very especially history *for*. The Cifesa series is a continuation of this rhetorical effort. As metaphors, they bring together the present and the past through iconic and symbolic links. This is embedded in the rhetoric of the film. In order to charge these metaphors with historical relevance, the films deploy a series of oppositions: the national v the foreign, the individual v the masses and the present v the past. To these we could add the gender symbolism (male v female) which is sometimes activated in the plots, but which has fewer political implications and often is dependent on the previous pairs. In each case, it is interesting to know not just how history is represented but also how the films themselves become history.

The national v the foreign

Perhaps the most clearly articulated opposition in the series is the one that sets up Spanish national identity against foreign influence and conquering interest. As we have noticed, this works at plot level in all of the examples by setting the films at moments in which the autonomy of Spain is in danger. Even when it is not, as in *Alba de América*, foreigners (the Jew Isaac, the French-leaning Armagnac) are still competing to gain from Columbus' enterprise, which is linked to Castile's Christian mission. The conflict in *La leona de Castilla* is internal, but again the role of external agents has to be noticed. As Fanés (1989) noted, this is a film that, precisely by placing the 'enemy' within, never solves its own contradictions and never works on an ideological level. The presence of external menace was considered as the best propeller to drive a plot that would construct a certain idea of Spain.

The reference in historical writing is what has been referred to as the 'purity' of the Spanish race. Américo Castro (1974) in particular has strongly challenged a version of Spanish history as 'depuration' of the foreign element. This process of depuration is nevertheless put in narrative terms in most of the Cifesa historical epics. The films

considered display the antagonism to the hero or, more often, heroine with 'foreign forces' in terms of plot and character as well as aesthetics. We have seen how the antagonism is central to some of these
plots. It is also an important element in character construction. In
Locura de amor, for instance, it is the Dutch who are attempting to
weaken the Spanish unity by committing the rightful queen to what
sounds like the equivalent of a mental institution. In order to achieve
this, they instigate a plot to make the queen jealous using Muslim
princess Aldara as a pawn. The Dutch are presented as devious and
Machiavellian against the loyal Spanish. Felipe is a foreigner, which,
following the rhetoric of the film, would explain his personality
flaws. Although Felipe's infidelities are there from the start, the film
carefully constructs the process of antagonization through the plots
of foreign agents: in the final account, Juana's husband is exonerated
from his philandering (he unaccountably repents on his deathbed);
after all he is a Spanish king. Finally, the same rhetorical opposition
is deployed in terms of aesthetics. The representation of the French
in both *Agustina de Aragón* and *Lola la piconera* illustrates again
what is understood by 'essential Spanishness', something to defend
against polluting influences. The first appearance of 'afrancesado'
('Gallicized') Luis (Agustina's fiancé) gives us the model of other
occurrences; a three-quarter shot of the actor, facing the camera but
looking sideways over his shoulder, twisted, foppish and dandified,
he represents the perfect picture of the excessive refinement the film
aesthetically disavows. Elsewhere, *Agustina de Aragón* shows the
simple beauty of village interiors and the charming spontaneity of
Spanish citizens. One potent aesthetic signifier of 'Frenchness' in
these films then will be effeminacy. The best example is maybe the
first sequence in *Lola la piconera*, in which the French invading army
is seen relaxing before the battle, playing around, drinking to excess
and cross-dressing. The aesthetic effeminacy of the French in these
films will contrast with the masculinity of the Spanish protagonist.
The virile looks of Aurora Bautista and her intense, aggressive
exhortations to her country folk contribute to the explicit association between virility and Spanishness.

The individual v the masses
The second opposition articulating each of these historical epics
sets the individual against the masses. This is a recurring opposition
in social films: the plot structure presents an individual fighting

unfairness as an agent of social change. Both in terms of society and in terms of historical process, this motive symbolizes change in terms of metonymic reduction: a series of different actual elements are projected on a character who then acquires a special importance. Heroes are dreamers, individuals with an exalted notion of what Spain should be. The central character in historical epics then becomes the elected hero without whom a state of decadence would have been perpetuated. In this sense, all heroes in historiographical narratives in this period are linked to Franco. The notion of an extraordinary agent of history had been activated in reference to Francisco Franco since the early years of the Civil War. Franco was 'el timonel de la dulce sonrisa', the charioteer of the nation. Rhetorically there are a number of operations taking place in this opposition as silently as effectively. First, the metonymy referred to above which equates the individual with the masses he or she leads; second, the notion of destiny as the vector for history; third, the insertion of the figure of the hero (or heroine) at the heart of the narrative. Traditionally this focalization has been a salient feature of idealistic historiography associated with Romanticism. A historical character (Queen Isabella, Christopher Columbus, Agustina de Aragón, Queen Juana) is made to represent essential virtues of the race and the spirit of the times as those virtues are tested by historical circumstances. Sometimes the masses are just inferior to the hero, uncomprehending; on other occasions, the main struggle of the hero is precisely against the masses. This account is valid both for historiographical fictions and essays, but it is the former model that we see more clearly realized in the films under consideration. Again this contributes to the identification of heroines and heroes in the film with the *caudillo*, who was represented as a good shepherd, benign towards the folk he was leading into victory. The legitimacy of a historiography that takes for granted the truth of this operation was criticized in the 1940s by historians such as Américo Castro, always aware of the ideological element present in such mode of representation. The emphasis on the key role of individuals is an example of what Castro would call 'the emotional approach to history' (Castro, 1974: 144–89). Rather than describing a situation, this approach advocates a strengthening of patriotic feelings through appeal to identification and emphasis on emotion.

There would be in principle two ways of articulating the idea assigning historical value to an individual. On the one hand, this could be done through synecdoche: the individual is a part of the whole. The second is metaphor: individuals are made to symbolize the spirit of the times due an identification in their destinies. The films under consideration clearly choose the latter. This allows the films to be emplotted in terms of a classic narrative opposition, that which sets the dialectical conflict between individuals and the masses as responsible for historical process. As in the previous case, this opposition is displayed in terms of plot, aesthetics and character. In this way, Juana la Loca is in conflict with her husband's followers. She is constructed to represent the virtues of the race put under pressure by historical circumstance. The plot progresses narratively through this opposition. Her madness is sad not only in individual terms, but because by the end of the film it is made to signify the destiny of Spain when it is left in the hands of the wrong people. Christopher Columbus and Queen Isabella are different symbols of the historical mission of the country, and in the conflict between the former and the establishment and its enemies audiences are meant to draw conclusions that affect the present. Isabella is the Christian spirit, Columbus is the flawed man (arrogant and over-ambitious, his dreams are dreams of personal glory) who will nevertheless become a tool in the hands of God to set Spain on her historical mission (as the editing in the final sequence suggests). Isabella and Columbus are in this film like the characters in medieval morality plays: they work as ideas and their conflict describes the state of the soul (in the case of *Alba de América*, Spain's soul).

The same opposition can be perceived in such films as *Lola la piconera* and *Agustina de Aragón*. Individuals are marked as saviours of an endangered Spain. In terms of character construction, the scripts insist on the special aura of the heroines. A clear example of this can be found in the way in which male characters keep on referring to Agustina as an 'extraordinary' woman even before she has done anything really extraordinary. Extraordinariness is in these cases something that is a marker of the role she is destined to play in history rather than something she does as a character. Again, the heightened, earnest performance of Aurora Bautista (as compared to the naturalness of Virgilio Teixeira, the foppishness of Eduardo Fajardo or the folksy straightforwardness of Manuel Luna) contributes to reinforce her moral superiority. One of the character traits that distinguishes the hero in many of these films is the sense of a mission. Both Columbus and Agustina seem to be driven by superior forces to act as they do, as if in their respective quests they were only tools of God. This articulation of individuality reinforces the sense of metaphysical necessity in the narratives. Together with this clear distinction between the elected individual and the masses there is an identification between them, as suggested above. The very first images of *Agustina de Aragón* show a dishevelled Aurora Bautista by her cannon, shooting and shouting at the French: '!No podéis vencernos nunca, cobardes, asesinos!' The use of the first person plural here and elsewhere in the film contributes to underline this identification between heroine and the masses in terms of a common destiny. Even more explicitly, the prologue describes Agustina as 'Símbolo de la gloria de la raza'.

Characterization in terms of metaphysics is also prominent in *Alba de América*. This narrative personifies the Golden Age through the figure of Queen Isabella, a metaphor for the eternal Spain. It is Isabella who seems to be the heart of the age of empire and its main propeller. This is emphatically articulated in the *mise-en-scène*. Her looks clearly imitate classic iconography in diverse images of the Virgin Mary. Her demeanour, her appearances (for instance, in a military hospital taking care of the wounded) all point towards sainthood. Her ideals are Christian ideals, and her view of Spain as a nation to fulfil a historical mission set out by God (both by fighting the Muslims and by bringing the Gospel to the undiscovered lands) is prominent throughout the film. Thus she is made to adopt a strong stance in supporting Columbus in his expedition. It is her words that close the film once the historical feat has been achieved, and they emphasize its metaphysical dimension. The rest of the films in the cycle are set in different periods, but the myth of the Golden Age still prevails as something to be achieved which identifies with Spanish virtues and Catholicism.

The past v the present

The terms in which the opposition between past and present is contextualised in Falangist discourse have been introduced earlier. It is the time to develop more fully its narrative articulation in the Cifesa epics. A recurring feature of the films under consideration is the flashback structure: most of them are framed by somebody remembering events in the past (Martín Alonso Pinzón in *Alba de América*, Alvar de Estúñiga in *Locura de amor*, Agustina in *Agustina de*

Aragón), the moment in which some great enterprise was in danger before the threat was averted by the hero or the heroine.

For instance, *Alba de América* starts with the loss of faith of sailors after long days of travel, despairing they will ever reach their destination. This could have strong echoes in the early 1950s of Spain's situation: the country was going through isolation and economic crisis and the temptation of despair was very real. Pinzón's story is intended to strengthen the faith in the nation's mission and exhort them to pull together to realize their destiny, symbolized by the benign figure of Isabella. In terms or narrative rhetoric, the choice of the flashback as a structural device is relevant: it endorses the mechanicist view of history commented on above, it tightens the causal relationship between the events being remembered and the present. Just as the sailors finally reached the promised land (something we see as the long flashback ends), Spain will finally get through the critical times. At the same time, there is a particular myth of the past that is always present, although sometimes it only appears latently. This area of the past is first constructed symbolically as a Golden Age, which is then described in some of its iconic features: political and cultural unity, Catholicism, racial purity. Of course not all of the films present this Golden Age explicitly, although there is always a gesture towards such a period in which the essential virtues of Spanishness were the natural state. *Locura de Amor* does not appear to exploit this myth of the Golden Age as deeply as it could. In fact, the main impulse of the narrative is melodrama, and it becomes so excessive that it drowns any explicit ideological agenda. Still the myth of a great historical moment which is endangered through scheming and foreign interference is carefully constructed in the film. Queen Juana is the 'pure' Spanish woman whose bubble will be burst by her husband, King Felipe, a foreigner in the hands of scheming foreigners. Even though she appears as frivolous in her early scenes, we are told that she was educated in the most pure Spanish tradition. Such stark contrast between such Spanishness and the perceived transgression of her husband is the cause for her madness: if she was actually the superficial woman she appears to be when surrounded by the court ladies, if foreign airs had actually affected her morals, we can infer, she would have found consolation in the arms of Estúñiga (Jorge Mistral). Historically she bridges the Golden Age of the Catholic Monarchs (unification, Catholicism) and the age of empire represented by her son Carlos I.

The end of an idealistic golden age of romance and purity is brought about by political scheming and courtly corruption. Through identification with the queen's sorrow there is a gesture towards elegy for this 'time of innocence'. What is relevant in the end is the implied narrative of historical redemption: thanks to the strong arm of Carlos I, dissidence is stifled and the empire is united again. The fact that narratives in this model eventually end in the restoration of balance and the essential Spain of the past prevails can be read as a reference to the outcome of the Civil War.

In *Alba de América* the myth of the Golden Age is constructed mostly as Queen Isabella's dream of a nation chosen by God to perform a unique mission in history. Again, this dream is echoed by Franco's own description of his role in Spanish history. Among the films in the series, this is perhaps the one which most explicitly gestures towards the Francoist present: Carrero Blanco was rumoured to have written substantial parts of the script and the very inception of the project was an attempt to set the record straight on the role of the Spanish in the 'discovery' of the new world. At the same time, as evidenced by the list of experts in the credits, it is also the film in which the iconic impulse is the strongest, and it is precisely the tension between the iconic and the ideological, between the reconstruction of events and the relevance in the present, that finally made the film into a failure. The rest of the films in the cycle are set in different periods, but the myth of the Golden Age still prevails as something to be achieved which identifies with Spanish virtues and Catholicism.

This is the case of the third major film in the cycle, *Agustina de Aragón*. Although set in the nineteenth century, the film constructs a past in which 'liberalism' is a four-letter word (the presence of Voltaire's complete works on the table of 'afrancesado' Luis definitely damns him in the eyes of Agustina) and in which, with a few occasional (and sometimes transitory) exceptions, all the 'real Spanish people' are pulling together to fight foreign influence. The myth of the Golden Age is therefore displaced from its proper time (the sixteenth century). References to the achievements of the 'essential' Spain abound. For instance, religion is everywhere in the lives of the villagers and the citizens of Zaragoza, there is no room without a crucifix presiding (they are absent when the lodgings of 'afrancesados' appear); the 'Virgen del Pilar' is also a constant presence in the film and focal point of the activities of Zaragozanos in time of crisis. Together with the prevalence of the Catholic religion, the film also presents the Francoist idea of nationalism as merely charming regional differences: two of the villagers are shown in friendly banter revolving around the superficial differences between Catalans and Aragonese ('Sardana' v 'Jota', 'Virgen del Pilar' v 'Virgen de Montserrat'). Spanish nationalism is aestheticized and depleted from political meaning. Apart from this, the Spanish are shown to be acting in unity, as led by the tireless Agustina and the absurdly heroic Palafox (Fernando Rey). Together with the emphasis on centralism and Catholicism as signifiers of essential Spain, the film connects with the present through its mistrust of the power of the press (and the lies it may spread).

Autarky, leadership and the historical role of Francoism are therefore represented and justified in the Cifesa films in terms of rhetorical tropes. The articulation of Francoist historiography in terms of fiction narratives is achieved through this particular set of oppositions which define the model and construct a symbolic version of the past that accounts for the present situation in general and for the triumph of Franco in particular. Whatever the ideological values of the Francoist account of Spanish history and its doubtful accuracy, it is important to emphasize its appropriateness for the construction of historical epics. This version of history is emplotted using symbolic motives which are very close to basic structures in the classic narrative cinema, although in some cases (e.g. *Alba de América*), the iconic impulse will dangerously unbalance the narrative structure. Otherwise, the consequences of the model created by these oppositions (such as causality, the role of fate, Manicheism or demonization, confrontation of individual and mass, narrative closure after a perceived threat is averted, identification, redemption, connection between the ideological and the emotional, etc.) suit perfectly the demands of the narrative model Spanish audiences were accustomed to. At the same time, it satisfied the ideological demands of the regime. For instance, by emphasizing the role of individuals and including an emotional version of history, the model encourages identification, so audiences were rhetorically 'invited' to share Franco's destiny. Through its emphasis on mechanicism and teleology, the model not only becomes relevant in the present, but also credible in terms of narrative plot, as it provides a clear ending where conflict is finally resolved. In turn, this could contribute to explaining why alternative historiographical models of Spanish history (such as the one proposed by Américo Castro) failed to provide, even when censorship was no impediment, a similarly popular cinematic model to represent history. A 'decentralized' version of Spanish history without heroes, based on dynamic relationships between classes or ethnic groups, that underplays drama and strong conflict is, without doubt, as cinematic as any other, but given audiences' viewing habits, it could hardly become popular.

Notes

1 For instance, the credits of *Alba de América* feature naval and historical experts to support the film's value as historical truth.
2 For different accounts of Francoist construction of history see Ramón López Facal, 'La nación ocultada', in Pérez Garzón, 2000.
3 Ibid.

Bibliography

Castro, Américo (1974) *Cervantes y los casticismos españoles*, Madrid: Alianza Editorial.
Fanés, Felix (1989) *Cifesa, la antorcha de los éxitos*, Valencia: Institución Alfonso El Magnánimo.
Heredero, Carlos F. (1993) *Las huellas del tiempo. Cine español, 1951–1961*, Valencia: Filmoteca Generalitat Valenciana.
López Facal, Ramón (2000) 'La nación ocultada', in Juan Sisinio Pérez Garzón, *La gestión de la memoria: la historia de España al servicio del poder*, Barcelona: Crítica.
Ortega y Gasset, José (1946) *España invertebrada: bosquejo de algunos pensamientos históricos*, Madrid: Revista de Occidente.
Pérez Garzón, Juan Sisinio (2000) *La gestión de la memoria: la historia de España al servicio del poder*, Barcelona: Crítica.
White, Hayden (1978) *Tropics of Discourse: Essays in Cultural Criticism*, Baltimore: Johns Hopkins University Press.

5

Re-framing the past: representations of the Spanish Civil War in popular Spanish cinema

David Archibald

Following the death of General Franco in November 1975, representations of the Spanish Civil War within popular Spanish cinema changed beyond all recognition. Under the dictatorship, the Civil War had almost exclusively been represented as a just and righteous crusade against atheism, communism and freemasonry, perhaps most notably in the film scripted by the dictator himself, *Raza / Race* (Sáenz de Heredia, 1941). However, Franco's death ushered in a period that permitted a cinematic re-examination of this traumatic period in Spain's past, free from the censorial control exercised by the right-wing regime.

This artistic freedom, coupled with a desire to cinematically re-represent a repressed and distorted historical period, has ensured that the country's recent past has become a rich historical seam for Spanish film-makers to mine. As Barry Jordan and Rikki Morgan-Tamosunas note, 'of the nearly three hundred historical films produced since the 1970s, more than half are set during the Second Republic, the Civil War and Francoism' (1998: 16).

In the period immediately following Franco's death some film-makers openly challenged early nationalist accounts of the Civil War, producing alternative histories of past events in documentaries such as *La vieja memoria / The Old Memory* (Camino, 1977) and *¿Por qué perdimos la guerra? / Why Did We Lose the War?* (Santillán, 1978). This initial move to debate the central political concerns of the Civil War was followed by a move away from detailed historical and political analyses. As Antonio Monegal points out, 'after the constraints of censorship were lifted, there have been many films made that were (supposedly) about the war, or about the tough times during the dictatorship. But the treatment of the topic was mediated by some form of indirection' (1998: 203). This is indeed the case, and from the late seventies onwards a number of fiction films examined the Civil War's impact on those caught in the cross-fire (e.g. *Soldados / Soldiers* (Ungría, 1978)), or focused on smaller, personal concerns (e.g. *Las bicicletas son para el verano / Bicycles Are for Summer* (Chávarri, 1984)).

Thus despite the turn to twentieth-century history by Spanish film-makers, there have been few films whose primary subject matter has been the Civil War itself; the film director Vicente Aranda suggests that 'apenas hay películas sobre la Guerra Civil ya que hay un deseo de olvidar este suceso histórico. (There are hardly any films about the Civil War as there is a desire to forget this historical event)' (Aranda in D'Lugo, 1997: 291). This is not a trend isolated in the world of cinema, but is reflective of a more widespread tendency in Spanish society itself. As the historian Paul Preston comments:

> Since the return of democracy to Spain, commemoration of the Civil War has been muted. The silence was partly a consequence of the legacy of fear deliberately created during the post-war repression and by Franco's consistent pursuit of a policy of glorifying the victors and humiliating the vanquished. It was also a result of what has come to be called the *pacto de olvido* (the pact of forgetfulness). An inadvertent effect of Franco's post-war policies was to imbue the bulk of the Spanish people with a determination never to undergo again either the violence experienced during the war or the repression thereafter. (2000: 21)

The tendency to produce films that elide much of the political and historical detail of the period has also been noted by Marvin D'Lugo who points to 'a Spanish nostalgia genre that regularly transforms the politically charged periods of the Civil War and immediate post-war periods into the *mise-en-scène* of narratives that have little to do with politics or history in the conventional sense' (1997: 289). This essay presents a brief analysis of three popular Spanish films from the 1990s that are set in the period leading up to and including the Civil War. It explores the way in which politics and history are represented in the films and also explores how film-makers using popular cinematic forms have appropriated the Civil War setting to comment on contemporary political and social issues.

My use of the term 'popular' is broadly in keeping with the definition outlined by the German playwright Bertolt Brecht who argues that '"popular" means intelligible to the broad masses, taking over their own forms of expression and enriching them' (1965: 108). Thus, rather than focusing on documentary cinema or art cinema, the three films examined here, *¡Ay, Carmela!* (Saura, 1990), *La lengua de las mariposas / Butterfly's Tongue* (Cuerda, 1999), and *Libertarias / Freedom Fighters* (Aranda, 1996) all employ conventional narrative techniques common to most popular cinemas.[1]

This focus on popular cinema raises further questions about the adequacy of conventional narrative cinema to adequately represent the past. In recent years a number of theorists working on film and history have rejected the use of narrative cinema as a means of representing modern events. Hayden White argues that 'the twentieth century is marked by the occurrence of certain 'holocaustal' events [. . .] These kinds of events do not lend themselves to explanation in terms of the categories of traditional humanistic historiography' (1996: 21). White cites as examples the two world wars, the great depression and the genocide of six million European Jews by the Nazis. For White, the Spanish Civil War, an internecine conflict that raged for a period of three years and resulted in up to 500,000 deaths would be a 'holocaustal' event, the scale of which would have been unimaginable before the advent of the twentieth century. Therefore, events like the Spanish Civil War defy understanding by conventional historiographical methods of enquiry. Furthermore, in terms of cinema, he argues that they are unrepresentable by conventional artistic modes. In calling for new forms of representation he states: 'This is not to say that such events are not representable, only that techniques of representation somewhat different from those developed at the height of artistic realism may be called for' (1996: 29).

White's position has been influential among theorists straddling the boundaries of film and history who call for modernist / postmodernist cinematic texts that foreground their own construction and problematize the telling and re-telling of history.[2] White may well have a point; however, for their own reasons many film-makers continue to utilize conventional narrative techniques, perhaps primarily to find a large audience for their films. White may well believe that new film forms are required to deal with the complexities of modern events, but what happens when film-makers continue to engage with modern events through popular cinema? What happens when events that White deems to be unrepresentable by conventional, popular forms are indeed represented by them? Does popular cinema have nothing to tell audiences about the past?

Until relatively recently most historians cared little about cinematic representations of past events. But in a world where the visual immediacy of the cinematic image increasingly works to displace traditional historiography, these representations have become increasingly important. It may be a commonly held belief that audiences do not visit the cinema for lessons in history, but when historical events that have been suppressed over generations are projected onto cinema screens, these representations become increasingly important for formulating how audiences conceptualize past events. This is certainly the case in relation to the Spanish Civil War.

La lengua de las mariposas

La lengua de las mariposas is a film that seems to be firmly locked in a past from which it does not attempt to escape. As the opening credits run, a montage sequence of black and white photographs presents a picture of a tranquil, rural Spain brought to life as the camera pans into the small Galician home of Moncho, the film's seven-year-old male protagonist. Set in the months immediately preceding Franco's rebellion on 18 July 1936, the turbulent politics of the pre-Civil War period are alluded to when a group of women discuss the political situation. Moncho's mother warmly welcomes women's enfranchisement, thus alluding to the Republic's progressive, reforming status. The subterranean dangers threatening to disturb the new regime are highlighted when another woman from the group states that 'they're burning churches in Barcelona'. These potential dangers are developed further when the local *cacique*, Don Avelino, states that 'things are bad' and suggests that the drastic solution is to 'set fire to Madrid'. The film's spring setting, perfectly captured in the cinematography of the green and golden countryside scenes, connotes a world with the potential to blossom; only careful nurturing, however, can ensure that it successfully avoids the profound dangers it faces.

Central to the plot is the relationship between Moncho and Don Gregorio, his ageing anarchist schoolteacher. Moncho can be seen as a metaphor for the Second Republic, established five years earlier, with his age and asthma indicative of its frail nature and his nickname, Sparrow, connotative of its status as a small harmless creature

preparing to spread its fledgling wings. After spending the spring
months teaching Moncho and his classmates, Don Gregorio retires
and, in his closing speech to an assembly of pupils and parents, states
that 'if we can allow one generation, just one generation, to grow up
free in Spain, then no-one will ever be able to take away their liberty'. Don Gregorio presents a belief in the enlightening potential of
education; his attempts to educate the children in the beauty of the
natural world, perspective painting in art and the knowledge to be
found in the world of literature, exemplifying a philosophical
approach which asserts that the study of art and literature can be utilized as a tool to construct better adults. Don Gregorio's choice of
subject matter in poetry, Antonio Machado's 'Childhood Memory',
with its references to the biblical tale of Cain and Abel, also illustrates Don Gregorio's use of literature as a weapon to forewarn of
the bitter consequences of fratricide.[3]

Moncho's metaphorical status is further represented in the struggle between the priest and Don Gregorio over the child's education.
When the priest complains to Don Gregorio that Moncho is forgetting his Latin, the boy stands as representative of a country struggling to break free from the rigid strictures of 1930s Spanish
Catholicism. Rather than Moncho entering some spiritual void, it is
the study of art, literature and nature that Don Gregorio hopes will
fill his spiritual needs.

Manuel Rivas, the writer of ¿Que me queres, amor? (What Do You
Want From Me, Love?) the title of the novel on which the film is
based, states that La lengua de las mariposas is 'about two types of
apprenticeship [. . .] Apprenticeship in love and apprenticeship in
freedom' (2000: 8). And Moncho's apprenticeship in freedom takes
place alongside his lessons in friendship with Roque, his fledgling
love with Aurora and the joys, or otherwise, of carnal pleasure when
he surreptitiously spies on the lustful romps of his father's illegitimate daughter, Carmina, and her amorous, drunken lover O'lis.
These lessons in friendship and freedom, however, sit astride
Moncho's experience of the darker side of human behaviour exemplified by the threatening presence of three of the key male characters: the corrupt businessman Don Avelino, the Chinese girl's
controlling husband and the personal manifestation of fascism
embodied in O'lis.

Moncho's asthma attack during a springtime nature trek prompts
Don Gregorio to 'save' him by plunging the young boy into the river,

thus signifying his 'baptism' into the waters of a somewhat muddy mix of anarchism and liberal humanism. The film suggests that if Don Gregorio had had sufficient time it would have been possible to completely inoculate the boy against the potentials of evil. In the concluding sequence, however, as Don Gregorio joins the other Republicans being led from their holding cell and loaded onto a cart, prompted by his parents, Moncho joins the crowd shouting insults at his teacher. His initial desperate cries of 'rojo' (red) and 'ateo' (atheist) are followed by the words he was so lovingly taught by Don Gregorio, culminating in an anguished cry of 'espiritrompa' (butterfly's tongue). His feelings of personal betrayal, coupled with his inability to comprehend the situation, fuel his confusion, and, like so many others in the hot summer days of 1936, he is thrust into a conflict which he is unable to understand. The closing, medium close-up, black-and-white still shot captures Moncho's perplexed gaze as he stares in the direction of the cart taking Don Gregorio to his death. Below is the caption, 'The Spanish Civil War had just begun', and this freeze frame can be equated with a freezing of time, poetically suggesting that time itself stood still with the coming to power of Franco.

This representation of Republican Spain is one seen through rose-tinted spectacles, a sugar-coated past set in a dream-like golden age; the beautiful cinematography and the melancholic music working to increase this nostalgic re-creation of a past that never was. Yet it is a past that audiences know will be destroyed by the impending nightmare of fascism. The stress that *La lengua de las mariposas* places on the transformative powers of education suggests that in contemporary Spain, with a generation of young people brought up free from the constrictive dictatorship and educated in the world of liberal democracy, it is a nightmare that need no longer haunt contemporary Spanish society. Thus the Civil War is represented as a period that can safely be consigned to the past. A troublesome event, yes, but one that Spanish audiences need not worry about too much in the present.

¡Ay, Carmela!

¡Ay, Carmela! recreates a quite different image of Spain as the Civil War draws to a close. The war setting is foregrounded in the opening sequence as the camera pans over a war-ravaged town where

depressed, dejected soldiers squat at street corners. An armoured Republican car sits immobilized. The walls are covered in torn and tattered left-wing posters. It is a world far removed from the rural tranquillity and childhood innocence of *La lengua de las mariposas*. Intertitles locate the film on the Aragón Front in 1938, not a pleasant place for Republican soldiers caught in a war that seems increasingly unwinnable. Yet the non-diegetic singing of '¡Ay, Carmela!', a popular song among Republican soldiers, introduces a lighter side, a contrast in tone that is developed continually until the film's tragic, but inevitable conclusion.

Director Carlos Saura's *oeuvre* includes a number of films touching on the Civil War and life under Franco, from *La caza / The Hunt* in 1965 to *Dulces horas / Sweet Hours* in 1982. His films tend to adopt a serious tone, often centring on the desire to remember and the fallibility of memory itself. But rather than examining the conflict head on, his films have often used metaphor and allusion to grapple with the politics of the period and its political and social fallout. By the time of *¡Ay, Carmela!*'s release, however, Saura's approach had clearly changed. 'I would have been incapable a few years ago of treating our Civil War with humour', he states, 'but now it is different, for sufficient time has passed to adopt a broader perspective, and there is no doubt that by employing humour it is possible to say things that it would be more difficult if not impossible to say in another way' (Saura in Edwards, 1995: 116).

A key use of humour in the film is in Saura's blurring of the lines between 'good' Republicans and 'evil' fascists. Carmela, Paulino and Gustavete, members of 'The Tip-Top Variety Show' who perform cabaret acts for Republican soldiers, are captured by Franco's troops as they flee the front. Their far from heroic departure involves Carmela offering sexual favours to distract a sleazy Republican driver while Paulino and Gustavete siphon much-needed petrol for their intended escape to Valencia. Thus, the central characters are seen as deserting the sinking ship while the Republican soldier who asks of Carmela, 'let me warm my hands on your titties', is represented as little more than a frustrated sex pest. 'Evil' may remain, illustrated when a group of prisoners are taken out and executed against a wall, but not all the fascists fall into this category. This is most clearly exemplified by the Italian officer, Lieutenant Amelio di Ripamonte, and his comically camp troupe of soldiers who are disparagingly described as a 'bunch of fairies' by a Spanish officer. In the past these representations may have attracted political condemnation; in a comic wrapper, Saura has the scope to break black-and-white categorizations, free from the risk of harsh political criticism.

¡Ay, Carmela! is no neutral, apolitical comedy and it clearly illustrates the foreign influences on Spain that helped shape the Civil War's outcome. Thus the conflict is not represented as a solely Spanish affair, but as an arena of international battle which preceded the larger conflagration of World War II.[4] This is hinted at initially in the opening theatre scene when the Republican soldiers sit in fear of the planes overhead and Paulino states: 'It sounds like one of those German turkeys'. The level of international involvement becomes crystal clear, however, in the closing theatre sequence where the audience comprises an international collection of German, Italian, Moroccan and Spanish soldiers. The military support Franco received from Germany and Italy is clear by the physical presence of their troops and highlighted further when Paulino extorts: 'three peoples, three cultures and one single victory'. On the other side of the divide sit the captured Polish International Brigaders, representative of the forty thousand international volunteers who travelled to Spain to fight fascism. By representing the Brigaders as Polish, the film also suggests a link with Germany's invasion of Poland in 1939, the event that marked the start of World War II. The Soviet Union's support for the Republican government is also suggested through Gustavete's hammer and sickle adorned red sweater that he wears in the theatrical sketch 'The Republic Goes to the Doctor'. Thus rather than representing the war as a primarily Spanish affair, it locates it within a wider international perspective.

The closing theatre sequence scene also raises questions about the role of artists living under dictatorship and presents two possible alternatives. Firstly, the practical pragmatism of Paulino, who may have Republican sympathies but moves relatively effortlessly between both sides and who earlier states, 'We're artists, we do as we're told'. On the other hand, Carmela may be prepared to compromise, but she has her limits. When she removes her militia costume to reveal a Republican flag wrapped around her body it provokes a cacophony of jeers and abuse from the fascist troops. As the Polish prisoners burst into a rendition of '¡Ay, Carmela!', she joins their defiant chorus and bares her breasts to the prisoners, their last sexual 'treat' before death. Her actions are not motivated by an obscure idealism, she is simply not prepared to see others humiliated and idly stand by. In contrast Paulino attempts to deflect the situation by resorting to 'The Farts', a comic routine which utilizes his flatulence to great effect. However, when a Spanish officer fires a solitary pistol shot from the theatre auditorium the camera cuts to a slow-motion shot of Carmela falling to the stage floor as the bullet strikes her forehead. The comic is instantly transformed into tragedy, with Carmela's death standing as representative of the many who died fighting fascism in this bloody conflict.

It is perhaps a weakness of the film that as the narrative moves towards its dramatic conclusion, Carmela's period is about to start, thus placing her heroism at the door of some kind of biologically induced emotionalism rather than the noble act of a traditional heroine. Despite this she is presented as a positive figure that cannot be bought and sold. She is not prepared to compromise her art and dies, Paulino toes the line and lives. *¡Ay, Carmela!* raises questions, however, about the quality of life that he will lead. Indeed, this is clearer in the original play by José Sanchís Sinisterra on which the film is based, where the story is told in flashback with Paulino sweeping the floors of an old theatre, his status reduced from that of proud performer to humble janitor. In the closing scene of the film, Paulino and Gustavete lay flowers at Carmela's graveside before they drive off into a barren land, a metaphorical wasteland made desolate by war and the impending conquest of fascism. The possibility of flowering, of building a new world lies hopelessly crushed. Yet the closing upbeat non-diegetic singing of '¡Ay, Carmela!' strives to break the potential despondency, suggesting that inspiration can be found from the example of those prepared to make a stand against oppression, regardless of the personal consequences. *¡Ay, Carmela!* clearly highlights how art and culture can be appropriated for political ends, with both Republicans and fascists keen to utilize theatre for propaganda purposes. While Spanish audiences may have moved on from the agitprop theatrical projects of the 1930s, Saura's film is an indication of the importance of cinematic images in creating an understanding of past events.

Libertarias

Libertarias explores the internal politics of the Republican movement by focusing on an assorted group of women, notably anarchist activists, prostitutes and a nun, fighting with Mujeres Libres (Free

Women), the women's section of Spain's anarchist movement. Through its focus on female protagonists, the film attempts to analyse the position of women in the war, but it also strives to recover, and indeed celebrate, the neglected history of Spain's anarchist movement. In doing so, it highlights the revolutionary dimensions of the conflict, which are laid bare in the introductory intertitles:

- Summer 1936
- 18 July. The Spanish army rises against the Republican government.
- 19 July. In Barcelona and Madrid the army is defeated thanks to the peoples' heroic efforts.
- 20 July. The masses demand a revolutionary state. The legal government is unable to control the situation.
- 21 July. The Spanish Civil War begins. The last idealistic war. The last dream of a people striving for the impossible. For Utopia.

The opening slow-motion montage sequence of men and women marching defiantly, their raised fists signifying their allegiance to the workers' movement, firmly locates the narrative in the turbulent public sphere of revolutionary Spain. A black-and-white shot of a church cross falling signifies the Republican movement's anti-clerical aspects. As the image is colourized, a black and red anarchist flag is flown proudly as groups of workers boldly proclaim, 'Down with capitalism! Death to priests! Long live Durruti! Long live the workers!' This is clearly not a representation of the Civil War as a conflict between good and evil subsumed within a simplistic democracy versus fascism equation. Instead, *Libertarias* grapples to visually represent a period that George Orwell graphically describes in his autobiographical account, *Homage to Catalonia*. Of his arrival in Barcelona in November 1936, Orwell famously states, 'It was the first time that I had ever been in a town where the working class was in the saddle' (1989: 9). Orwell refuses to ignore the revolutionary nature of the conflict when he comments that 'in Catalonia, for the first few months, most of the actual power was in the hands of the Anarcho-Syndicalists, who controlled most of the key industries. The thing that had happened in Spain was, in fact, not merely a civil war, but the beginning of a revolution' (1989: 192). The class nature of the conflict was highlighted not only by those on the left, but also by Franco himself when he stated, 'Our Crusade is the only struggle in which the rich who went to war came out richer than when they started' (in Preston, 2000: 64). The revolutionary nature of the conflict and the class struggles at the heart of it are further alluded to in *Libertarias* when one of the militiamen shouts across the trenches to nationalist soldiers on the other side of the barricades, 'You are trying to defend the interests of your millionaire generals'.

The political issues at stake are summed up in the speech given to the 'liberated' prostitutes by the chronically caricatured anarchist Concha who croaks to the cynical hookers, 'Our country is now in revolt. The symbols of repression are burning. The workers have occupied the factories and barracks [. . .] freedom has broken out. A word is heard repeatedly in homes, factories and workshops: revolution'. Whilst Concha's political polemic falls on deaf ears, Pilar, her fellow militiawoman, skilfully wins them over to the side of the revolution with a more basic appeal to their immediate self-interest when she states, 'What do you want? To be whores all your life? To have cocks stuck up you 10 or 15 times a day? And all for a bowl of stew'.

Over and above exploring issues of war and revolution, *Libertarias*'s particular focus is on the role of women in the war and the film progresses from the somewhat cynical attitudes expressed by the initial response of the freshly liberated prostitutes to a genuine comradeship that develops amongst the female protagonists. However, as the women prepare to fight at the front, they are forced to endure sexist ridicule from some of the militiamen, one of whom shouts, 'Comrades don't your tits get in the way when you shoot?' The initial sexism they face lays the ground for a more generalized assault on the position of women fighting at the front. The anarchists leaders' willingness to forego their principles is initially suggested when the anarchist leader Durruti asserts that 'if it's necessary we'll impose an iron discipline. I'm willing to renounce everything except victory'. He later decrees that women are to be banned from fighting: 'Of ten militiawomen examined five have gonorrhoea and three are pregnant. We have more casualties from the clap than from enemy bullets [. . .] I want no women at the front'. Thus the liberation movement is seen to be incapable of accommodating half of those sympathetic to the aims of the revolution. The rolling back of the progressive nature of the revolution becomes even more clear when one of the prostitutes reads out a letter from one of her co-workers from Barcelona: 'We were amazed to see that the pussy game was more popular than ever. The union guys gave us a house and we've set ourselves up. There is a constant line of militiamen'. Thus the initial gains of the revolution prove to be short-lived as the sexual division of labour and 'natural' order begins to be re-imposed in the rear, as it is at the front.

Libertarias's central character, the aptly named nun, María, highlights the potentially liberating qualities of the anarchist movement and the narrative charts her spiritual journey from Christianity and convents, through brothels, trenches and her appropriation of a quasi-anarcho-spirituality, before she reaches her ultimate destination in a fascist detention centre. Her spiritual transformation begins when she encounters the medium, Floren, who when asked, 'Are you an anarchist too?' replies that she is both anarchist and spiritualist and links the two apparently contradictory philosophical outlooks by asserting that 'Jesus was the first anarchist'. The sexual politics at play are also developed when Floren asserts that 'Jesus isn't a man, she's a woman'. María's transition from Catholic nun to nun of the revolution begins; she moves rapidly from the word of God to the word of the anarchist theoretician Kropotkin, citing his writings as she persuades peasants to feed the militia and appeals to the nationalist troops to come over to the Republican side.

This religious theme is further developed, and the biblical symbolism obvious, when, as the militia prepare to slaughter a lamb, a group of Moroccan troops arrive and brutally attack the militia. The closing sequence attempts to tie the strands of anarchism and spiritualism clearly together. Pilar lies dying, her throat slashed in the previous scene. As María cradles her almost lifeless head, non-diegetic, angelic choral music fills the air and María states:

> One day in the time of the Lord, this planet will no longer be called Earth. It will be called Freedom. That day the exploiters of the people will be cast into the outer darkness where there will be wailing and gnashing of teeth and the angels of heaven on the most high will sing in joy as they behold the star Freedom, more blue and more radiant than ever. Because peace and justice will reign there. Because paradise will always be there and death will no longer exist.

Thus *Libertarias* concludes on a utopian, spiritual note, continuing the thread that has been developed throughout the film's narrative. Aranda states, 'There are many examples in history of events that seemed impossible, but have happened. That's why we have to keep on believing in utopia. The film talks about two utopias: women's and society's. They both end tragically, but there is still hope enough to keep fighting'.[5] *Libertarias*'s utopian spiritual thread, however, somewhat dissipates this hope and weakens its political analysis, formulating possible solutions to contemporary problems in religious utopian strivings, rather than utopian strivings in the material world.[6] Fredric Jameson asserts that the role of political art is 'to convey the sense of a hermeneutic relationship to the past which is able to grasp its own present as history only on condition it manages to keep the idea of the future, and of radical and utopian transformation, alive' (1979: 72). It is a role that *Libertarias* fails to fulfil. As previously stated, the opening titles describe the Civil War as 'The last idealistic war. The last dream of a people striving for the impossible. For Utopia'. But despite Aranda's assertions, *Libertarias* appears to suggest that the 'impossible' aspirations of the anarchists were inevitably doomed to failure on Earth and are only possible within some non-tangible ethereal space.

So how far do these films fit into D'Lugo's assertion that Spanish films set in this period often have little to say about politics or history in the conventional sense? They may not all contain the central political analyses of earlier documentaries, but nevertheless in all three films the settings operate as more than convenient backdrops. Even *La lengua de las mariposas*, which seems the most apolitical, contains specific historical and political material, for instance, in relation to women's enfranchisement, religion and corruption, although it clearly finds comfort in suggesting that the nightmare of the Civil War is a past that will never be returned to. *¡Ay, Carmela!* refocuses attention on the international dimensions of the conflict which are rarely addressed cinematically, but also raises more general political concerns surrounding the role of artists in society. The most overt political and historical study is contained in *Libertarias*; by locating the reasons for the defeat of the anarchist revolution within the anarchist movement itself, it clearly presents a different political focus than *¡Ay, Carmela!*'s concentration on international forces. These films, perhaps with the solitary exception of *Libertarias*, do not offer detailed political analyses of the Civil War. Yet, in their own way, they each have their political points to make, both about the war and about broader issues. There exist different, often contradictory, representations of the Spanish Civil War in popular cinema, and perhaps it is not possible to mark out a simple definitive trend as D'Lugo asserts, but to recognize a diversity of uses for the past. That this period increasingly attracts cinematic attention suggests unease about a past that has not been settled.[7] But perhaps it is better to argue about the past than to forget it. The Colombian novelist Gabriel García Márquez describes the deteriorating condition of an amnesiac: 'The recollection of his childhood began to be erased from his memory, then the name and notion of things, and finally the identity of people, and even the awareness of his own being [. . .] until he sank into a kind of idiocy that had no past' (1970: 46). In bringing the Spanish Civil War to the cinema screen, despite their limitations, all these films work to break down the silence of the *pacto de olvido*, forcing spectators not to forget, but to actively remember. These three popular Spanish films are not the experimental self-reflexive modernist texts that Hayden White and other theorists demand. However, they clearly reveal that seemingly unrepresentable events continue to be represented by popular artistic forms. Furthermore, these films do have a role to play in salvaging a sense of history and struggling to ensure that Spain does not live in a perpetual present, but comes to terms with a problematic past, all the better to encounter the problems that it faces in the present.

Notes

1 For an introduction to the aesthetics of cinema see David Bordwell and Kristin Thompson (1993).

2 For an introduction to recent debates about cinema and history see Robert A. Rosenstone (1995).

3 In *Cain on Screen: Contemporary Spanish Cinema* (1993), Deveney uses the theoretical framework of *Cainismo*, which he describes as 'a fraternal antagonism within Spanish society' (1993: 5) to analyse a number of films located during the Civil War, quoting Unamuno's assertion that the concept of Civil War 'began with the fraternal assassination of Abel by his brother Cain' (1993: 6). *La lengua de las mariposas* is not the first film set in this period to recall the poem; indeed, Deveney cites its use in *Las largas vacaciones del '36* / *The Long Vacation of '36* (Camino, 1976). This may be a theme touched on by Spanish film-makers; however, the 'theory' of *Cainismo* itself, rather than providing illuminating analyses of the films it examines, represents a flawed theoretical approach that flows from an understanding of the nation state as a collective unit with its population sharing a communal interest. The theoretical model of *Cainismo* unsuccessfully attempts to

transcend barriers of class, gender and national identity, to name only the most central, leaving it unable to deal with the complexities of the films it strives to analyse.

4 A number of historians view the Spanish Civil War as the first chapter in a large conflagration. For an introduction see Paul Preston (1996), where Preston describes the events in Spain as 'a rehearsal for the bigger world war to come' (1996: 5).

5 Quoted in 'Viva la revolucion! Viva la mujeras! [sic]', www.green-left.org.au, 12 February 2000.

6 Some historians have pointed to this association between anarchism and religion, citing anarchism as the response of people who feel betrayed by the Church and whose vision is akin to an early Jewish–Christian utopia. See Gerald Brennan (1990: 188–9).

7 *Land and Freedom* (Loach, 1995), perhaps one of the most famous films of recent years to deal with the Civil War, offers an interesting and plausible mix of reasons for the defeat of the Republic – reasons both internal to Spain, and external – by focusing on the role of the communists and the Soviet Union in the suppression of the revolutionary movement. An analysis of Loach's film is beyond the boundaries of this article.

Bibliography

Bordwell, David and Kristin Thompson (1993) *Film Art: An Introduction*, London and New York: McGraw-Hill.

Brecht, Bertolt (1965) *Brecht on Theatre: The Development of an Aesthetic*, London: Methuen.

Brennan, Gerald (1990) *The Spanish Labyrinth: An Account of the Social and Political Background to the Spanish Civil War*, Cambridge: Cambridge University Press.

Deveney, Thomas G. (1993) *Cain on Screen: Contemporary Spanish Cinema*, Methuen, N.J. & London: The Scarecrow Press, Inc.

D'Lugo, Marvin (1997) *Guide to the Cinema of Spain*, Westport: Greenwood Press.

—— (1998) 'Vicente Aranda's *Amantes*: History as Cultural Style in Spanish Cinema', in Jenaro Talens and Santos Zunzunegui (eds.), *Modes of Representation in Spanish Cinema*, Minnesota: University of Minnesota Press.

Edwards, Gwynneth (1995) *Indecent Exposures: Buñuel, Saura, Erice and Almodóvar*, London: Marion Boyars Publishers.

García Márquez, Gabriel (1970) *One Hundred Years of Solitude*, London: Cape.

Jameson, Fredric (1979) 'Marxism and Historicism', *New Literary History*, 11: 1, Autumn.

Jordan, Barry and Rikki Morgan-Tamosunas (1998) *Contemporary Spanish Cinema*, Manchester: Manchester University Press.

Monegal, Antonio (1998) 'Images of War: Hunting the Metaphor', in Jenaro Talens and Santos Zunzunegui (eds.), *Modes of Representation in Spanish Cinema*, Minnesota: University of Minnesota Press.

Orwell, George (1989) *Homage to Catalonia*, London: Penguin.

Preston, Paul (1996) *A Concise History of the Spanish Civil War*, London: HarperCollins.

—— (2000) *Comrades! Portraits From the Spanish Civil War*, London: HarperCollins.

Rosenstone, Robert A. (ed.) (1995) *Revisioning History: Film and the Construction of a New Past*, Princeton: Princeton University Press.

White, Hayden (1996) 'The Modernist Event', in Vivian Sobnack (ed.), *The Persistence of History: Cinema, Television and the Modern Event*, London and New York: Routledge.

www.greenleft.org.au 'Viva la revolucion! Viva las mujeras!' [*sic*]. Accessed on 12 February 2000.

6

'Palaces of Seeds': from an experience of local cinemas in post-war Madrid to a suggested approach to film audiences

Esther Gómez-Sierra

The purpose of this chapter is to study the testimony of a female filmgoer and her experience of regular attendance at a *cine de barrio* (double-bill local cinema) in a central and popular quarter of Madrid, the *barrio* of Maravillas or Malasaña, in post-war Spain. Her account took the shape of an informal talk given in March 1996 to a class of final year students in the Department of Spanish and Portuguese at Manchester University. In what follows, I review this testimony in relation to the material, the emotional and the intellectual aspects of film reception. I am aware that my choice of this point of departure is not without problems; I will return to these later. Nevertheless, the aim of my analysis is to stress the need in the field of film studies today for ethnographical research on the audience, and to suggest a possible way of carrying it out. The ultimate implications of such research are yet to be seen, but I shall argue from this case study that if we want to be faithful to the realities of film-watching, we must rethink 'audience studies' as 'audiences studies'. Audiences are more than the inert object of different kinds of theoretical analysis; they have individual voices. In this chapter I seek to underline their importance.[1]

A viewer's tale

The subject of this account is Matilde Sierra Fernández, a woman born in Madrid in 1930. The period she recalls is mainly the decade between 1945 and 1955, with some mentions of later films. During those years, Spain slowly left behind the hardest stages of post-war rationing, repression and isolation, and started to open its borders to international relations and commerce, with the relative softening of the general climate of public punishment characteristic of the aftermath of the war. The viewer belongs to the city's working class. What follows is a word-for-word translation of the transcript of her testimony, which can be read in the appendix. I try to keep the idio-syncrasies of the original; to preserve the flow of her account, my occasional interjections and questions have been ommitted. In both original and translation I have supplied words in square brackets when their lack was likely to obscure understanding of the given passage. I also include the dates of the films mentioned.

There was nothing else, back then. There was no television; cinema was the people's pastime . . . I did not like horror films, and as they never told you what the film was about, I would be in agony until it started . . . As the plot unfolded I could relax.

We used to go to a cinema called *Dos de Mayo*, but we called it 'The Palace of [Sunflower] Seeds'. Everybody ate them all the time. I used to go on Sundays to the first showing, at four o'clock. I would arrive at the cinema at three to wait until they opened, and I would queue until four to grab a good seat. We all went . . . we all went. The cinema was in Dos de Mayo street, in the centre of town, what is now the area of Maravillas, a very pop-ular area because the *movida* of Madrid started there. The ticket cost was one and a half pesetas; I was eighteen years old when I started working (in 1949), I earned sixty-five pesetas per week. Of course, you had to make an effort to save the money for the ticket. . . .

The first thing on was the *NO-DO*, a news bulletin of the Francoist regime that told you what [Franco] wanted people to know; and because it was the only direct information we had, we liked it. As there was nothing else; we accepted what they gave us. [In the *NO-DO*, Franco] opened all the water reservoirs under the sun, with those ceremonies, all those things. It was also very important that he gave prizes to big families of fourteen and fifteen children; a pity. It wasn't at all like the news bulletins now; then there was only national news, very restricted. There wasn't anything else, we didn't really know whether it was any good or if there was anything better. There were two films, it was a double-bill session. The first one was a filler, the second was the main feature. The first film entertained us a lot; there was an interval between the first and the second, and there was a sign that said: 'Bar service'. We were very patient, but when the film could not be heard because the equipment was very poor, [people] used to protest by stamping their feet and screaming: 'sound, sound!' If the film was very bad, people had no other option than to put up with it or leave; sometimes – not very often – they left. There was nothing else to do.

The first film I ever saw was *Goyescas* (1942). In general, the Spanish films they used to show were the *españoladas*, very patriotic: there was one called

Raza / Race (1941), Franco wrote the script under a pseudonym, and it was incredible. Also *Locura de amor / Love Madness* (1948), the story of Juana la Loca, the wife of Philip of Hapsburg: he had been very unfaithful, and after that he dies, and she was madly in love with him and spent her life in exile [from the Court] around Spain with the husband's coffin until she decided to bury him – or they made her bury him. The actresses of the time were Aurora Bautista and Sara Montiel, very young. There were other kinds of Spanish films, like *Surcos / Furrows* (1951), which deals with the beginning of migration from the countryside to the cities, how families would break up because of having gone in search of a better life that turned out to be not so good; they left the furrows for a better life they never attained.

But the films I liked most were, of course, the American ones: *Gilda* (1946). As censorship was so terrible then, with *Gilda* it happened that imagination went beyond reality; well, do you remember when Gilda takes her glove off? Everyone assumed that the censors had cut that scene because she went on stripping; imagine, it never was like that, because later on I have seen the uncut version and it did not happen, it was the glove and nothing else. And then, to slap a woman's face so brutally . . . There were people against it and they used to go to the cinema doors and protest, saying it was against nature, against public morals. There were a lot of prudes in favour of what Franco said, but it was also due to the very strong repression at the time. *Gone with the Wind* (1939): that was wonderful, it was the best of all; I loved American films, and I still do. *Gone with the wind*: lots of people saw it, it lasted a very long time on release, lots of people; it was the cinema event of the day, a great film. There were films that, because of censorship, were unintelligible, for instance *Mogambo* (1953). They were all in the jungle, on a safari; one of the actors was Clark Gable – there were people who called him 'cable face'.[2] Dialogues were unbelievable; in order not to have adultery on screen they ended up with incest! Grace Kelly was married, but for the husband to see the love affair between her and Clark Gable unfolding before his very eyes was too strong, so they changed it so that the husband became a brother.

There were very successful [Spanish] musical films: *El último cuplé / The Last Couplet* (1957), a very good film with all the true Madrid popular songs, with barrel-organs, popular celebrations; she was very young, Sara Montiel . . . There was also Imperio Argentina, who did *Goyescas*, and during the Spanish War was in a lot of films in Germany, and that's why there were rumours that she was a Nazi. And Hitler treated her like a goddess; she was an international star. That film also stars Rafael Rivelles, a famous theatre actor, the husband of María Fernanda Ladrón de Guevara. Theatre was very good, but it too was tightly censored; Buero Vallejo wrote very good plays, like *Historia de una escalera*, but censorship was also present there.

And, of course, *¡Bienvenido, Mr. Marshall! / Welcome Mr. Marshall!* (1952). This film was a success, but not as it should have been. Franco sold us to the Americans, and it was really a parody of how much we had had to pay: the military bases of Zaragoza, Rota y Torrejón, and all that for milk powder, cheese made of plastic and American tinned meat. And this film is an example of true reality, but people did not understand the scope of the true story. Only later, when I saw it on television, when I was really an adult, did I understand what it was, but when I saw it in the cinema I didn't. It is an amazing satire – Berlanga is one of the best directors we have. [In *¡Bienvenido, Mr. Marshall!*] there is a very poor village deep in Castile. An impresario arrives with a female Andalusian folklore star, and seizes the opportunity to give the villagers the idea for a scam to great the Americans: everyone invests money they didn't even have in order to contribute and set up the Andalusian folk decors, with the typical props of tambourine, Córdoba hat and frills. Imagine, [Castilian] peasants with frilly dresses and Córdoba hats and ruffled shirts: a pity.

The post-war was more terrible than wartime itself, and you can see that in *La colmena / The Beehive* (1982), which is a true film where every character is true, everything is very well portrayed.

Local cinemas disappeared because of speculators; also, the arrival of television finished them off.

Some considerations

The cinema frequented by the viewer, the popular *Dos de Mayo*, was situated at 32 *Espíritu Santo* Street. It opened in 1928 with a showing of *Viva Madrid, que es mi pueblo* (1928). It had 1,474 seats and offered films in continuous session; despite the lack of air conditioning, it attracted large audiences. It was bought in 1929 by the firm Julio César for a million pesetas; in 1969 a fire put an end to its activities. The house was rebuilt and the cinema disappeared to give way to other businesses.[3]

Several points of interest are raised by the viewer's testimony. In the first place, there is a clear sense of community, linked to the ritual of film attendance and stressed by the very act of giving the account: the frequent use of 'we', and the insistence on the fact that 'we all went', mark the experience of cinema-going as essentially shared. The space of the *cine de barrio* becomes a gigantic games room, an impossible extension of the home and at the same time an affordable alternative to it. If food and fuel rationing were an everyday home reality, the cinema offered the chance for the compulsive consumption of the available snack – sunflower seeds – and the warmth of the human congregation. There was a general passion for films: when new releases arrived, crowds queued around cinemas with such anticipation that the police had sometimes to intervene, and weekend tickets had to be booked in advance.[4] The feeling of heightened expectation was enhanced not only by the wait outside 'in order to grab a good seat', as the viewer says, but also by the lack of previous information as to the genre or plot of the film. The spectator was kept in the dark in more than the literal sense, as there was an element of surprise in the act of film-watching, and also a potential for disappointment when the picture in question did not respond to particular expectations: 'I did not like horror films, and as they never told you what the film was about, I would be in agony until it started . . . As the plot unfolded I could relax'. There is a strong contrast with modern spectators, who are inundated with trailers and printed information weeks before premières take place and in the cinema itself before the film even starts, and are therefore rarely able to watch a movie without a predetermined idea about it.[5]

A second aspect of interest has to do with the materiality of film projection. Cinemas situated in the commercially ebullient centre of Madrid, the streets of *Gran Vía* and *Fuencarral*, were for premières. Then there would be a re-release in a lesser cinema followed by a spell in a local cinema, a second re-release, and then the film finally arrived to the double-bill local cinema. The number of cinemas increased rapidly: in 1941 there were 63 in the city of Madrid, and 29 in the province; 94 in 1942, and around 100 in 1945. By 1951, the number had reached 124: 11 of these would have been for premières and 15 for re-releases. About 110 cinemas would be showing films in continuous session and 100 offered a double bill. Such diversity allowed people to see a film even after it had been removed from the release or re-release circuit (Cebollada and Santa Eulalia, 2000: 212). It also meant that the overwhelming majority of projection spaces catered for a growing demand for inexpensive access to films. Following a widespread architectural trend, première cinemas, above all those on *Gran Vía*, were conceived as 'picture palaces', lavish theatres with striking decors, and consequently some of them would include the word in their commercial name, for instance, *Palacio de la Prensa* or *Palacio de la Música* (Cebollada and Santa Eulalia, 2000: 193–7). The double-bill local cinemas were at the opposite end of the commercial scale: what was shown in them would already have done the rounds of the city but, in compensation, they could be enjoyed for a tenth of the original price. The public was certainly aware of the difference between these kinds of cinemas and expressed it with sarcastic and self-deprecating humour, as the account shows: 'we called it "The Palace of the [Sunflower] Seeds"'.[6] This irony is noteworthy. It is a sort of discursive seesaw which makes fun of material limitations by the almost surreal association between a magnificent building and the humblest of snacks, raising expectations of luxury with the first element and crushing them with the second. But it also produces an opposite pull, the acknowledgement that, for those who frequent it, the place is still a picture palace of a certain kind: one invested with familiarity, defined by the behaviour of its patrons, marked by a popular habit and located almost in a parallel universe to the real palaces, sometimes built not many streets away.

The humorous title given to the space where films were shown entails a complex sort of acceptance, a compound feeling that also pervades other moments of the testimony. If on the one hand there is a passing mention of the limitations of the technology, i.e. problems with faulty sound, it is not really an obstacle to the success of the show, as material shortcomings are stoically endured ('We were very patient'). On the other hand, the viewer's understanding of the strategies of programming, with first films working as 'fillers', do not prevent her from enjoying them for what they are, and from stating *a basic need for entertainment* that is collectively met: 'The first film entertained us a lot'. Such acceptance is not acritical: the testimony shows a simultaneous awareness of the socio-political *status quo* and of the power, purposes and limits of propaganda: 'There were people against it [*Gilda*] and they used to go to the cinema doors and protest, saying that it was against nature, against public morals. There were a lot of prudes in favour of what Franco said, but it was also due to the very strong repression at the time'.[7] The official news bulletin is described as a product which 'told you what [Franco] wanted people to know', and there is an ironic perception of its choice of materials, with the reference to 'all the water reservoirs under the sun' opened by the dictator or to the regime's unashamed promotion of large families. Still, the complexity lies again in the acceptance of those news bulletins for what they are, and in the acknowledgement that they have become the only source of information available and therefore have an unspecified and at the same time restricted value: 'There wasn't anything else, we didn't really know whether it was any good or if there was anything better'.[8] It would be easy, and probably too hasty, to reject this attitude as simple conformism. This particular member of that audience, instinctively acting as its representative, states her immediate awareness of the manipulation effected by censorship, and views the messages within those parameters; in contrast, present-day viewers with enormous amounts of information at their fingertips sometimes have neither the chance nor the sophistication to distance themselves from more subtle forms of manipulation in news and cinema.

Politics go hand in hand with the statement of aesthetic preferences. The testimony rejects the 'incredible' and dislocated patriotism (*patrioterismo*) of the *españoladas*. This label was applied either to hysterically epic films imbued with Francoist ideology and filled with characters that spoke in characteristic high-sounding mode, or to inanely folkloric pictures with Andalusian overtones. A similar attitude is expressed by the film director Jaime de Armiñán: 'During those difficult years (1943) we kids who were cinema fans [. . .] had an Olympian disdain for national films. It was enough to say with disgust "That's Spanish" and run away [. . .] from the Padilla, Salamanca or Vitoria, which were my local cinemas'.[9] In contrast, the testimony states a limitless and unproblematic admiration for American films, because they opened spaces of difference in several ways: they were finished products of a buoyant cinematic industry, they offered geographical, cultural and romantic escapism and entertainment, and at the same time they drew, by their mere existence, the horizon of another life. The preference for foreign (mostly American) productions already existed before the war and the misguided protectionism of the post-war period managed to do very little to curb it.[10] It is worth noting that the testimony is not totally dismissive of Spanish films, as it praises *El último cuplé* (1957) and *Surcos* (1951), and gives considerable space – albeit with a certain disengagement – to the melodramatic plot of *Locura de amor* (1948), becoming a distant precedent of recent histories of film which try to vindicate the quality of a section of post-war Spanish cinema.[11]

The mental space created mainly by American films becomes not only a refuge, but also a field of quiet resistance against the larger space of Spain as manufactured by the dictatorship's propaganda and reflected in films such as *Raza*.[12] In this confrontation, censorship backfired and provoked derision in different ways, perverting spectators' attitudes and even inadvertently training them in the ways of deconstruction. As stated in the testimony, the ridiculous changes to *Mogambo* affected the verisimilitude and intelligibility of the plot. Under censorship, allegedly created to preserve innocence and purity, the spectator becomes distrustful and assumes that what is shown on screen will always be a mutilated version of the original. The reservations that were applied to NO-DO intended portrayal of the real news contributed, in their extreme form, to the assumption that an alternative – i.e. complete – film existed in which shocking contents were more prominent than they really were. The rumours about *Gilda* were untrue; but such was their power of conviction, supported by the (uncut) violence of the famous slap given by Glenn Ford to Rita Hayworth, that in this testimony they have to be disproved by an argument from experience, that of double-checking: 'Everyone assumed that the censors had cut that scene because she went on stripping; imagine, it never was like that, because later on *I have seen the uncut version and it did not happen*, it was the glove and nothing else' (my italics).[13]

In the testimony, the viewer shows her analytical ability to identify the difference between herself as a young spectator in the 'palace' and as a more mature individual with repeated access to films later on in life. We have also seen her early skill at keeping a sceptical distance from the contents of the screen. This stands in stark contrast to the physical involvement of the audience at a *cine de verano* in Segovia attended by the writer Laurie Lee (my italics):

I was invited out into the plaza to watch a midnight ciné. Here, once again, the aqueduct came into use, with a cotton sheet strung from one of its pillars, on to which a pale beam of light, filtering from an opposite window, projected an ancient and jittery melodrama. Half the town, it seemed, had turned out for the show, carrying footstools and little chairs, while children swarmed on the rooftops and hung in clusters from the trees, their dark heads shining like elderberries.

The films's epic simplicity flickered across the Roman wall, vague and dim as a legend, but each turn of the plot was followed with gusto, *people jumping up and down in their seats, bombarding the distant shadows with advice and warning, mixed with occasional shouts of outrage. The appearance of the villain was met by darts and stones*, the doltish hero by exasperation, while a tide of seething concern was reserved for the plight of the heroine who spent a vigorously distressful time. During most of the film she hung from ropes in a tower, subject to the tireless affronts of the villain, but then the hero finally bestirred himself and disembowelled the villain with a knife, the audience was satisfied and went to bed.[14]

Regarding the relationship between spectator and screen stars, the testimony hints at the viewer's affinity with some famous actresses of her generation, such as Sara Montiel ('very young', as she was); it also provides an added insight into the link between cinema and politics, with its reference to the rumoured relationship between Imperio Argentina and the Nazi establishment. Above all, it illustrates another form of heightened collective experience, which in this case does not consist exactly of the ritual of cinema-going, as we saw before, but in the enjoyment of a specific highly entertaining product that was sweeping through box offices: 'Gone with the Wind: that was wonderful, it was the best of all; I loved American films, and I still do. Gone with the Wind: lots of people saw it, it lasted a very long time on release, lots of people; it was the cinema event of the day, a great film'. The film, precisely shot at the same time as the Francoist troops entered Barcelona, was not shown in Madrid until November 1950, with double passes and matinées during weekends to meet the demand it generated. Despite the fact that tickets were dear – the cheapest cost fifteen pesetas – they had to be booked in advance (Cebollada and Santa Eulalia, 2000: 212). The Spanish release of the film had been delayed due to World War II and also to the electricity restrictions imposed in post-war Spain. At the time it was made, its main protagonist's non-conformist resistance and opposition to imposed rules seemed to match the climate of increasing world hostilities; but when it was released in Spain, America had taken a turn towards the promotion of female domesticity after the end of the war and the return of men from the front, an ideology not at all dissimilar to the one held by the Francoist regime. The ideological décalage caused by this time-gap raises the question of how the message of the film would have been perceived in Spain, a question to which I return at the end of this article in note 20.

Cinematic and political complexities, together with the limitations imposed on the individual by the influence of context, are shown in the viewer's take on ¡Bienvenido, Mr. Marshall! On the one hand, she acknowledges that the extent of the film's socio-political critique escaped her at the time of first viewing, given that she was still in a state of what she herself describes as a sort of infancy – despite the fact that when the film was released she was a twenty-two year old woman. Only in a later stage of 'adulthood', that is to say, of more defined and developed political awareness, could she apprehend the extent of the film's satire and its hidden critique of the way in which

Spain had carried out the negotiations of the 1952 *Convenio* with the USA. On the other hand, even at this point she does not succeed in making a crucial connection: both the films, those entertainment products so enthusiastically and openly loved by her, and the surrender of strategic military bases to the United States – in exchange for the paltry foodstuffs she so much resents – were a result of the American ethos. She cites post-Franco films such as *La colmena* as 'true', and she also refers to the 'truthfulness' that she finally perceived in *¡Bienvenido, Mr. Marshall!* What is succinctly meant is that, for her, both films are on a par as reliable representations of the socio-political reality of the post-war era. In this respect, the testimony shows an interesting, even if delayed, reversal of the workings of escapism: the fictions on screen are a heightened revelation of the state of affairs in the country, not an alternative to it.[15] As John Hartley explains, 'not only do pictures dramatise and teach the democratic process, but also, for vast readerships, they are the very form in which that process is performed' (1992: 3).

The concept of 'audience', as such, is perhaps an impossible one. It is currently acknowledged that it is no longer possible to speak of the viewing public as a homogeneous entity: 'The spectator can no longer be seen as the single construct of an ideological apparatus. Audiences are multiplicitous. There is not a 'female' or 'male' spectator but different socio-cultural individuals all busy producing reality as the films rolls by. Age, gender, race, class, sexuality affect reception and meaning production' (Hayward, 2000: 124).

Until now, however, the attempts to define audiences in detail or describe them extensively have not progressed from plan to practice.[16] Precisely because the audience is neither a universal abstraction nor a passive object, there is a compelling need for empirical and ethnographical research on the topic.[17] At the beginning I mentioned that I was aware of the problems arising from my choice of case study. Small ethnographic snapshots such as the one examined here are obviously error-prone.[18] No minimally stable generalization can be made from them: in this particular case, several objections spring easily to mind. For instance, some of the points made in it could be applicable not only to audiences defined by the space of the Madrid double-bill local cinema, but also to other spectators outside Madrid or even outside Spain. It can also be argued that the site of viewing does not totally define an audience, because its members could occasionally switch places in the hierarchy of cinemas or because the relationship between individual and site cannot ultimately be fixed. In addition, a single sample of this sort is subject *per se* to a variety of limitations, from the influence of the individual personality to the tricks played by memory; from the unpredictable state of mind at the time of the account to the selection and creation of narratives for a given interlocutor (in this case, a group of foreign students); from the constraints established by factors such as gender and social class to the boundary-blurring influence of nostalgia. Precisely because of their limitations, snapshots such as this call for the creation and development of a wider database of testimonies. Fortunately, a considerable part of the generation concerned is still alive to tell the story; but this will not always be the case. As has been said in another context, 'film history is slipping away, before our very eyes, from the status of contemporary to that of near past' (Talens and Zunzunegui, 1998: 8n.5).

There have been different European recreations of the world of old and post-war cinemas: the Italian film *Cinema Paradiso* (Giuseppe Tornatore, 1989), the Catalan *Anita no perd el tren* (Ventura Pons, 2000), the play *La raya del pelo de William Holden* (José Sanchís Sinisterra, 2001), the autobiographical books of Terenci Moix and Guillermo Cabrera Infante.[19] For my purposes, despite their intrinsic value and the important information they contain – especially the writings of Moix and Cabrera – these works are limited precisely by their artistic intention. In the study of audiences there is a wide gap between these kinds of product and what we could see as their opposite, the abstract assertions made by some critics. To reconstruct the state of affairs of which the testimony examined here is a sample, i.e. to map the Spanish post-war audience, we must go beyond the particular, the speculative and the fictional.

This research has inevitable links with several intertwined disciplines such as the history of private life, oral history, ethnography, anthropology and others. Unfortunately, we cannot interrogate the recipients of the cultural products of our ancient past: written accounts are the only means available to find out about the people's expectations, behaviour and general reception of, for instance, a mass-entertainment product characteristic of the Spanish Golden Age, the *comedia*, whose development took place in the seventeenth-century theatres of Madrid. In the case of film, however, the possibility of direct contact with spectators grants us entry to an almost untapped field of research, which can allow us to retrace Spanish audiences of the past with the help of the unmediated present testimonies of their members. Some similar projects are already available, such as the CD *The Flicks. A Social History Project: Reminiscences of Cinema in Rural Chorley, Lancashire*, funded and assisted by the Heritage Lottery Fund, CDAA, The Projected Picture Trust, North West Sound Archive and Astley Hall Education and Outreach.[20]

Interviews and questionnaires, and participant observations, if available, would be the principal means to carry out such research. Secondary material can be found in written sources: journalistic accounts, autobiographies and diaries, etc (with the proviso that these genres are likely to include an element of elaboration, inherent in any human discourse, greater than the potential elaboration of answers in interviews and questionnaires). A project such as this would first require an identification of a significant group of potential interviewees and the earmarking of enough funds to carry the work out. According to the Communication, Cultural and Media Studies panel in the last (UK) national research assessment exercise, the overwhelming preponderance of text-based work over empirical research and fieldwork in this area of study can be explained by the lack of significant funding, as 'textual analysis can be more readily combined with other academic work commitments than sustained or intensive fieldwork'.[21] A possible objection to a project of this kind might be that there is nothing that a member of an audience can say that has not been said, perhaps in a better and more articulate way, by film critics. One may counter that each member of an audience is a critic with a defined experience of film viewing, and that it is in the act of conveying and establishing such experience and in the potential for new openings of meaning that the importance of individual accounts lies. All the necessary restrictions notwithstanding, the testimony studied here gives us an important insight into the emotional and social meaning of cinema, as viewed in a specific site, for a given individual who presents herself as a member of a Spanish generation united, albeit temporarily, by a single medium, instead of being defined from the outset, like later generations, by the availability and influence of a choice of alternatives to cinema such as television and video.[22] Her account reveals a need for entertainment, but also an understanding, sometimes gradual, of the realities of her time, an understanding that takes place beyond, around and through what is seen on screen. A certain scepticism and an ability to avoid taking the messages of Francoist propaganda at face value are also present, as is the sense of a lost community united both by pleasure and

by a capacity to overcome material restrictions by escapism or humour.
Such a community worked as an undeclared counterbalance to the one
defined by the pro-government Church of the time, full of strict rules
and constrictions and based on dynamics of submission. The local
cinema could therefore be seen as a space of physical and psychological shelter, a sort of church – and Church – of entertainment, some of
whose members would be capable of a *jouissance* tempered by the partial realization of the problematic relationship between reality and its
representation.[23] In this framework, accounts such as the one analysed
become a particular kind of defining confession, 'requiring, in
response to the public confessions of screen and page, constant private
soul-searching, comparison, internal interrogation and realignment of
the self', resulting in the creation of the self as a social other, that is to
say, as "the public"'(Hartley, 1993: 4).[24]

(To Andrew Miles Swarbrick)

Appendix: a viewer's tale (Spanish original)

En aquella época no había otra cosa, no había televisión; el cine era el
pasatiempo de la gente . . . No me gustaban las películas de miedo: como no
te informaban de qué iba, hasta que no empezaba yo estaba sufriendo . . .
Luego ya cuando se desarrollaba ya me relajaba.

Íbamos a un cine que se llamaba *Dos de Mayo*, pero lo llamábamos '*El
palacio de las pipas*'. Todo el mundo comía pipas todo el tiempo. Iba los
domingos, a la primera sesión, a las cuatro. Llegaba al cine a las tres para
esperar a que abrieran, y hacía cola hasta las cuatro para coger buen sitio.
Íbamos todos . . . íbamos todos. El cine estaba en la Calle Dos de Mayo [en
realidad, en la Calle Espíritu Santo], en el centro, que ahora es el barrio de
Maravillas [o Malasaña], un barrio muy popular porque de ahí viene la
movida madrileña . . . El cine costaba una peseta cincuenta por sesión;
cuando yo empecé a trabajar, a los dieciocho años [es decir, en 1949],
ganaba sesenta y cinco pesetas a la semana. Desde luego, el dinero había que
juntarlo con esfuerzo . . .

Lo primero que salía era el NO-DO, un informativo del régimen franquista que te contaba lo que [Franco] quería que supiera el pueblo, y como
era la única información directa que teníamos pues nos gustaba todo,
porque no teníamos otra cosa; y lo que nos echaran . . . [En el NO-DO,
Franco] inauguraba todos los pantanos del mundo en esas ceremonias, todas
esas cosas. También era muy importante que premiaba a familias numerosas
de catorce y quince hijos; una pena. No era para nada como el telediario
ahora; entonces sólo eran noticias locales y muy restringidas. No había otra

cosa; tampoco estábamos muy informados de si eso era lo bueno o había algo mejor. Echaban dos películas, era programa doble. La primera era de relleno, y la segunda era la importante. La primera película nos entretenía mucho; entre la primera y la segunda había un intermedio, y allí en el cine salía un letrero que ponía 'Servicio en el ambigú'. Nosotros, aparte de ser muy resignados, cuando la película se oía muy mal porque el material era de lo más deficiente, pateaban y decían 'isonoro, sonoro!'. Si la película era muy mala la gente no tenía más opción que quedarse o marcharse; a veces se marchaba, pero pocas; no había nada más que hacer.

La primera película que vi fue *Goyescas* (1942). Las películas españolas que nos ponían eran las españoladas; eran muy patrióticas: había una que se llamaba *Raza*; el guión lo escribió Franco con seudónimo, y era increíble. También [era muy famosa] *Locura de amor*, con la historia de Juana la Loca, la mujer de Felipe el Hermoso, que le había sido muy infiel, y se muere, y ella estaba loca de amor por él, y se pasó la vida desterrada [de la corte] por toda España con el ataúd del marido hasta que quiso que lo enterraran o la obligaron a enterrarlo. Las actrices del momento eran Aurora Bautista y Sara Montiel, muy jovencita . . . Había otro tipo de películas españolas, como *Surcos*, que cuenta cuándo empezó la emigración de pueblos a ciudades, cómo se desmoronaban las familias por ir a otra vida mejor que después no era tan buena; dejaban los surcos por otra vida mejor que jamás consiguieron.

Pero las películas que a mí más me gustaban eran, desde luego, las americanas: *Gilda*. Con *Gilda* pasó que como la censura era tan terrible, pues la imaginación iba más allá de la realidad: entonces ¿os acordáis de cuando se quitaba Gilda el guante? Se suponía todo el mundo que ahí la censura lo había cortado porque al final acababa desnudándose; imagínate, que eso no ha existido, porque yo luego he visto la versión íntegra y eso no pasó, se quedó en el guante nada más. Y luego, pegar una bofetada así, tan tremenda . . . Había gente que estaba en contra de eso e iba a la puerta del cine y se manifestaba porque decían que eso era contra natura, contra la moral; había muchos beatos a favor de lo que Franco decía, pero también era por la represión tan grande que había. *Lo que el viento se llevó*: eso fue una maravilla, estaba por encima de todo, es que el cine americano a mí me chiflaba, y aún es el que más me gusta. *Lo que el viento se llevó*: iba muchísima gente, duró mucho tiempo en el cine, iba mucha gente, fue un acontecimiento cinematográfico, entonces era una gran película. Había películas que por la censura eran incomprensibles, por ejemplo, *Mogambo*. Estaban todos en una selva, en un safari; uno de los actores era Clark Gable – había quien le llamaba 'cara de cable'. Los diálogos eran increíbles: ¡para que no hubiera adulterio lo cambiaron de tal forma que terminó siendo un incesto! Grace Kelly estaba casada, pero como era muy duro que el marido estuviera delante, prácticamente, porque ella acaba con Clark Gable, pues entonces lo cambiaron de tal forma que el marido era su hermano.

Había películas musicales que tuvieron mucho éxito: *El último cuplé*, una película muy buena con todos los cuplés de la época y del Madrid clásico, con organillos, fiestas populares; era muy jovencita Sara Montiel . . . También estaba Imperio Argentina, que hizo *Goyescas*, y en la guerra española hizo mucho cine en Alemania y por eso decían que era nazi. Y Hitler la tenía como a una diosa, era una estrella internacional. Y en esa película también aparece Rafael Rivelles, una primera figura del teatro, marido de María Fernanda Ladrón de Guevara. El teatro era muy bueno pero – igual – estaba muy censurado; porque Buero Vallejo sacaba unas obras buenísimas, *Historia de una escalera*, pero ahí estaba la censura.

Y, desde luego, *¡Bienvenido, Mr. Marshall!* Esa película fue un éxito pero no al nivel que tenía que haber sido. Franco nos vendió a los americanos, y era, verdaderamente, la parodia de lo que nos había costado: las bases de Zaragoza, Rota y Torrejón, y eso a cambio de leche en polvo, un queso de plástico y carne americana de bote; y entonces esa película es el ejemplo de la verdadera realidad, pero la gente no comprendió el alcance de la verdadera historia. Porque luego yo ya cuando la he visto en televisión cuando ya he sido adulta es cuando he comprendido lo que era y entonces, cuando la vi en el cine, no. Es una sátira increíble – Berlanga es de lo mejorcito que tenemos. Es un pueblo castellano de tierra adentro de los más pobres, y entonces como en las fiestas del pueblo se presentó un empresario que llevaba a una estrella de folklore, pues entonces aprovechó el momento para darles la idea del montaje que tenían que hacer para recibir a los americanos. Todos empeñaron lo que no tenían para poner un poquito y poner los decorados folklóricos andaluces, la clásica historia de la pandereta y el sombrero cordobés y los volantes. Imagínate a la gente campesina vestida de faralaes y con sombrero cordobés y con chorreras y todo eso: una pena.

La posguerra era una época más terrible que la propia guerra, y eso se ve en *La colmena*, que es una película auténtica en la que cada personaje es auténtico; todo está muy bien reflejado.

Los cines de barrio desaparecieron por la especulación; la televisión también acabó con ellos.

Notes

1   A great deal of research on the topic has been carried out within USA and the UK, with significant emphasis on television audiences. David Morley highlights a guiding principle for the present article: the need to reconsider the relation of micro and macro processes and to 'sort the winks from the twitches' (1997: 137) in the development of ethnographies. Staiger (1992) and Butsch (2000) offer historical perspectives on the American domain. In the UK, Kuhn (2002) studies English film-goers of the thirties; Jancovich, Faire, and Stubbings (2003) look at the history of film-going in Nottingham.

2 An irreverent pun based on the phonetic similarity between Clark Gable and 'cara de cable' (i.e. 'cable face').

3 Cebollada and Santa Eulalia (2000: 275). This is the most complete work about the cinemas of Madrid. A parallel study on a Catalan cinema can be found in Colomer Amat (1995).

4 Cebollada and Santa Eulalia (2000: 210–11).

5 About this lack of information, we need to assume that the viewer's assertion refers to the B-movies and 'fillers', as the famous releases were the object of much talk, and in some cases word of mouth would have been enough. There is, to the best of my knowledge, an untapped territory for research in the advertising angle: who had access to film magazines? How much information was given in them or in the modest leaflets printed by some cinemas? Were there policies on advertising? (and if so where did they come from: the intuition of the impresario on how to whet the appetite of the public, or the influence of censorship?) To what extent and on what contexts was word-of-mouth operative? The writer Terenci Moix speaks in his memoirs about his privileged access to film publicity, as his family owned a modest business where advertisements would be sent to be disseminated amongst clients or displayed at the shop: 'Pasquines amarillentos, impresos a toda prisa en cualquier imprenta barata de las cercanías. Tipografías tristonas que anunciaban, en letras rudimentarias y carentes de imaginación, los títulos de las dos películas de la semana, amén de las frases de publicidad destinadas a potenciar sus atractivos. En medio de aquella composición desangelada, aparecían does recuadros que contenían a su vez dos folletos de colores. Eran los inolvidables "programas", que los demás mortales obtenían en los cines, previo pago de su localidad' (1990: 82). His account reveals a similar sense of a shared experience and the same passion for cinema as the testimony studied here: 'La costumbre del cine de barrio no implicaba una elección. Íbamos semanalmente, pusieran lo que pusiesen', that is to say: attendance to the local cinema, far from being the product of choice, was indiscriminate (1990: 85).

6 The denomination does not seem to have been exclusive: it was also applied to other cinemas such as the *Doré*, now Filmoteca Española, when its initial prestige dwindled, or to the *Padilla*, where it was the favourite snack of its (mainly juvenile) public; Cebollada and Santa Eulalia (2000: 274, 330). The film director José Luis Garci recalls the cinema *Alcalá* which he calls the most aristocratic *Palicio de las pipas* (1997: 8).

7 Falangist demonstrations took to the street in 1947, when the film arrived in Spain: images of Rita Hayworth were covered in ink, and priests threatened damnation for those watching it (Vernon, 1997).

8 In 1942, NO-DO (*Noticiarios y documentales cinematográficos*) was made compulsory in every programme, while the activities of indepen-

dent reporters and documentary-makers were suppressed. See Rodríguez (1999); Tranche and Sánchez-Biosca (2001).

9   'En aquellos difíciles años [1943] los niños que éramos entonces aficiona-dos al cine ... despreciábamos olímpicamente las películas nacionales. Bastaba decir con asco "ésa es española" para huir ... del Padilla, el Sala-manca o el Victoria, que eran las salas que yo tenía a mano' (Armiñán, 1993: 214). The author goes on to praise American films, such as *Inter-mezzo*, *Wings* or *Suspicion*, all of them shown in Spain during 1943.

10 Fernández Blanco (1998: 10–13).

11 'Me gustaría colaborar para erradicar por completo el injusto desprecio creado durante los años más duros de la posguerra [*sic*] entre los int-electuales y la gente de izquierdas contra el cine español, y que en buena medida todavía sigue vigente, para que, de una vez por todas, se dejaran los viejos prejuicios a un lado y se comenzase a apreciar el auténtico valor de una buena parte de su produción' (1997: 12). In 1955, the film director Juan Antonio Bardem had declared that Spanish cinema was 'politically ineffectual, socially fake, intellectually negligible, aestheti-cally useless and industrially stunted' (Caparrós Lera, 1999: 88).

12 The utopianism of entertainment is connected to social needs: the reason why entertainment works is because 'it is not just left-overs from history, it is not just what show business, or "they", force on the rest of us, it is not simply the expression of eternal needs – it responds to eternal needs created by society' (Dyer, 1985: 228).

13 Here arises a fascinating topic: that of the power of cinema's make-believe nature and its ability to manipulate the collective unconscious. Viewers of Bette Davis' *Jezebel*, totally shot in black and white, recall *having seen* her dressed in red, as this is a key plot element, frequently and significantly spoken about in the film. The viewer in our testimony, with whom I had recently the chance to check this point, is under the same belief.

14 This excerpt comes from Lee's novel *As I Walked Out One Midsummer Morning*, as quoted in Morris (1980: 5).

15 'The charge of escapism which is often levelled at film is probably based on the sense of separation from reality, which is highlighted as we leave the cinema [. . .]'. Cinema offers a vicarious involvement where 'representation appears as perception' (Turner, 1988: 109–11). Conversely, this part of the testimony illustrates the fact that the viewer finally comes to discern the film's perception of and rap-prochement with reality beyond its representation. *¡Bienvenido, Mr. Marshall!* was originally commissioned to be one more *españolada* with the accustomed Andalusian elements (see Besas, 1985: 35–6). The film managed to turn the conventions of the genre inside out with enormous wit, and thus convey an allegorical political message which

passed the censors and, as attested by our viewer, remained latent in some spectators. Others reacted in a very different way: when the picture was shown at the Cannes festival, the president of the jury, the American actor Edward G. Robinson, tried to ban the film as he considered it an insult to USA (see Caparrós Lera, 1999: 86).

16   Meers (2001: 141).

17   Meers (2001: 140, 142). This idea was present in the 2002 Oscars Ceremony: for the first time, a clip with the opinions about cinema of different members of the audience was shown. Despite its elaboration, following advertising techniques, with the presence of celebrities and a carefully selected sample of individuals made to look deliberately representative, it illustrated the general need to hear the voice of the spectators.

18   Meers (2001: 141).

19   Terenci Moix, *El cine de los sábados. Memorias. El peso de la paja/1* (Barcelona: Planeta, 1990); Guillermo Cabrera Infante, *Cine o sardina* [1997] (Madrid: Suma de Letras, 2001).

20   This CD includes an introduction, followed by accounts of cinema-viewing by members of the audience in the villages of Adlington, Brinscall, Coppull, Croston, Eccleston, Mawdesley and Whittle-le-Woods. The recordings were made during the summer of 2001 and are introduced by the radio and television presenter Judy Merry. I thank Ian Robinson, chairman of the Chorley Film Society, for letting me know about the existence of this project.

21   As reported by Ruth Pott-Negrine in 'A bleak future for research?, *Student Direct. Mancunian edition*, 18 March 2002, p. 20.

22   The potential of contemporary audiences for extreme disgregation does not escape those in charge of film projection: 'What does Chris [Stracham, from Harwich *Electric Palace*] consider his audience to be? "It's not an audience. You've got 20-odd audiences, and there can be very little crossover between them. Occasionally, you'll get two different audiences going to a film and there can be antipathy between them"' ('Reel Lives', by Simon Hattenstone, *The Guardian. Friday Review*, 1 March 2002, p. 3).

23   'Since people vary according to their gender, race, religion, age, class, nationality, politics, tastes, etc., the same movie will often provoke different reactions. While the persuasive rhetoric of most mainstream films is designed to elicit a common response or "preferred reading" from viewers no matter what their politics, politically-conscious viewers are capable of so-called "oppositional" or "aberrant" decodings' (Walker and Chaplin, 1997: 75). The ideology of Francoism as expressed in films such as *Raza* has been labelled a 'paranoid discourse' (González Requena, 1998: 88); its lack of definition – specially during its early stages – and its

inability to produce a historical project or a relevant connection to the country's present situation have also been pointed out (González Requena, 1998: 83). These matters are illustrated by the recent finding of a re-editing of *Raza*. It shows how the 1941 version, anti-American and openly fascist, was arranged in 1951 to look pro-American and anti-communist, in order to accommodate the state of international affairs generated by the cold war and the new friendship between Spain and the States (Talens, 1998: 68). The new copy was substituted for the original one in the archives; it is impossible to determine which version would have been the one seen by the viewer in our testimony.

24 An economic analysis of Spanish audiences from 1968 to 1995 can be found in Fernández Blanco (1998). *Nickelodeón: Madrid y el cine*, pp. 109–19, offers the results of a survey carried out amongst Spanish film-makers (directors, producers, actors), critics and writers, about the film that represented better the city of Madrid. The result was *Surcos*. What follows is a proposal for a research method. The testimony analysed could be part of a project entitled, for instance, 'Popular Cinema of the Spanish Post-War: Spaces and Audiences'. The following points should appear in the interviews with spectators regarding the time-span studied:
   • Quantifiable: (1) Origin: cities (with a distinction between big cities such as Madrid and Barcelona, provincial capitals and smaller towns), villages, countryside; (2) Gender; (3) Age (with the possibility of estab-lishing age groups in each generation); (4) Class; (5) Level of educa-tion; (6) Ideological leanings; (7) Religious beliefs; (8) Cinemas visited; (9) Frequency of cinema-going; (10) Genre preferences and/or dislikes.
   • Non quantifiable (left for the researcher to evaluate after a compar-ative study of results): (11) Level of *jouissance*; (12) Critical output; (13) Awareness of context; (14) Consciousness of being part of a col-lective; (15) Ability for double perspective (this last point is of extreme importance, as it affects almost all the quantifiable ones, i.e. the spectator may have belonged to one class during the post-war and to a different one at the time of the testimony; in what ways can this influence the account given?).
This list does not pretend to be exhaustive: there are other factors that could be seen as important – for instance, speaking another national lan-guage at a time when linguistic diversity was politically persecuted, etc.
      If we had a representative number of answers to the preceding points, we could attempt, for instance, to confirm or disqualify a couple of hypotheses arising from the study of the present testimony. Would audiences have perceived the heroine of *Gone with the Wind* as an outlet for feelings of alienation from or rebellion against the dicta-torship? Could the popularity of the film – besides its value as an enter-tainment product – have been based on such a perception? Could its

viewing have been in some instances a vicarious and symbolic statement of political opposition? Would this process have been conscious? Would it have been active in the minds of both men and women? Could it have taken place in the picture palace as well as in the double-bill local cinema? Or again, which spectators would have perceived the full extent of the critique involved in *¡Bienvenido, Mr. Marshall!*: those with a higher level of education, those of a certain age, those with a definite ideological adscription? The research proposed would also allow us to explore an issue linked to the former two points: whether the lack of problematization in the reception of American cinema is a feature particular to the testimony studied, or whether it was common to a cross-section of the spectatorship at the time. This is just a sample of the topics that could be illuminated by an ethnographic approach.

The result of such research should entail a wider understanding of audiences in their social, historical, political and cultural contexts. Hopefully, it could also give clues about other European audiences while defining the specificity of Spanish spectators at the time. Last but not least, the possibility of reconstructing the life of the spaces where films were shown from the point of view of the audience appears an enticing one. The ultimate objective of this research could be twofold: the creation of a recorded archive of spectatorship, and the formulation of its analysis, evaluations and conclusions in a general study.

I would like to thank Peter Evans, Jo Labanyi, Jeremy Lawrance and Óscar Varona for all their helpful suggestions.

Bibliography

Armiñán, Jaime de (1993) *El cine de la Flor*, Madrid: Nickelodeón.

Besas, Peter (1985) *Behind the Spanish Lens: Spanish Cinema under Fascism and Democracy*, Denver: Arden Press.

Butsch, Richard (2000) *The Making of American Audiences*, Cambridge: Cambridge University Press.

Caparrós Lera, J. M. (1999) *Historia crítica del cine español: desde 1897 hasta hoy*, Barcelona: Ariel.

Cebollada, Pascual and Mary G. Santa Eulalia (2000) *Madrid y el cine. Panorama filmográfico de cien años de historia*, Madrid: Comunidad de Madrid.

Colomer Amat, E. (1995) *Saló Imperial, un cinema històric a Sabadell*, Sabadell: Societat Cinematogràfica del Saló Imperial.

Dyer, Richard (1985) 'Entertainment and Utopia', in Bill Nichols (ed.) *Movies and Methods, II*, Berkeley: University of California Press, 220–32.

Fernández Blanco, Víctor (1998) *El cine y su público en España. Un análisis económico*, Madrid: Fundación Autor.

Garci, José Luis (1997) 'Madrid y el cine', in *Nickelodéon. Revista trimestral de cine: Madrid y el cine*, 7.

González Requena, Jesús (1998) 'Vida en Sombras: The *Recusado*'s Shadow in Spanish Postwar Cinema', in Jenaro Talens and Santos Zunzunegui (eds.) *Modes of Representation in Spanish Cinema*, Minnesota: University of Minnesota Press, 83–103.

Hartley, John (1992) *The Politics of Pictures: The Creation of the Public in the Age of Popular Media*, London: Routledge.

Hayward, Susan (2000) *Cinema Studies: The Key Concepts*, London: Routledge.

Jancovich, Mark and Lucy Faire with Sarah Stubbings (2003) *The Place of the Audience: The Cultural Geographies of Film Consumption*, London: British Film Institute.

Kuhn, Annette (2002) *An Everyday Magic: Cinema and Cultural Memory*, London: I.B. Tauris.

Meers, Phillippe (2001) 'Is There an Audience in the House?', in *Journal of Popular Film and Television*, 29, Autumn, 138–44.

Morley, David (1997) 'Theoretical Orthodoxies: Textualism, Constructivism and the "New Ethnography"', in Marjorie Ferguson and Peter Golding (eds) *Cultural Studies in Question*, London: Sage, 121–37.

Morris, C. B. (1980) *This Loving Darkness: The Cinema and Spanish Writers 1920–1936*, Oxford: Oxford University Press–University of Hull.

Rodríguez, Saturnino (1999) *El NO-DO. Catecismo social de una época*, Madrid: Editorial Complutense.

Staiger, Janet (1992) *Interpreting Films: Studies in the Historical Reception of American Cinema*, Princeton: Princeton University Press.

Talens, Jenaro (1998) 'The Referential Effect: Writing the Image of the War', in Jenaro Talens and Santos Zunzunegui (eds.) *Modes of Representation in Spanish Cinema*, Minnesota: University of Minnesota Press, 58–72.

Talens, Jenaro and Santos Zunzunegui (1998) 'Introduction: History as Narration. Rethinking Film History from Spanish Cinema', in Jenaro Talens and Santos Zunzunegui (eds.) *Modes of Representation in Spanish Cinema*, Minnesota: University of Minnesota Press, 1–45.

Torres, Augusto M. (1997) *El cine español en 119 películas*, Madrid: Alianza Editorial.

Tranche, Rafael R. and Vicente Sánchez-Biosca (2001) *NO-DO. El tiempo y la memoria*, Serie Mayor, Madrid: Cátedra / Filmoteca Española.

Turner, Graeme (1988) *Film as Social Practice*, London: Routledge.

Vernon, Kathleen M. (1997) 'Reading Hollywood in/and Spanish Cinema: From Trade Wars to Transculturation', in Marsha Kinder (ed.) *Refiguring Spain: Cinema/Media/Representation*, Durham: Duke University Press.

Walker, John A. and Sarah Chaplin (1997) *Visual Culture: An Introduction* Manchester: Manchester University Press.

7

Populism, the national-popular and the politics of Luis García Berlanga

Steven Marsh

The cinema of Luis García Berlanga presents a problem. Berlanga, who announced his retirement in 1999 after the release of his latest film *Paris-Tombuctú*, is a constant disruptive presence in Spanish culture of the second half of the twentieth century. If Buñuel has been the historical and aesthetic benchmark for critics of Spanish cinema and the marketing of Pedro Almodóvar has provided its international launching pad, the attention paid to Berlanga has faced problems intimately related to politics and particularly those of national identity. His lack of success outside Spain has frequently been attributed to some sort of untranslatable Spanishness. Since the death of Franco he has been the subject of several books in Spanish which have all tended to follow the same format: a lengthy and highly entertaining interview with the director followed by synopses of his films. In this vein, there has been a successful endeavour to construct a *persona* called Luis García Berlanga that has very little to do with his cinema: Berlanga the eroticist, Berlanga the professional *Valenciano*, the (safely) apolitical anarchist, the raconteur, the compulsive liar, the mercurial doubter. However, just as there is agreement on Berlanga the *persona*, there is no such consensus on whether his cinema is subversive or not. Indeed, like the genre of comedy itself, he is often considered a conservative (Cañique and Grau, 1993: 275).

   In this chapter I will argue that the problems surrounding criticism of Berlanga, and the source of his complexity, revolve around a contested notion both of the 'popular' and the nation: that he is to be located at a slippery juncture somewhere between popular culture and cultural populism. What is indeed constant in Berlanga's work is his drawing upon popular traditions and practices: the fairground, the *fiesta*, the street parade and the crowd. It is precisely his fidelity to a peculiar vision of popular comedy, woven within the interstices of national and international culture, which never ends well, that has confused critics and confounded efforts to make of him an auteur. It is noteworthy that while Berlanga has been inextricably linked to a discourse on Spanishness, he remains the most vigorous and acerbic critic of Spanish *alegría* (joy). Much of this critique, like that of Fellini (the director with whom he has been most closely identified), concerns Berlanga's particular vision of the grotesque and the body.

Italian communist leader Antonio Gramsci proposed a means by which apparently conventional beliefs and ideologies can prove contestatory. Analysing Mussolini's Italian state, he identified the securing of *consent* as a key feature in the popular success of fascism from which leftists had much to learn. Gramsci's thinking, nonetheless, is keen to distinguish between the uncritical exaltation and consequent instrumentalization of 'the people' that constitutes populism – which in the case of Spain often foregrounds *alegría* – and his own theory of 'the national-popular' that recognizes the complexity of 'the people'. 'The people', he says, 'are not a homogenous cultural collectivity but present numerous and variously combined cultural stratifications which, in their pure form, cannot always be identified within specific historical popular collectivities' (1985: 189). The popular for Gramsci is thus a resource and not an end in itself. The point lies in the potential of the 'humus of popular culture' (1985: 102) with regard to a political project.

Closely connected to this is Mikhail Bakhtin's term *heteroglossia*. While Gramsci describes the ideological battleground within which the different discourses of civil society engage as hegemony, heteroglossia is Bakhtin's definition of socially stratified language in which an 'official' dialect has established dominance but it is one that strives in permanent dialogue with alternative or opposing languages. In Gramscian thinking, the struggle for hegemony is exemplified by his comment that 'the jargons of various professions, of specific societies innovate in a molecular way' (1985: 178). In Bakhtin, meanwhile, there is a similar contest of competing voices that extends beyond linguistics to the matrix of power relations. Elsewhere Bakhtin delineates the inverted hierarchy of mediaeval festivity in ways that I hope to demonstrate are relevant to Berlanga. In Bakhtin downward movement and low positioning and its concomitant upward and superior opposites are disrupted by the comicity of carnival (1984:

370). To this end, Bakhtin theorizes a positive representation of the grotesque body marked by a cycle of consumption and defecation that proves germane to the work of Berlanga.

One of the distinctive features of the work of Berlanga is the chorality that connects national tradition with subaltern practices and tactics. The chorus in Berlanga is always cacophonic, never harmonious. A stream of elements much cherished by authority come off badly in his films amid the discord provoked by the popular, from the institution of marriage and the family to the state itself. It is my view that the mature work of Berlanga stands at the crux of the Spanish native tradition, and *Plácido* (1961) and *El verdugo* (1963), together with the earlier *¡Bienvenido, Mr. Marshall!* (1952), are generally accepted as constituting his finest movies. In the following discussion of these films, I will suggest that the key to Berlanga's work lies in an exploration of how the shifting sands of sedimented and emergent discourses are both reproduced and reworked in individuals and communities. Furthermore, the objective of this chapter is to discuss and develop a theory of film comedy within which Berlanga can be located and thenceforth examine how the cinema of Berlanga acts subversively upon our received notions of how we perceive the nation-state and its subjects once subjected to comic interrogation.

Plácido is a film in which unitary notions of society are exposed, often debunked and frequently re-aligned. A Christmas film with a direct relationship to Frank Capra's *It's a Wonderful Life* (1946), it follows the day-long odyssey of the eponymous Plácido and his family. Pressed for money and time, desperate to pay an instalment on the motorized cart that provides him with a livelihood before sundown, Plácido and his clan to and fro across a provincial town. Cajoled and coerced by the overweening Gabino Quintanilla (the organizer of the event), they act as messengers, gophers and providers of public transport for the reluctant bourgeois hosts of a displaced crew of tramps and minor cinema stars who are relocated one Christmas Eve to the dinner tables of the local well-to-do under the auspices of a charitable campaign whose slogan reads: *Sit a Poor Person at Your Dining Table* (a richly significant echo of similar Francoist events of the period).[1]

Slogans are important to Berlanga. While generally they are populist instruments employed by dominant groups and designed to weld 'the people' within a cross-class, seamless and fixed consensus, in Berlanga slogans prove to be anything but straightforward or immutable. Invariably slogans are misinterpreted and distorted. The comicity of this film lies, not so much in the exposure of Catholic hypocrisy, as in the dismemberment of hierarchy by means of adjacency and closeness. In sloganizing there exists the proposition of a sociological unity which in turn provokes its own disfunction and fragmentation.

Plácido's wife, Emilia, administers the municipal toilets, located in the town's main square, which also provide the place where the entire family congregate and, at first, appear to live. There is in this a scatalogical framework which determines the parameters of the film. In a movie elaborated largely around a series of dining tables, it is in the spirit of Bakhtinian set-piece that the initial terms of the film should be established within the environment of public evacuation. This is a sequence poised around the duality of the body. For Bakhtin, who draws attention to the direct correspondence in folk culture between the face and the buttocks, debasement involves renewal.

Plácido's brother Julián, furthermore, introduces an element that will become central to the film: that of the infirm body. When Plácido asks him to lend him money to pay the instalment on his motorized cart Julián responds with some pride: 'You've a business. I am an invalid'. The literal body complete with deficiencies and disfunctions – and Julián is lame and limping – often undoes dominant metaphors of a unitary body politic. Further, the body is pointedly central to the disruption of gender oppositions. Plácido marches straight into the toilets to Quintanilla's cry of: 'Watch out! That's the door to the Ladies'. Moments later when Quintanilla himself enters by the same door, Emilia shrieks: 'You! Through the door to the Gents, scoundrel!'

One of the clearest Bakhtinian-like sequences in the film occurs shortly after the scene in the municipal toilets. The festive parade (or *cabalgata*) sets off towards the town from the railway station and meets a funeral cortege midway on the hill. If the key to Bakhtin's biocorporal world lies in the proximity of life and death, as symbolized in the duality of bodily functions, the head-on collision of carnivalesque floats and the hearse reinforces it. Moreover, the disputed discourses of the film manifest themselves through the shroud of established order in the production of excess. Quintanilla in a moment of overzealous piety chides the military band for not having removed their caps as a mark of respect for the deceased and is rewarded with a lesson in military etiquette, to which he replies by resort to *alegría*: 'Ah you did it in military style. I didn't know that. Very well then now, let's see some *alegría*, more *alegría*! *Alegría*!'

Plácido is a film promiscuously strewn with coy references to the symbols of established order. Moments previous to the parade, amid the chaos of the railway station, the *guardia civil* are seen escorting a line of grim-faced women through the crowd awaiting the arrival of the starlets. Their function as prisoners' relatives becomes clear when a woman comments: 'Poor men, having to spend these days in gaol'. Just as notions of 'charity' or slogans are open-ended and vulnerable to plural interpretation, the crowd provides a kind of camouflage for political comment. The comic mode thrives on this kind of contiguity.

The much commented technique that Berlanga employs to achieve this cacophonic effect is the long take. The long take or sequence shot allows for a fluidity between individuals and the crowd, it both sets one off against the other and locates individual agency in a collective context. It is a representation of excess and multiple difference. Technically it is the absolute opposite of the shot-counter-shot, which Berlanga almost never uses. The shot-counter-shot (very much favoured in classical Hollywood) is both a means of generating suspense between two individuals and a convention for representing dialogue. The long take, on the other hand, allows Quintanilla to leap from the float to berate the band members and Plácido to descend and negotiate with the man to whom he owes money. It permits a flow of different persons across the same 'space' within the same 'time'. This synchronicity expands space while also allowing individuals to voice their specific concerns without removing them from the crowd from which they emerge. This permits the representation of two (or more) completely different contexts to be represented simultaneously, as is the case of the processesion and the funeral cortege or of the arrival of the actors and the line of prisoners relatives. Furthermore, it enables the Bakhtinian schema of *up* and *down* to be complicated. The starlets who are raised *up* at the train window and on steps are sneered at by the haughty Señora Galán, the campaign president, who says of one of the actresses: 'She must be a hussy'. Meanwhile, in a shot that echoes the previous toilet scene, we catch a brief glimpse of a man on the train urinating in the toilet compartment.[2] The reception committee, on the other hand, consisting of the coalition of religious and business representatives are *down* among the crowd adjacent to the prisoners' relatives and the *guardia civil* escorting them. There is a certain subversive politics in the proximity, in the physical adjacency of these sequences that is cinematically reinforced by the sequence shot. Moreover, it is precisely in this type of shot that other critics have indulged in the rhetoric of national affiliation. What has been enclosed within an essentialist view of collective and unitary Spanishness is, in my view, precisely the means by which the fissures surrounding the discourse of the nation are produced.

There is a sheen of legal, medical, military and religious discourse enshrouding this film that is punctured by the comedy. The porous discourse of civic cohesion established at the beginning of the film through the campaign slogan is multi-layered and sustained by discourses of medicine and law as is made clear by the central sequences at the dinner tables. These sequences are all long takes, technically the same as the *cabalgata*/funeral cortege in clustered and claustrophobic miniature. What is envisaged as unchanging in the slogan, moreover, is problematized in references to medicine and law. The radio journalist, engaged as a master of ceremonies to publically convey this impression, sees his populist efforts consistently undone in similar terms to those of Quintanilla whose notion of *alegría* sits ill with military etiquette. Faced with one guest's curmudgeonly relish – the old man diagnoses himself as suffering from cancer while interviewed live and is disgusted by the notion of eating langoustines – the radio reporter desperately hisses: '*Alegría, alegría*'.

Immediately following this scene, the camera shifts to another residence where one of the poor guests, Pascual, has been taken genuinely ill. Álvaro, the son-in-law of the Helguera family household, takes his pulse. As is apparent in almost all of Álvaro's ignominious interventions he knows nothing yet claims to be an expert on everything, but particularly matters concerning law and medicine. His expertise is continually exposed. Solemnly he takes Pascual's wrist and fails to find the pulse. Pascual's moving head, nonetheless, demonstrates that he is patently alive.

The interesting feature of the legal and medical discourses is that, in spite of efforts to bind them together and of the fact that they sit well as accoutrements of respectability, they continually produce disjunctions. Álvaro is some kind of lawyer who is exposed by the legalistic vocabulary he employs. His expertise – in law as well as in medicine – relies exclusively upon gesture and rhetoric. He goes through the motions of finding Pascual's pulse and brandishes a thermometer. It is within this flimsy framework of the vacuous jargon of *experts*, moreover, that military and religious doctrine emerges.

Álvaro's quackery is repeated, as we will see, in the figure of the dentist Don Poli, the neighbour from downstairs who is summoned to administer to Pascual. There is a doubling here of both legal and medical discourses and a consequent disjunction that is further reinforced by the dentist's accompanying poor person, Rivas, who makes the medical diagnosis of Pascual's illness. Similarly, it is upon the testimony of Rivas that Álvaro makes a dubious legal diagnosis 'They live in a state of concubinage!' Álvaro's outrage is legally flawed; the Spanish word *concubinaje* was the legal term for male adultery not for unmarried cohabitation; just as Rivas makes a correct diagnosis of Pascual's illness, he also employs a legally more correct term to describe the nature of Pascual and Concheta's domestic arrangement when he says simply that they are 'together'.

The language of *appearance* is the gelling material of these formal discourses (legal and medical) but they also prove their undoing. Appearances not only justify authority, they come to undermine reliable diagnosis. They both sustain authority and demonstrate its falaciousness. Don Poli is revealed as an oddity by virtue of the fact that he dines with his guest Rivas and his dog at the table while being waited upon by his devoted sisters. When the Helguera family call downstairs to Don Poli for medical assistance, it is Rivas who makes the observation: 'But aren't you a dentist?' The arch response he receives from one of the sisters is that her brother is an *orthodontist*. She too employs the hollow jargon of science. Don Poli's medical knowledge is pure performance. As he has already confessed, his experience of bodies amounts to little more than failed attempts to insert a *protesis* in the mouth of his pampered dog. Armed with the accoutrements of medicine – stethoscope and white coat – his *appearance* in the Helguera household is not only dependent upon the paraphernalia of the profession but the diagnosis also depends on the privileged information provided by Rivas. Just as Rivas is a better lawyer than Álvaro he is also a better doctor than Don Poli. Furthermore, his transparent gluttony embellishes and reinforces his subversive function. He provides a link between the dining table and death while exposing the fragile authority of the bourgeois family whose status is balanced upon the delicate discourse of civic respectability which is uneasily sustained by a combination of appearance and medical, legal, military and religious verbiage.

The characters of Plácido and Quintanilla represent appurtenances of their own respective classes. In part they are foils to one another, but they are also condemned to share the same space for much of the film. Their adjacence sets them apart from their respective social groups. Quintanilla prides himself on his family connections and those to come (he is engaged to Martita Galán, the daughter of the campaign president). He introduces himself to establishment figures (the notary and the bank manager) as being of the same class as them. His prospects as a son-in-law place him close to Álvaro (it is Álvaro's status to which he aspires) and this is an alliance reinforced by the complicity arising out of the discourse on medicine. On learning that Quintanilla has caught a cold, Álvaro lends him a thermometer and later produces a contraption for steaming out congested chests.

Meanwhile, Plácido wages a battle to accommodate himself to legal requirement. Just as Álvaro is fond of spouting legal statute, Plácido is the innocent victim of the same discourse. The narrative thread of the film is provided in Plácido's terror of losing his means to a living by failing to pay the instalment on his motorized cart before sundown as the law demands. It is noteworthy that falacious interpretation of the law is both an instrument that threatens to deny Plácido his livelihood while simultaneously swirling around the death of Pascual (the instalment and *concubinage* respectively). In both instances, these are discourses clumsily perpetuated by figures of authority: Álvaro, the bank manager and the notary. They are discourses which Plácido, from the very start of the film, uncritically accepts. The requirement to pay is phrased by him, for most of the film, not only as legal obligation but as civic duty. Confounded time and time again by bureaucratic exigence, he goes from humbly explaining to the notary's clerks at an early stage in the film, 'I want to pay, I am a serious person' to – when he is finally able to pay – outright rebellion upon learning that his creditor's name does not figure on the documents and thus he is not legally obliged to honour the agreement. It is at this point when the notary supplants his legal status to question Plácido's morality. The legal discourse upon which civic cohesion is sustained is promptly replaced by recourse to morality when it suits the dominant group. The question of 'ethics' only becomes a factor when contestation emerges in Plácido's reaction.

The cleavage between medical and legal discourse that occurred earlier in the figures of Álvaro and Don Poli is further complicated here. Legal discourse is, once more, exposed as a rhetorical nicety, as jargon designed as enforcement. In this sense power works, as both Bakhtin and Gramsci maintain, in the employment of technical euphemism (which forms a basis for consent) but once that fails coercion comes into play.

Adjacence arises at other moments in the film. Rivas who dines with the fake doctor / dentist is the contiguous link to Concheta and Pascual: he is their neighbour. As we will see later, it transpires that the couple are also neighbours to the *guardia civil*. Señor Helguera lives in fear of his neighbours, such as the dentist himself who attends to the dying Pascual. More than anything else the proximity of life to death and death to eating helps bind the ambivalence of the word *alegría* that reverberates throughout the film. 'No meal can be sad', writes Bakhtin:

> Sadness and food are incompatible (while death and food are perfectly compatible). The banquet always celebrates a victory and this is part of its very nature. Further, the triumphal banquet is always universal. It is the triumph of life over death. In this respect it is equivalent to conception and birth. (1984: 283)

Mari Luz, who hosts Concheta, has taken advantage of the situation to invite her lover, Ramiro, to dine. In this sequence we see the man doing the washing-up, consigned to the kitchen, in a reversal of the earlier sequence in which the dentist dines with his dog and Rivas while attended to by his sisters. The spatial differences in this sequence are the product of panopticism (Ramiro lives in fear of a visit from the civic committee) but they also produce a kind of adjacence, an appurtenance of authoritarian discourse that clarifies the boundaries of power – those which are crossed. Ramiro crosses traditional gender roles (he is doing the washing-up in the kitchen) and is separated from the women in the dining room. The window through to the kitchen provides both a means of communication and separation. Moreover, on the one occasion he dares to pass into the dining room is when his worst fears are realized. There is a knock on the door and he dives into the wardrobe to hide, carrying a bottle of champagne. This marks the arrival of Gabino Quintanilla come to fetch Concheta to be forcibly married to Pascual. At this moment we hear a loud pop (as the champagne cork detaches itself from the bottle) and then the following conversation which takes a similar turn to the earlier one in which Quintanilla, tellingly but erring once more, posited *alegría* as adjacent to the military:

> Quintanilla: A shot! I heard a shot!
> Mari Luz: No, no . . . just the seasonal *alegría*.

The panoptic legal discourse concerning *concubinage* (the presence of Concheta, the prying inspection of Quintanilla and the fact that Ramiro and Mari Luz are terrified illicit lovers) swirls with that of the vocabulary of war and the discourse of medicine and illness (Ramón's eye has been injured by the cork) and does so in a scenario in which both death (the forthcoming death of Pascual) and eating are prominent features (Concheta is seated at the dinner table). Within this loop the significance of the word *alegría* – which has similarly been used on previous occasions with a degree of joyless desperation – is one that stretches beyond the screen. If the different contiguities mark ambivalent hybrids emerging amid competing discourses, then *alegría* is the fracturing impulse that pervades the 'national' discourse. The Spanish party animal (the *juerguista*) is a stock figure of the national discourse and was one put into play virtually at the very moment when *Plácido* was being filmed by the then Tourism and Information Minister Manuel Fraga Iribarne, whose slogan 'Spain is different' was designed to attract foreign tourists. *Alegría* connects, moreover, to the breakdown of comic convention and locates it within national discourse.

In *Plácido* – and, as we shall see, in *El verdugo* – the figure of the *guardia civil* makes a significant appearance. The state at its most menacing – rifle raised and cocked – and the family merge into a disjunctive moment marked by death in both films. Plácido's family and Concheta are challenged in the language of the battlefield by the *guardia civil* on the roof when they carry Pascual's lifeless body back to his dwelling. This is a critical moment. At this point Plácido is not acting for money or even under duress, he is acting out of genuine charitable concern for Concheta. His 'charity' positions him quite literally in a battlefield – similar, in fact, to a real spatial border. The metaphorical notion of a leaking border between discourses is given literal representation here. Two contiguous points meet in a familiarly Bakhtinian representation: the *guardia civil* is *up* on the roof and Plácido's clan is *down* below making their way up the stairs. The *guardia civil* has a *panoptic* function. Just as many Spanish towns and cities were ringed by barracks, it seems apt that Concheta and Pascual live in contiguous closeness to the *cuartel*. The up / down positioning of the *guardia civil* / Plácido and company also has a corresponding side-by-side consequence. Much of this film can be read as an exposure of social difference between classes and gender. Yet, as has already been established in the sequence that takes place in the public toilets, the notion of *dwelling* is ambivalent. A dwelling is also a place of refuge, beyond the scope of panoptic power. Plácido's actions – as if he were crossing a kind of no-man's land – reproduce the pattern of his movements between the territories of the bourgeois families, Concheta and Pascual's hovel and the public toilets that complicates and contests a notion of *place*. Place is an adjunct, a liminal dwelling often located at the very centre of power. Just as Concheta and Pascual's home is both beneath and beside the barracks so too the public toilets, used by Plácido's family as a base, are in the central square of the town. Adjacence is not always physically marginal to the loci of power. Sometimes it is at its heart, insinuating – at times discreetly, at others explicitly – from within. It is from within 'place' that the contingent signs of history often peep through to caress the contiguous signifiers of location.

Berlanga breaks with the tradition of comedy which ends in reconciliation, happy endings and often marriage. Berlanga's endings are rarely happy, indeed his protagonists usually end up on their own. *El verdugo* (*The Executioner*) is Berlanga's bleakest and most sustained film and yet its strength lies in being precisely a comedy. The conflicts here are waged along and within the boundaries of middle society, but particularly occupy that terrain where the state and civil society meet. This is a film organized around that relationship and turns on the performance of a representative of the state at its most lethal, the executioner (José Isbert). Isbert plays Amadeo who, in the words of his future son-in-law José Luis (Nino Manfredi): 'seems like a normal person [. . .] you'd never imagine he was an executioner'. His normality, his amiable bonhomie vies with the macabre nature of his trade, symbolized by the ubiquitous briefcase containing the garrotte that terrifies everyone he meets. Isbert's performance is fundamental to this effect, grandfatherly, *inimically* Spanish, concerned with food, commonsensical and pragmatic with a shrewd line in comic observation. Of José Luis' job in the funeral parlour he remarks on its security, guaranteed against recession. Apparently malleable, Amadeo is also completely manipulative: a representative of the state but by no means fully of the state.

It is from within this combination of pragmatic common sense and superstition that the film unravels into an anatomy of Francoist society of the early 1960s. *El verdugo* explores the nation as inter-action, as a society riven with coexisting differences. The ways in which this uneven, partial and unstable alliance between state and civil society is achieved depend, in large degree, upon the figure of Isbert. Isbert's performance functions at the juncture of a series of non-discursive elements which, as in *Plácido*, form the vertices of this film. If death in Bakhtin is an ambivalent representation then rarely has a film expressed this ambivalence better than *El verdugo*.

The music backing the title shots of *El verdugo* captures this per-tinently. As the drawings and captions come up on the screen we hear a cheerful rendition of the twist which moments later fades into the first sequence and fuses with a *martinete* (a gypsy prison song) murmured against the dialogue, which in turn takes place simulta-neously with an execution. The funeral parlour is the inappropriate scenario for a jam session of the funeral band who play the same twist while Amadeo's daughter Carmen lingers at the doorway to announce her pregnancy to José Luis. As in the previous discussion of *Plácido,* the simultaneous presence of death and birth is of Bakhtinian significance. At the very end of the film, just after José Luis has carried out his first execution, precisely when he is in the midst of the grimmest depression, a group of foreign tourists arrive and the music (the same twist we hear earlier) bursts into life once more. In all these instances death stamps its emblematic imprint on modernity. *El verdugo* appropriates the twist to invoke both the Americanization of youth culture and the arrival of 'libidinous' tourism (the unanticipated result of Fraga's sloganizing) from out-side the borders of the nation.

The Bakhtinian significance of the music becomes politicized when music fuses with dress. Invariably it is on these occasions when the state and civil society meet. In an extraordinary sequence when José Luis is finally summoned to Mallorca to perform an execution, the uniformed *guardia civil* track him down to the Drach caves and tannoy him with a megaphone that sheers against the Offenbach being played for the tourists.

One of the most eloquent and enduring images in Spanish cinema occurs in the penultimate sequence of *El verdugo* as José Luis is dragged through the prison hall, half-unconscious and vomiting to perform the execution. His straw hat, with which he had been enjoying his holiday, falls abandoned on the floor. The uniformed warders oblige him to wear a tie, forcing it upon him, as if it were the garrotte. The two groups of people walking slowly through the long white room to the small door at the far end are the perfect culmination of the previous moments when José Luis had been comforted by the prison governor and the priest. Desperately expectant of an imminent pardon José Luis is attended to by the priest. From the moment of his arrival on the island José Luis is transformed into the condemned man. From his parodic 'arrest' by the *guardia civil* when the family step off the boat to this remarkable sequence he is propelled inexorably towards the scaffold. Strikingly, this shot is filmed without music, against the murmuring of the priest's prayers.

Just as José Luis as state executioner becomes the *condenado*, the sequence of events that leads to José Luis from Madrid to Mallorca constitutes a parody of the institution of the family. Carmen actually refers to it as a kind of honeymoon. When José Luis is summoned to Palma de Mallorca she says, 'At the end of the day we never had a honeymoon'. Within this context, the accompanying presence of a new born baby and the father-in-law disturbs the symbolic locus at the heart of traditional discourse and becomes the raw material of a critique of the state at its most repressive.

The wedding as a comic scenario is important. Far from being the point of reconciliation, in both *Plácido* and *El verdugo* the wedding marks the most desperate and disjunctive of solutions. This is more than just a reversal. This departure from conventional comedy marks a particular reworking of the discourses of law and family. If in *Plácido* the wedding marks an act of Christian conscription, the press-ganging of a couple into dubious legality, the enforcement of a doctrine in which the totalizing intention of discourse breaks down, in *El verdugo* this coercion intimately links the family to the state.

It is noteworthy, moreover, that in *Plácido* and *El verdugo* Berlanga's hapless heroes are both the fathers of new-born children who live in close proximity to death. Death and birth are molecular symptoms of the closeness of the state and civil society. José Luis, upon finding himself in a similarly adjacent position (that is to say, a character both inside and outside the institution of the family) of son-in-law to those characters in *Plácido*, resorts to his condition as a means of denying his discomforting inheritance. On being introduced by Amadeo to a hack writer he admires for his book *Garrote vil* and who exalts the profession of execution and dedicates the book, 'To the future executioner, maintainer of a family tradition', José Luis retorts, 'I'm only the son-in-law, I am not a part of the dynasty'. José Luis, condemned by his condition as son-in-law, is able to exploit this marginal status as an alibi; just as Álvaro and Quintanilla in *Plácido* make use of their positions as sons-in-law to bind discourse, with José Luis they also prove the key figures in its undoing.

As in *Plácido*, it is in the spirit of Bakhtin that each time 'death' arises in this film somebody is eating. At the very first execution that Isbert performs, the prison warden is put off his food by Amadeo's case, José Luis is plied with food and drink in the prison just as he is about to embark on his execution and at the very end of the film when José Luis returns to the departing ship and says he will never perform another execution again the only comment his wife makes is to offer him a sandwich.

Hopewell echoes a lot of other critics when he comments on the 'failure' of Berlanga's characters: 'Chance, mishap, chaos and compromise sweep mild-mannered José Luis [. . .] from being caught in bed with the executioner's daughter to being dragged to an execution chamber, as the state's official garrotte expert. José Luis has joined the system' (1986: 62). I think that this is more complicated than Hopewell claims. It is true that outrageous misfortune deals José Luis a poor hand. But what is questioned here is more the state itself than any individual. The state is not the system; civil society bursts with dissenting voices, fears and misgivings. The representatives of the state are 'normal' human beings. *El verdugo* is a powerful indictment of the death penalty, not a tale of individual misfortune; it is an investigation of how the state makes victims of its closest allies with the objective of consensus starkly undermined by the coercive impulse. Chance is not what is allowed to count in this film. In almost all the cases of apparent misfortune that occur to José Luis lies the manipulative hand of Isbert / Amadeo, yet he is the most attractive character in the film. Amadeo leaves his case in the funeral parlour van (deliberately?) and thereby introduces José Luis to his daughter. On finding José Luis in bed with his daughter, Amadeo employs traditional morality – echoing the rhetoric of a Catholicism he clearly doesn't practise – to oblige José Luis to propose marriage, and once there is a child and the possibility of a house involved Amadeo and Carmen morally blackmail José Luis into acceptance of his role as the state's executioner. Amadeo is in some ways the personification of the state, sufficiently benign to be acceptable but perfectly capable of ruthlessness. He is a kind of 'son-in-law' to the state; an adjacent figure, socially marginalized by his job but for that very reason possessed of an additional mobility. He is a figure that moves on the frontier between state and civil society, between the family and the scaffold, a borderline character at the centre of the Bakhtinian schema of death and rebirth. His Spanishness (the same kind of Spanishness often cited today to explain Berlanga and to construct him as an auteur) is made parodic by his performance, precisely by his pragmatism, his employment of common sense, his handling of the more dedicated state servants and most importantly by his 'timelessness'. Isbert is always old. This 'timelessness' is similar to other facets of popular culture; *pasodobles*, flamenco and carnival persist in their popularity outside of marketed time. What happens with Isbert is that his Spanishness eludes total incorporation by the state. Difference not only oozes from the kaleidoscopic set of foreigners, costumes and family disputes but in the otherness of Amadeo / Isbert himself. Isbert's performance, which is as much verbal as physical, is crucially the clearest example of the tacit agreement between state and civil society. Isbert's *inimical* Spanishness becomes a parody of Spanishness. I am reminded of Judith Butler's comment:

> The loss of the sense of 'the normal' [. . .] can be its own occasion for laughter, especially when 'the normal', 'the original' is revealed to be a copy, and an inevitably failed one, an ideal that no one can embody. In this sense, laughter emerges in the realization that all along the original was derived. (Butler, 1990: 139)

Isbert plays a type Spaniard, he is always referred to as 'normal', and undoes Spanishness in the playing of it. His parody hits at the heart of the appropriative objectives of the Spanish state; the attempts to identify Spain with the state are rendered redundant by Isbert's exposure of the manufactured nature of the Spanish state itself. In this way Isbert transpires to be the most subversive character in the film. Intrinsic Spanishness doesn't exist and Isbert's performance is crucial to the unmasking of the 'original'. Connected to this is what I originally conceived of as a problem arising out of Nino Manfredi's performance. Manfredi also plays a stock Spanish character, the *calzonazos* – the brow-beaten hen-pecked man of many of Spain's 1950s and 1960s films and one of Berlanga's favourite types. Manfredi, however, is

Italian, a fact well known to Spanish audiences. His foreignness is very different to that of other actors from abroad starring in Spanish films. Manfredi does not play an outsider, he plays the most typical stereotyped Spanish man. Here, while Isbert's voice is distinctively his, Manfredi's is dubbed into Spanish. At first I attributed this to miscasting (it is an ideal role for Fernando Fernán Gómez) yet in the light of Butler's comment Manfredi's performance becomes more interesting. Disturbance is caused over the very question of Spanishness, not only in the parodic performance of Isbert but also in the casting. More than that the excellence of the typecasting of Isbert helps to define the comedy of Manfredi, helps to establish that 'all along the original was derived'.

Notes

1 Berlanga claims that this was the name of a real campaign in Valencia (Cañique and Grau, 1993: 36).
2 This echoes the traditional Catalan nativity scene which features *el caganer* defecating in one corner of the *belén*. Something that is repeated in *El verdugo*.

Bibliography

Bakhtin, Mikhail (1984) *Rabelais and his World*, Bloomington: Indiana University Press.
—— (1996) *The Dialogic Imagination*, Austin: University of Texas Press.
Butler, Judith (1990) *Gender Trouble, Feminism, and the Subversion of Identity*, London: Routledge.
Cañique, Carlos and Maite Grau (1993) *¡Bienvenido Mr. Berlanga!*, Barcelona: Destino.
Gramsci, Antonio (1971) *Selections from the Prison Notebooks*, London: Lawrence and Wishart.
—— (1985) *Selections from Cultural Writings*, London: Lawrence and Wishart.
Hopewell, John (1986) *Out of the Past: Spanish Cinema After Franco*, London: British Film Institute.

8

Marisol: the Spanish Cinderella

Peter W. Evans

The most famous of all Spanish child stars, Marisol has attracted relentless press scrutiny but virtually no critical attention. This chapter offers the beginnings of a critical biography of a manufactured star who, from childhood to adolescence and beyond, mediated the feminine ideals and fantasies of a generation of Spanish girls. Discovered and transformed by Manuel J. Goyanes, the film producer, into the enormously lucrative, chirpy, dyed-blonde diminutive singing and dancing image of an officially sanctioned tourist-friendly and Costa del Sol-dominated 1960s Spain, Marisol can also be read now as a raucous, assertive child and adolescent with an ambivalent relationship to the Law-of-the-Father-fixated films in which she starred. Among child stars, less proletarian than Joselito, and more knowing than Pablito Calvo; among adolescents, more sexually self-conscious than Pili and Mili, Marisol refracted in her all-singing, all-dancing, all-talking vivacity the hectic expression of a nation's sham illusion of utopian festivity.

A star is born

'Marisol' was born Josefa Flores González (also known as Pepa Flores) in a humble neighbourhood of Málaga in 1948. Growing up listening, on radio, at the cinema, and elsewhere, to the music of Lola Flores, Imperio Argentina, Antonio Molina and others, she began to sing and dance herself, soon attracting the attention of the organizers of the Coros y Danzas de la Obra Sindical de Educación y Descanso, the State-approved society for girls of slender means, the poorer relation of the middle-class Coros y Danzas de la Sección Femenina. These performances, while she was still only eight years old or so, led to appearances with various groups in Madrid and elsewhere, and eventually to radio broadcasts and TV shows where, in 1959, she was spotted by Mari Carmen Goyanes, the famous film producer's daughter.

In return for their agreement to put their daughter under contract for film work with Goyanes' company, her parents were offered 40,000 pesetas and reassured that Pepa would be allowed to continue with her studies. She would be expected to remain in Madrid – accompanied by her mother – while tests were made. As these were extremely positive, production went ahead and, accordingly, Luis Lucia, a major director, who had already had successes with child stars, was engaged, and the film *Un rayo de luz* (1960) was under way. The publicity machinery was already in full swing: TV appearances were organized and the decision made to give their new star a new name, 'Marisol'. The brainchild of Goyanes himself, the name chimed in with the film's title combining, as Javier Barreiro argues, ordinariness ('Marisol' was not, even then, an uncommon name in Spain) with difference (invoked by the elemental suggestions of sea and sun):

> Era un nombre ni especialmente raro ni demasiado usual y se avenía muy bien con la luminosidad que proyectaban el rostro y el aura de la protagonista. (Barreiro, 1999: 40)

> (The name was not especially odd or rare, and suited the luminosity of face and aura of the protagonist.)

The 1960s were anyway still a Church-dominated decade when almost every female child was being baptized Mari something or other, their parents no longer able – even those without religious convictions – as had obviously been possible in pre-war times, to opt for more secular first names like Salud, Higiene, Libertad or Constitución (Torres, 1996: 27). Celestino Deleyto argues that the name was an apt choice for mediating the aspirations of Spain's political masters of the day: 'Marisol (note the Spanishness of her artistic name: *Mari* and *Sol*) came to epitomise the new Spain, looking optimistically into the future . . . ' (Deleyto, 1994: 243).

Of course, as was to be expected, Barreiro also notes (1999: 40), the name 'Marisol' acquired greater popularity after her screen debut. The film was a huge success – with photography by Manuel Berenguer and a script loosely based on Frances Hodgson Burnett's *Little Lord Fauntleroy* – taking 30 million pesetas at the box office in

Spain. Goyanes' knack for publicity – including allowing her to appear as the protagonist of stories about her life and friends in various comics and magazines like *La revista de los amigos de Marisol* – ensured that henceforward Marisol was committed to heavy-duty involvement in the promotion of her films. She advertised Lux soap, the 'jabón de las estrellas', gave countless interviews to magazines like *Lecturas*, which sold millions on the back of her fame, and sang to the Spanish *gastarbeiter* in Germany, engagements, of course, carefully recorded on *No-Do* newsreels of the day. Despite the material rewards of her screen success, the hectic pace of this life contributed to her increasingly uncomfortable relations with the Goyanes family, difficulties she has repeatedly referred to subsequently, sometimes going so far as to claim that her childhood was sacrificed in their mission to transform her into the Spanish Shirley Temple. To measure up to the Goyanes ideal, Marisol endured the refinement of her *andaluz* accent, was converted from brunette to blonde, and twice underwent surgery on her nose, a fate not dissimilar to that experienced by her Hollywood child star precursors. Her film work over the next five years was prolific, producing at least one film a year: *Ha llegado un ángel* (Luis Lucia, 1961), *Tómbola* (Luis Lucia, 1962), *Marisol rumbo a Río* (Fernando Palacios, 1963), *La nueva Cenicienta* (George Sherman, 1964), *La historia de Bienvenido* (Augusto Fenollar, 1964), *Búsqueme a esa chica* (Fernando Palacios, 1964), *Cabriola* (1965). From *Un rayo de luz* to *Cabriola*, Marisol was gradually maturing from child star to adolescent, from lovable, even if occasionally wilful, infant to desirable teenager and future bride, and by the time of the screening of *Cabriola* her on-screen nubile potential was being transformed into the off-screen engagement with Goyanes' son Carlos.

He was not, however, the first of her *novios*, among whom had numbered the famous Flamenco dancer, Antonio. The marriage was solemnized on the 16 May 1969, a union by all accounts less of love than of convenience and protection of the Goyanes' commercial interests in their prodigy. These were soon confirmed when Carlos took over his wife's business affairs. But the marriage lost no time in beginning to founder, its difficulties to some extent mirroring Marisol's growing frustrations, in changing social and political circumstances, with the ideologized image of her child star past. The marriage was over by 1972 (although not dissolved until 1975), and with it all vestige of pretence at gratitude to the family that had created the Marisol myth. She reclaimed her identity as Pepa Flores, refusing to be referred to professionally and privately as 'Marisol'. In tune with the rejection of her Francoist-constructed screen past, as ultimately complaisant child or adolescent in traditional happy-end narratives, Pepa Flores began to be identified with left-wing political agendas, took on theatre work, and became romantically involved with dissident figures like the radical *cantautor* Juan Manuel Serrat, and then with Antonio Gades, the dancer and choreographer, the father of her daughters María (born, while she was still legally married to Goyanes, 1974), Tamara (born 1976) and Celia (born 1981). A clear early sign of this atempted flight from 'Marisol' appeared during the filming of *La corrupción de Chris Miller* (1972), where eventually, though, box-office considerations overrode the star's desire to appear in the credits not as 'Marisol' but as 'Pepa Flores' (Barreiro, 1999: 107). Made by Juan Antonio Bardem, one of the iconic directors of the 'Conversaciones de Salamanca' generation, the film is interesting in its adherence to the child / parent narrative patterns of many Marisol films. The heavy-handed treatment accounted for the film's critical failure, but its importance for Marisol / Pepa Flores lies in its provision of an opportunity through which to escape from some of the cruder forms of the persona's construction. While some of the ground gained in this film was lost in her next, *La chica del Molino Rojo* (1973), made not by a dissident like Bardem, but by the popular genre director Eugenio Martín, the momentum that was now driving Pepa Flores away from 'Marisol' was unstoppable. The assault on her gradually disowned earlier persona was given a further nuance through the publication on the cover and in the inside pages of the 1976 September issue of *Interviú* of Pepa Flores in nude poses. Though these contributed further, as Celestino Deleyto argues (Deleyto, 1994: 244), to the deconstruction of a 1960s icon, they were in fact at least six years out of date, and had been taken by her husband Carlos who had hoped through these to persuade an Italian producer to finance a film starring Marisol and Alain Delon. The publication – without her consent – of the photos caused a furore leading, since the legacy of Franquismo had not been totally exhausted, to the arrest of the photographer, against whom charges were later dropped. While her film career went steadily into decline – the one exception being *Los días del pasado* (Camus, 1977), her most interesting film in maturity – her political convictions rose ever higher, leading in 1978 to public affirmation of support for the PCE, the Spanish Communist Party. It was fitting, therefore, that after finally getting his divorce from Marujita Díaz, Antonio Gades and Pepa Flores chose to get married in Cuba. In 1986, this marriage would also end. Her last film, *Caso cerrado* (Juan Caño, 1985) had already been made by then, but the impact of this, as well as the bit parts in her work for Saura, *Bodas de sangre* (1981), *Carmen* (1983), which also, as Rob Stone argues (2001: 203), further highlighted her Communist allegiances and attempted distance from her ideologized past, in no way threatened the iconic significance of the star who in the 1960s, as Barreiro puts it (1999: 197) was, alongside the bullfighter El Cordobés and Spain's premier football club, Real Madrid, the cultural measure of the times.

The good daughter

Had Graham Greene seen any of the earliest Marisol films he might have written a piece about her of the sort that landed him in the law courts. Greene's offence was to write about *Wee Willie Winkie* (John Ford, 1937) in a way that drew attention to the sexuality of its child star, Shirley Temple. On the surface, *Wee Willie Winkie* is a film for children, a nursery room tale appealing to innocent audiences; underneath, the film was in Greene's estimation an exposure of child sexuality and of interest to more than innocent audiences. Those who forced Greene and his publishers to withdraw the review were guided by the desire to protect the commercial interests of the studio that made the film, a judgement in no way informed by theories of child sexuality, never mind paedophilia. To overplay the sexual frisson of the first Marisol films would undeniably be to detract from their many other engrossing features, to underestimate their appeal to innocence, their flickerings of rebellion as well as their endorsement of tradition. Yet to neglect such problematical issues would also be to simplify them.

In *Un rayo de luz* the narrative follows a little girl's developing relationship with various members of her family, above all her grandfather, who discovers that his son, dying in an air crash early on in the film, has married beneath him. Marisol's mission in this, as in most of the other early films, lies in smoothing away difficulties before family reconciliation. So, for instance, in *Ha llegado un ángel* she is an outsider figure who through her timely intervention in a somewhat dysfunctional family resembles in some ways Paco Martínez Soria who in *La ciudad no es para mí* (1965) solves his own troubled family's problems through a mixture of an old man's *paleto* drive, energy, goodness and cunning. These two early Marisol films, though, gesture beyond the immediate pleasures of simple comedy. In *Un rayo de luz* the credits seem designed for child audiences, introducing Marisol herself as a cartoon character, yet even here suspicions are aroused. Not unlike Tinkerbell in Disney's *Peter Pan* (1953), whose unmistakably voluptuous outlines compromise innocent caricature, Marisol even in cartoon form shows the peek-a-boo fringes of her underpants beneath a skimpy dress. Once the film proper gets underway her costumes often preserve this coquettish pattern. As befits the projected ideological synecdoche of an Andalusia-defined 1960s Spain, she alternates between modern European dress styles and traditional Andalusian outfits. In modern dress she is characteristically more exposed: for instance, one of her dresses, white with red spots, tied in at the waist, barely covers her bottom and sanctions generous display of bare legs. The child of the narrative is said to be ten, but Marisol was going on for thirteen when the film was in production. Inevitably the budding adolescence of the young Marisol colours the representation of the child, and the voyeurism of the spectacle is further nuanced through the repeated pattern, certainly noticeable in this film, of narratives hinging on father or father surrogate / daughter relationships. There would be little point asking whether Luis Lucia, or the writers on these films (including the dramatist Alfonso Paso on four of the early films), had read Freud.

In a period dominated by the conservative theories of child and adult psychology developed by figures such as Juan José López Ibor, the chances are pretty slim, but the fact nevertheless remains that although the promotion of the Marisol films mediated the values of a majority audience brought up on Franquismo, the underlying premise opened up more awkward questions. At the very least Marisol's parents' eagerness to submit their daughter to the glamour and publicity process of the Goyanes family could be read as an example of Münchausen syndrome by proxy abuse. On this reading, Marisol is the typical example of the child from a lower socio-economic group whose parents surrender her to a parent substitute, who may abuse the child – as the parents turn a blind eye – in the supposed interests of transforming her life through the rewards of stardom. The many father-substitute characters in the Marisol films highlight the fine line between the fate of the star both on- and off-screen.

For all the pleasure she gives audiences through her remarkable performances in these films, the child star loses control over her own life, becoming, as Ian Tofler puts it,[1] 'an instrument for the implementation of the parent's agenda', providing 'a second chance to achieve lifelong parental goals and unfulfilled dreams' (2000: 219). In real-life case histories children whose pain in such circumstances has been ignored may 'distance themselves from their own feelings and collude in this objectification of themselves' (Tofler, 2000: 222). In the Marisol films the visible pain derives from the often melodramatic situations of the narratives: for instance, the death of the father in *Un rayo de luz*, orphanhood in *Ha llegado un ángel*, a blind father in *Búsqueme a esa chica*, poverty in *La nueva Cenicienta*. But beyond these safe expressions of ultimately assuaged emotions, minor resistances to the controlling ideology of the film emerge from the very force of Marisol's extraordinary performances, especially in her musical numbers, which are characterized by precocious assertiveness and almost hoydenish authority. What is clearly intended as a spectacular phenomenon of adult bravura emanating from the body of a child actually also becomes a complex site of resistance, of sexual self-consciousness and psychological aggression, the screen projection of the conscious and unconscious drives of her biological and commercial creators. In this respect her fiery dancing and powerful, adult vocal tones (through over-use in her early films leading, as Jesús Rodríguez notes (1999: 26), to its coarseness in middle age), to some extent resemble the unwitting rebellion of the *petardista*, the firework-crazed child in the *Gran familia* films, whose explosions provide perhaps unintended commentary on the conservative values of the 1960s moral majority in Spain. There is nothing here, of course, of the direct challenge to the prevailing attitudes that may be found in the work of 1960s and 1970s dissident Spanish film-makers. Marisol's behaviour is worlds apart from, say, the baleful insubordination of an Ana Torrent in *El espíritu de la colmena* (Erice, 1973) or *Cría cuervos* (Saura, 1975). But the conciliable, good daughterly qualities which above all characterize the Marisol persona may be further inspected through reflection on what may be regarded as her own Cinderella complex.

Cinderella

La nueva Cenicienta is an apt title not just for the narrative of this particular film but also for elucidating marked features of the Marisol persona. Here, she is the daughter of the impoverished owner of a *pensión* (Fernando Rey), stuffed with members of a circus act, all out of work and for whom Marisol eventually turns out to be a saviour. She becomes involved with two men, Antonio, a famous Spanish dancer of the times and Paul Clarke, an American singer (Robert Conrad, mainly a TV actor whose most famous series was *The Wild Wild West,* 1964–68). By the time of the making of this film Marisol was sixteen years old, even though the fairytale ambience tries to have the best of both worlds by reminding its audience of her recent child star past. The voice-over at the beginning of the film emphasizes the marketable essence of the persona: 'Rubia, dulce, chatilla, y con una alegría en el cuerpo y en el alma capaz de espantar a todas las brujas y a todos los lobos que salgan en el camino'.

The remark's allusion to the fairytale world of the film, emphasized throughout by the voice-over, inevitably draws attention to its sexual connotations. The reference to the Big Bad Wolf recalls Bruno Bettelheim's reading of the story of Little Red Riding Hood as commentary on the female child's journey towards sexual independence and maturity (1988: 166–83), where a choice must be made between the reality and pleasure principles, between the safeness of home and the thrill and danger of the unknown, a decision that in the process confronts the child with her own libidinal desires. These matters lie also at the heart of the Cinderella fairytale. Even though some of the narrative and characterological features of the tale are missing in *La nueva Cenicienta* – such as, for instance, the Ugly Sisters – enough of the original is retained to make a significant connection. Cinderella / Marisol begins the narrative in a degraded state, the poverty-stricken world of her father's *pensión.* While Bettelheim's analysis of the degradation of Cinderella's situation as a recognition of Oedipal desires is interesting from the point of view of Marisol's constant attachment to fathers or father figures in most of the films, the further point about the fitting of the foot to the glass slipper as a sign of sexual maturity is even more significant in *La nueva Cenicienta.* The film includes a modified version of this incident both as a necessary component of the narrative and as self-conscious commentary on the transition of Marisol from innocent child to, like, for example, Gigi before her, sexualized adolescent. In this narrative, after witnessing the impressive dancing of the young girl played by Marisol, Antonio picks up a shoe she leaves behind while hurrying away and sets off to find its owner. In the meantime she has also become involved with the American singer played by Robert Conrad. She is eventually found by Antonio, so that in the rousing big production number finale the hybrid essence of Marisol as affirmation of traditional Spanishness as well as of American-style modernity can – as in all the films – once more be proclaimed. Her father's insistence on her being photographed at first with Antonio and then with Paul produces in a sense a cultural *ménage à trois* at the end of the film. As she leaves the stage she again loses her shoe, this time to be picked up, we suspect, not by Antonio but by Paul, in a gesture that would consolidate the US / Spanish ties hoped for in *¡Bienvenido, Mr. Marshall!* (1952) and subsequently realized in the air base / economic accords between the two countries. (The Spanish / US topos is repeated in *Búsqueme a esa chica*, where Robert Horton plays the American entrepreneur on whom Marisol has a crush.) But the fitting of the shoe – whether by Antonio or by Paul – also marks the daughter's quest for independence from the father. Clinging on to the best in one's past – symbolized by the Andalusian and flamenco traditions – and looking for difference and novelty in the modern world represented by the American may, from one point of view, be entirely desirable elements of the maturing process. But here both the attachments to the past and the search for the new seem, at the deepest levels, ultimately regressive since they confirm in the construction of the Antonio and Paul characters the values of the father and the conformist order to which he belongs. Cinderella must be taught to be true to herself, but what if all around her offers little scope for authenticity?

Nevertheless, the twice repeated incident of the lost or discarded shoe seems to indicate that, at the very least, sexual maturity has been achieved for, as Bettelheim argues, the meaning of the glass slipper episode in the fairytale is ultimately sexual:

> male acceptance of the vagina and love for the woman is the ultimate male validation of the desirability of her femininity. But nobody, not even a fairy-tale princess, can hand such acceptance to her – not even his love can do it. Only Cinderella herself can finally welcome her femininity, although she is helped by the prince's love. (Bettelheim, 1988: 271)

As in the original story, where Cinderella has to accept her degraded condition before she can progress to a mature and fulfilling relationship with the Prince, so here Marisol / Cenicienta has to accept her traditional Spanishness – with all that this implies for 1960s Spain – before she can know herself and be worthy of the love of the foreign Prince Charming, the American Paul Clarke.

Mothers and daughters

The sexual and social acculturation of the Marisol persona is further complicated through her relations with mother or mother-surrogate characters in these films. Mothers appear, for instance, in *Un rayo de luz* and *Tómbola* (1962), but in others, such as *Búsqueme a esa chica*, the rather frumpy maiden aunt persona of Isabel Garcés turns up in one of her many mother-surrogate roles as a chaperone of not unmitigatedly benign influence. The older woman here functions in two ways: firstly, as someone through whom the film sets out its Oedipal agenda; secondly, as an alternative choice of womanhood for the male. In the case of films like *Lolita* (Kubrick, 1962) and *Gigi* (Minnelli, 1958), two famous Hollywood films that also adopt this pattern, the older woman is a grotesque version of the eroticized female monstrous from whom the male is in flight. What the older male seeks in young maidens like Lolita or Gigi, and flees in horror from in Lolita's mother or Gigi's aunt, is release through innocence from experience. The male sees in the older woman an all-devouring social and sexual other. In *Búsqueme a esa chica*, an adolescent-targeted film with little interest in directly addressing questions of social or sexual complexity, the older woman is not monstrous but nevertheless devalued. Moreover, unlike *Lolita* or *Gigi*, and as the film is not made according to the traditions of a culture traumatized by 'Momism', the Marisol film projects the older woman, in contrast to the roles played by Shelley Winters and Hermione Gingold in the Hollywood equivalents, as more harmless, reassuring and de-eroticized. The difference to some extent also partly lies in Franquismo's sanctification of motherhood. In *Tómbola* the almost evangelical narrative turns on the theft of a painting of the Madonna, who through Marisol's devotion eventually redeems the penitent thieves. Marisol's relations in these films with mothers or mother-substitutes raises questions not only about the attitudes of daughters towards their mothers but also about the psycho-social nature of the creative impulse itself, here exemplified by Marisol's singing and dancing. As Valerie Walkerdine argues in a general discussion of female stars, being a performer offers a means of escape, from socio-economic as well as from other forms of disadvantage. For 1960s Spanish girls, for whom opportunities for self-fulfilment were clearly more limited than in modern times, being a performer provided an especially attractive means of escape. Valerie Walkerdine comments:

> Being looked at presents still one of the only ways in which working-class girls can escape from the routines of domestic drudgery or poorly paid work into the dubious glamour industries so despised by feminists. I want to argue that being the object of that eroticised gaze is far more socially contradictory than Laura Mulvey (1974) and others (for example, *Screen*, 1992) would admit. 'Patriarchy' is not to be understood as some simple overarching phenomenon, but practices of sexuality and eroticism can literally afford to operate differently for different social groups with differing degrees of privilege. Subjectivity is not constituted only as the object of the gaze, but subjects are formed in a large number of different practices with different opportunities and possibilities open to them. Fame is one of the few promises and hopes open to many of these girls. It is one of the few ways that they can stop being a schoolgirl. (1997: 142–3)

For all its Münchausen by proxy syndrome elements, Marisol's specularization achieved at least this much: the transportation of a working-class *andaluza* from routine drudgery into a world of tangible rewards, acting in films where she was imaged as a blend of conformity and rebellion, a daddy's daughter who was also a rebel, the cheeky *chica* who often took the initiative in solving crimes (e.g. in *Tómbola*) or fraudulent designs (e.g. in *Búsqueme a esa chica*). Now a sexualized nymphet, now an action girl, she was also the daughter who, in Melanie Klein's terms, may have sought to repair through her performing art the damage to the sometimes present, but more often absent, mother.

Melanie Klein's work with children focuses on the split between good and bad objects (in reality the same, but maintained as such in the child's mind, though they are eventually reunited). Eventually, too, external objects become internalized, exemplifying in the process the constant interplay of projection and introjection from early life. The child later becomes aware of the separation of the object, and recognizes that the good and the bad object are the same, an awareness that leads to anxiety over the safety of the former. Guilt and concern lead to reparation and, for Klein, creativity, or art, is inspired by the reparative impulse and the need to repair the damaged object. As a theory of art, Klein's argument has its problematical side, since the creative impulse is regarded as something exclusively reparative and not, precisely, creative. Nevertheless, the stress on reparation would seem to be particularly relevant to the Marisol films. Seen in this light, Marisol's musical and other performative moments in these films are readable not just as examples of attention-seeking, or of attachment to the father, or as celebrations of Spanish culture and accommodations with American modernity, but as an appeal to the mother, even if the mother is often a more shadowy figure. Interestingly, Marisol has commented in inteview that she was closer to her grandmother (Barreiro, 1999: 82), a confession that might offer further substance to the Kleinian reading of her perhaps guilt-ridden, reparative self-consciously creative impulses.

Finale

The constant tension between the manufactured elements of the Marisol persona and the resurgent drives of Pepa Flores' own authenticity are noticeable throughout her career. In a slightly later film, *Carola de día, Carola de noche* (Armiñán, 1968) this split is reflected in the double life the heroine leads as an exiled East European princess and the ordinary young woman who seeks romance in the night life of Barcelona. Her song 'Soy una muchacha igual que todas', as she wanders around the city before ending up in a restaurant where she cannot pay the bill, seems like a girl's lament for her kidnapped childhood. The point is further stressed when former liberties and current entrapments form the elegiac content of her next song, 'Recuerdo mi niñez'. In Barcelona the image of Marisol as an Eastern European princess not only constrained by her entourage but also pursued by her political enemies creates an apt self-conscious image of the star whose slim Aryan blondeness mixed with the dark Andalusian ethnicity of voice and gesture brought pleasure to millions of adoring fans who never knew the pain that such packaging involved. The girl from far away, who was also somehow the young assistant you might expect to meet in the shop around the corner, was a cocktail a little more potent than that imagined by the middle-class mothers out hunting for safe daughters-in-law, and for whom she provided the seemingly perfect model.

Note

1   I am grateful to Professor Christopher Cordess for the reference to Ian
    Tofler's article on Münchausen syndrome by proxy abuse.

Bibliography

Barreiro, Javier (1999) *Marisol frente a Pepa Flores*, Barcelona: Plaza &
    Janés.
Bettelheim, Bruno (1988) *The Uses of Enchantment: the Meaning and
    Importance of Fairy Tales*, Harmondsworth: Penguin Books.
Deleyto, Celestino (1994) 'Rewriting Spain; Metafiction and Intertextuality
    in Saura's *Carmen*', in *Journal of Hispanic Research*, 2: 2, 237–47.
Klein, Melanie (1997) *Envy and Gratitude and Other Works 1946–1963*,
    London: Vintage.
Rodríguez, Jesús (18 July 1999) 'Buscando a Pepa Flores', *El País Semanal*,
    26–34.
Stone, Rob (2001) 'Through a Glass Darkly: Ritual and Transition in Carlos
    Saura's *Bodas de sangre*', in *Bulletin of Hispanic Studies*, 78, 199–215.
Tofler, Ian (2000) 'Parental and Adult Professional Gain from Exceptional
    Children: Achievement by Proxy', in Mary Eminson and R. J. Postleth-
    waite (eds.) *Münchausen Syndrome by Proxy Abuse: A Practical Approach*,
    Oxford: Butterworth Heinemann, 215–30.
Torres, Rafael (1996) *La vida amorosa en tiempos de Franco*, Madrid:
    Temas de Hoy.
Walkerdine, Valerie (1997) *Daddy's Girl: Young Girls and Popular Culture*,
    London: Macmillan.

1A Promotional material for *La Lola se va a los puertos* (1947)

1B Promotional material for *La Lola se va a los puertos* (1947)

2 Image of Imperio Argentina

3A & 3B Promotional material for *Alba de América* (1951)

4A Promotional material for *Agustina de Aragón* (1950)

EMPRESA QUINTANA, S. A.

LUNES
16
OCTUBRE

CINE
DORADO

¡UN ACONTE-
CIMIENTO
INOLVIDABLE!

AURORA BAUTISTA

EN LA MAS GRANDE SUPERPRODUCCION
DEL CINE ESPAÑOL

Agustina de Aragón

FERNANDO REY - VIRGILIO TEIXEIRA
EDUARDO FAJARDO - MANUEL LUNA

Jesús Tordesillas - Guillermo Marín - Juan Espantaleón
Fernando Fernández de Córdoba - Fernando Sancho
Raúl Cancio - Fernando Nogueras - José Bodaló
Manuel Arbo - Antonia Plana - Maruja
Asquerino - María Cañete - Pilar
Muñoz.

DIRECTOR: **JUAN DE ORDUÑA**

LA NUMANTINA EPOPEYA DE LOS SITIOS, REVIVIDA EN
LA MEJOR PELICULA DE HABLA ESPAÑOLA

TOLERADA PARA MENORES

Gráficas Vasconia - Teléfono 4021

4B Promotional material for *Agustina de Aragón* (1950)

5 Image from *Plácido* (1961)

6 Promotional image for *Ha llegado un ángel* (1961) starring Marisol

7 Narciso Ibáñez Serrador on the set of *La residencia* (1969)

8 Promotional material for *Las eróticas vacaciones de Stela* (1978)

9 Eduardo Noriega in *Abre los ojos* (1997)

10 María Galiana and Carlos Álvarez-Novoa in *Solas* (1999)

11 María Galiana and Ana Fernández in *Solas* (1999)

EMMA
VILARASAU

KARRA
ELEJALDE

TRISTÁN
ULLOA

Trying to reach
the limits of evil...

But evil has
no limits.

BASED ON THE NOVEL BY RAMSEY CAMPBELL

THE NAMELESS

12 English language promotional material for *Los sin nombre* (1999)

Screening 'Chicho': the horror ventures of Narciso Ibáñez Serrador[1]

Antonio Lázaro-Reboll

Any account of Spanish television history must include the horror-suspense series *Historias para no dormir* (1966-68) and the household notoriety of its Master of Ceremonies Narciso Ibáñez Serrador, or, as he continues to be familiarly known to Spanish audiences, 'Chicho'. Likewise any history of Spanish cinema must take into account the commercial popular success of his first horror film *La residencia* (aka *The Finishing School*, *The House That Screamed*, 1969), a commercial venture formulated with the express purpose of breaking into the international market.

The extent to which Ibáñez Serrador's successful transition from the household to the big screen responded to his image as a TV entertainer is part of a broader discussion in this chapter on the cultural politics that underpin popular genres. Chicho's popular standing among audiences is equal only to an almost uniform critical devaluation of *La residencia* as a horror genre product in specialist film journal reviews of the period (*Cinestudio*, *Film Ideal*, *Nuestro Cine* or *Reseña*); though the polarized critical response to *La residencia* needs to be considered within the historical context of an industry in crisis. Many reviewers criticized Ibáñez Serrador's production on the grounds of the director's formative years in television and the tastelessly excessive budget made available to him, more than fifty million pesetas, unheard of in the history of the Spanish film industry: how, when the industry was in dire financial debt, could a first-time director have at his disposal such a considerable amount? After the dismissal of José María García Escudero in 1967 and the economic failure of the 'New Spanish Cinema', the costly protection system introduced by the then Undersecretary of Cinema in August 1964 had led to delays in the payment of government subsidies to producers and exhibitors, leaving the administration with a debt of more than 300 million pesetas (see Hopewell, 1986: 64–5, 80). As Hopewell has pointed out, 'only a few forms of film-life survived and festered in such an economic climate' (1986: 80) – the so-called degenerate 'genres' or 'subgeneric' cinemas, horror films among them. As part of the rise of the horror genre in terms of production and exhibition during the decade of the 1960s in the American and European markets, Spanish horror was a dominant and indeed crucial part of the film culture available in the period. During the last part of the 1960s and the early 1970s, the production of horror films in Spain was one of the most commercially successful areas of Spanish cinema; in Spain the horror 'boom' really began with *La marca del hombre lobo* (*Mark of the Werewolf*, Enrique Eguiluz, 1967) and was consolidated with *La residencia* (1969) and *La noche de Walpurgis* (aka *The Werewolf's Shadow*, *The Werewolf Versus the Vampire*, León Klimovsky, 1970). However, the simple association of *La residencia* with other low-budget productions, of which Eguiluz and Klimovky's films are examples, requires further clarification.

The discrepancy between *La residencia*'s spectacular success and the critical response surrounding the film calls for analysis. Given Chicho's already firmly established persona as a brand name for horror and suspense among audiences, it is arguably this very association that underlies the critical prejudices of the 'serious' reviewers against a (dis)reputable generic figure within horror. This 'screening out' of what did not fit the aesthetic standards and interpretive rules of specialist film journalists who were safeguarding the 'interests' of Spanish audiences and, by extension, Spanish cinema is the main focus of this chapter. But before I move into an examination of the critical operations and institutional preoccupations at work in these contemporary reviews, let us follow the development of Chicho's artistic persona in the world of TV and the subsequent promotional force of that horror fame.

From *Obras maestras de terror* to *Historias para no dormir*

Ibáñez Serrador's connection with the horror genre lies in Argentina. But his life started on the other side of Río de la Plata, in Montevideo, Uruguay in 1935, since both his parents Narciso Ibáñez Menta and Pepita Serrador were part of the Spanish theatre groups that toured around Spain and Latin America. Like the Isbert or the Bardem family, the Serrador's belong to that familial artistic pedigree characteristic of Spanish show business, in particular of the world of theatre and cinema. Chicho's father, Narciso, was a child prodigy à la Shirley Temple or Freddy Bartholomew; as a teenager, tired of his repertoire and life as a child prodigy, he went to Hollywood and the story goes that he ended up carrying Lon Chaney's make-up case. From the master of disguise he learned not only make-up and interpretation techniques but also Lon Chaney's characterizations of monsters: Dr Jekyll and Mr Hyde, the Hunchback of Notre-Dame, the Phantom of the Opera, and so on. From child prodigy to 'monster', Ibáñez Menta adapted popular horror classics (Poe's tales, Bram Stoker, Bradbury, Lovecraft) for the theatre during the 1940s and 1950s.[2] When Narciso Ibáñez Menta and Pepita Serrador divorced, Chicho, who was four, stayed with his mother whilst touring and eventually moved to Spain in 1947. It was not until the late 1950s that Chicho arrived in Argentina with the intention of persuading his father to adapt for television the repertoire that had proved so successful on stage. In Argentina he learned his trade while making *Obras maestras de terror* (Masterworks of Horror) between 1958 and 1960 under the supervision of American and Dutch technicians. Following the demand of the market – in this instance the sale of TV sets – companies like Philips sent their technicians to developing countries such as Argentina in order to train future television directors. When an offer from TVE (Spanish Television) to do a remake of the programme *Mañana puede ser verdad* brought Ibáñez Serrador back to Spain in 1963,[3] his knowledge of the medium was soon to be put into practice in *Historias para no dormir* (Stories To Keep You Awake), a series of horror and suspense programmes based on *Obras maestras de terror* whose main protagonist was his father Narciso Ibáñez Menta.

The success of *Historias para no dormir* not only marks a shift in the then incipient history of Spanish television, which had only been founded in 1956, but would also be formative for a generation of Spanish spectators. And Ibáñez Serrador's TV productions would continue to be among the favourites of subsequent generations who, no doubt, will remember watching the censorious *Historias de la frivolidad* (1969),[4] the internationally and critically acclaimed *El televisor* (1974),[5] that familiar landmark in the history of Spanish television *Un, dos, tres* (which would change the concept of the

game show across European TV and become the launching pad for
Spanish artists such as the actress Victoria Abril),[6] and the more ped-
agogically oriented *Los Premios Nobel* (1968), *Waku Waku* (1989)
or *Hablemos de sexo* (1990) to name only a few. Referring to *Historias para no dormir*, Sara Torres writes that for 'the vast majority
of Spanish television spectators who are now in their forties and
fifties, the name Chicho Ibáñez Serrador is inevitably linked to
horror stories (1999: 232); while the philosopher Fernando Savater,
writing from the perspective of a horror fan, observes:

> I can understand those great contemporary creators such as Spielberg,
> Lucas or Landis when they acknowledge their debt to old TV series
> like *The Twilight Zone* that indelibly stimulated their imagination:
> Spanish audiences of that time experienced the same thanks to 'Histo-
> rias para no dormir'. (1999: 195)

And interestingly Savater emphasizes the word 'popular' when
referring to Chicho:

> Chicho Ibáñez Serrador showed a good nose for the macabre and the
> unusual, that is to say for what is popular and interesting ['lo "intere-
> sante" popular'], as well as a good sense of filmic narration that man-
> aged to rescue the generic conventions from the mediocrity imposed
> by limited resources and dictatorial hypocrisy. (1999: 195)

The significance of Savater's words should not be understimated, in
particular his comparison of Chicho to American film directors who
found their inspiration in such classics of popular culture and who
similarly made their reputation working in television before moving
into movie production; nor should we overlook his arguably playful
use of the phrase 'lo interesante popular', to which I shall return.

Historias para no dormir consisted of thirteen episodes that had
spectators glued to their television sets.[7] The stories were either
adaptations from supernatural or horror classics or original scripts
written by Luis Peñafiel (Ibáñez Serrador's literary pseudonym). The
first episode of the series, 'El cumpleaños', appeared on Spanish TV
sets in black and white on the night of 4 February 1966, introduced
by Ibáñez Serrador himself, and rated with two diamonds or rhom-
buses ('dos rombos'), TVE's distinctive sign of classification warning
contemporary audiences about the (pernicious) contents of a programme. By 1982 with the revival of the series, which this time featured four episodes in colour and in a longer format,[8] parents did
not have to screen the programme in advance of their children – no

trace now of the dreaded 'dos rombos'. Popular response to the 1966–68 version made in Spain was comparable to the spectacular impact of *Obras maestras de terror* in Argentina. Used to a 'costumbrista' aesthetics – the popular cultural tradition of *sainete* (farce) and *zarzuela* (Spanish operetta), Spanish television audiences had never seen any horror or science fiction on their screens before 1966 (García Serrano, 1996: 77). 'In those days', Savater notes, 'the fantastic genre, horror and science-fiction seemed to be luxuries that only Anglo-Saxon spectators could afford' (1999: 31). Following the tradition of American TV series of the 1950s and 1960s on sci-fi, horror, mystery or suspense which were introduced by a charismatic host, each episode was presented by Chicho himself. While Chicho's programme obviously partakes of the tradition of such revered series as *The Twilight Zone* (CBS, 1959–64), created and introduced by Rod Serling, or *The Outer Limits* (ABC–TV, 1963–65), with its more more mysterious host – the 'control voice', the opening to *Historias para no dormir* also actively promotes a Hitchcockian association, namely the *Alfred Hitchcock Presents* (CBS) TV series launched in 1955. The 'Spanish Hitchcock', comfortably seated, would advance the thematic skeleton of the tale to be told, the staple audiovisual of a creaking door slowly opening to reveal a superimposed and capitalized 'NARCISO IBAÑEZ SERRADOR' against the streaming white light. The name and surname of the director punctuated by a fierce drum was followed by 'presenta' and the title 'Historias para no dormir'. The token scream followed, the creaking door closed and the horror would begin.

In *Hitchcock: The Making of a Reputation* (1992) Robert E. Kapsis describes how 'a close analysis of the opening sequence of each programme vividly conveys the probable impact that the opening had on audiences and suggests the force of Hitchcock's image on the viewer' (1992: 31). 'By intensifying media interest in him,' Kapsis observes, 'the enormous success of "Alfred Hitchcock Presents" solidified Hitchcock's reputation as a popular entertainer and media personality' (1992: 35), enabling him to be 'the first Hollywood director to become a bonafide TV star' (1992: 26). Any comparison between Hitchcock and Ibáñez Serrador is unsustainable in terms of context and oeuvre; what interests me here is the self-conscious promotion-by-association of Ibáñez Serrador's name with the by then acknowledged master of suspense. Moreover, by the time *La residencia* was released in 1969 the name Narciso Ibáñez Serrador was readily tied in the public's mind with the horror genre. In the Spain of the 1960s, Chicho's pioneering transition from television to cinema was a unique phenomenon understandable only in terms of the institution of the author, of authorial reputation. The Hitchcockian link would in fact be played up – or down – by contemporary reviewers: Hitchcock's cinematic 'influence' would be a common source of outrage and derision among specialist film journalists, whereas trade journal publications and daily press reviewers would emphasize the TV persona link.

In the same way that Hitchcock with his TV shows 'had been able to establish a generic contract with his TV audience' (Kapsis, 1992: 42),[9] Chicho drafted and honoured his by catering to audiences' needs and expectations. The popularity of *Historias para no dormir* led to the publication between 1967 and 1974 of a collection of books with the same title, whose editor was Ibáñez Serrador – a marketing operation reminiscent of the *Alfred Hitchcock's Mystery Magazine* as well as other anthology collections. Classics of horror and science fiction, together with stories based on his own scripts for television, were introduced by Ibáñez Serrador, his familiar face in the top corner of the front cover, and the Master's ceremonial words on the back: 'the most scary horror stories of the past, the present and the future, horror that scares some, amuses others, entertains others, but that bores nobody'. Thus the interest and financial performance of the collection was constructed around the figurehead 'Chicho'. Other horror and science fiction publications followed in the late 1960s and early 1970s looking to find their own niche in the market: anthologies like *Narraciones genéricas de terror* (1968) or *Relatos de terror y espanto* (1972), the science fiction magazine *Nueva Dimensión* (1972), horror publications such as *Terror Extra* (1969) and *Terror Fantastic* (1971). The proliferation of comics, fanzines and magazines devoted to the genre attests not only to its growing commercial importance, but also to the significance of horror in the popular culture of the period. By the end of the 1960s 'Chicho' had become the most culturally prominent image of horror in Spain.

La residencia

In the words of the director the film was 'terribly promoted, promoted with clichés'.[10] Whatever its promotional failings, Ibáñez

Serrador's playing of the modesty card belies the force of authorial reputation, which surely operated as a 'must-see' principle. In the July 1970 issue of the trade journal *Cineinforme*, an advertisement written in English draws attention to *La residencia* in the following terms: 'Annabel Films S. A. presents *The Finishing School* (*La residencia*). The film that breaks all public and box-office records'. Ibáñez Serrador's name occupies the centre of the page, below which the reader is offered some figures relating to the takings in four major cities (Madrid, Barcelona, Zaragoza and Valencia), an overall of 44,879,482 million pesetas in the first six months. The October issue of the same year presents a double page advertisement that reads: 'the first Spanish boom in the world's box-office'; on this occasion the information on takings is given in dollars – '916.732 $ USA in the first 8½ months (in only 25 cities). Pic. is due for release in 27 more cities in the country'. *La residencia* appears at the top of a list of films being shown on Spanish screens between 1 September 1969 and 31 July 1970, even though it was only released in January – the first showing took place in Madrid on 12 January (cinema Roxy B); still running at the time when the list was published, the film is ahead of movies such as the American *Irma la Douce* (Billy Wilder, 1963) and *Funny Girl* (William Wyler, 1968) as well as the James Bond vehicle *On Her Majesty's Secret Service* (Peter Hunt, 1969). Under the heading '*La residencia*. A new Spanish Cinema?', *Cineinforme* proudly announces a welcome though unforeseen event: 'a home production occupies first place over the last few months' (1970: 31). The deliberately polemic question that opens the piece of news is matched by the probing closing lines: 'will this example be followed?' (1970: 32). Such framing raises questions about the ongoing debate around the 'New Spanish Cinema' promoted by García Escudero between 1962 and 1967. The figures show that *La residencia* is the most commercially successful film of all time – certainly since box-office control was installed in 1966, and further enthuses, unabashedly, that we are probably facing 'one of the most important films in the cinematography of the world' (1970: 31). This was the first Spanish picture to be shot in English; as the director stated in the press-book, producers and distributors had in mind the exportability of the film: *La residencia* was conceived as 'a stepping-stone from which we can break into the international market'. Unfortunately, the film was a failure on the international front since American International Pictures' promotion and distribution failed to reach contemporary American audiences.[11]

I would like to focus now on the advertising campaign that took place in Zaragoza, a city considered within the Spanish film industry as a testing ground for distributors and exhibitors. *La residencia* arrived in Zaragoza a week after its general release in Madrid on 12 January. The advertising campaign in the local newspaper *Heraldo de Aragón*, which lasted a week (13–20 January), drummed up interest around the figure of the director in news and posters, culminating in an interview with Ibáñez Serrador on the day of the film's release. In the cinema pages of *Heraldo de Aragón* the poster for the 13 January superlatively hails *La residencia* as 'the first great Spanish horror and "suspense" film'; it depicts the loosely drawn figure of a naked woman standing with her back to us and surrounded by a circle of threatening female silhouettes, well conveying the idea of enclosure and claustrophobia. Two names are emphasized: the director Narciso Ibáñez Serrador and the internationally renowned German actress Lilli Palmer. Next to this advertisement, there is another promoting Jesús Franco's *99 mujeres* (99 Women) which plays with imagery from the sub-genre of women-in-prison films – the attractive and probably wrongly-jailed young woman, the menacing warden, and the no less menacing aggressive inmate. Friday's newspaper edition featured a version of the same publicity poster for *La residencia*, though this time much bigger in size, while the Saturday readers (and prospective filmgoers) were introduced to the key protagonists in a photographic image that foregrounded the (suggestively protective) mother-son relationship, as well as a sadistic scene in which a woman tied to a bed is being whipped by another. Flicking through the cinema section of contemporary editions of *Heraldo de Aragón*, one might note, for instance, that although the most important message on the Saturday poster is that the director and some of the cast would be attending the première in Zaragoza, the poster clearly interpellates the male spectator by its positioning in the sports pages. The sexual suggestiveness conveyed in the advertisements – the spectacle of the female body and, more specifically, the display of female sexuality – must in turn be related to the commercial exploitation of female sexuality (sexploitation) that followed the relaxation of censorship during the late 1960s (Hopewell, 1986: 63–71). The hints of lesbianism at play within *La residencia*'s poster, and in the advertising of Franco's *99 mujeres*, are just two examples of film advertising campaigns which resort to the same representational codes. And yet while *La residencia* draws on 'the openly exploitative nature of much horror' (Hutchings, 1993: 3), this was no low-budget production, the exceptional production support at Ibáñez Serrador's disposal disturbing received ideas of contemporary Spanish horror film.

Moving away from the large number of cheap productions and co-productions made by directors such as Jesús Franco, León Klimovsky or Amando de Ossorio, Ibáñez Serrador's filmic project might be said to model itself on a spate of respectable horror films made during the early 1960s in Great Britain. *The Innocents* (Jack Clayton, 1961), adapted from William Archibald's play of the same title and based on Henry James's *Turn of the Screw*, starring Deborah Kerr, and *The Haunting* (Robert Wise, 1963), based on Shirley Jackson's *The Haunting of Hill House*, starring Claire Bloom and Julie Harris[12] – or even the American *What Ever Happened to Baby Jane* (Robert Aldrich, 1962), with Bette Davis and Joan Crawford – present aesthetic and narrative similarities with Ibáñez Serrador's venture: the use of Technicolor, literary adaptations in a legitimate attempt of the genre to clean up its act, stories centred around the figure of a governess (cinematic projects that resuscitated the careers of some actresses), and excellent period settings.[13] Therefore in its formal qualities Ibáñez Serrador's film appears to be more American or European than Spanish. Based on a story written by Juan Tébar and adapted by the director under his pseudonym Luis Peñafiel, *La residencia* is set in a French boarding school for difficult girls at the end of the nineteenth century. The headmistress Madame Fourneau (Lilli Palmer) exerts repressive control over her adolescent son Luis (John Moulder Brown), whom she forbids any contact with her pupils – none of them being quite good enough for her boy. Hence her ruthlessly authoritarian treatment of the boarders. When a series of mysterious disappearances – murders – take place, including that of the latest boarder Teresa (Cristina Galbó), and Madame Fourneau's right-hand girl Irene (Mary Maude), Fourneau, always a main suspect for the audience, decides to investigate. Her investigations lead her to the author of the crimes in the final sequence up in the attic; Luis has been dismembering his victims in order to stitch together his 'ideal' woman. Luis locks up his mother with his monstrous creation.

Unlike Jesús Franco, León Klimovsky or Amando de Ossorio, Ibáñez Serrador's reputation had been forged in an environment different from that of Spanish (and European) low-budget film-making.[14]

His background in television, his quality products for the small screen earned him a reputation in international TV festivals and placed him in a privileged position in relation to cultural policies emanating from the Ministry of Information and Tourism. In the same way that the 'New Spanish Cinema' was 'an attempt to "Europeanise" the Spanish cinema in accord with the general Europeanising of the Development Plan' (Hopewell, 1986: 65) of the 1960s, contemporary Spanish television programmes of the same period partook of this propagandistic operation, which was aimed at the international confirmation of Spanish film and television productions. It is at this juncture that I return to Fernando Savater's 'lo interesante popular' in order to understand the relevance of the cultural politics of the 'New Spanish Cinema' to a contextual understanding of Ibáñez Serrador's commercial enterprise. Apart from the protectionist measures outlined in the introduction, García Escudero's policy involved the promotion of what was to be named New Spanish Cinema. His protectionist measures entailed the restructuring of the economy of commercial cinema and an improvement in the quality of Spanish film through the production of artistic or cultural filmic products (the so-called 'Cine de Interés Especial' [Special Interest Film]) intended to promote a liberal image of Spain abroad. *La residencia* was classified as 'interés especial' and rated for over eighteens by the Film Censorship Board [Junta de Apreciación de la Dirección General de Cultura Popular y Espectáculos].[15] Trade journals – for instance, the enthusiastic piece of news featured in *Cineinforme* – as well as the daily press emphasized not only Chicho's phenomenal success in television but also the possibility *of La residencia* being the incarnation of 'A New Spanish Cinema'. Joaquín Aranda in *Heraldo de Aragón* follows this line of argument in his review: 'if Spanish Cinema produced more "Residencias", it is possible that it could produce the odd "Milky Way" or "Strada"' (1970: 3). The critical élite did not subscribe to such high praise; *Cinestudio, Film Ideal, Nuestro Cine* and *Reseña* rehearsed the typical criticism towards the horror genre, but more importantly, they framed their discussions of the film within wider considerations about the state of the national film industry and the directions that Spanish cinema ought to be taking. It is to these crucial aspects of the critics' discourse – generic prejudices and institutional preoccupations – that I move in the last part of this chapter.

Critical response

As Angel Pérez Gómez acknowledges in *Reseña*, the release of *La residencia* has been 'surrounded by a tense atmosphere that has had a notable influence on critical assessment' (1970: 172) of the film, and adds that critical opinion was polarized – the film 'has been the object of either furious or enthusiastic assessments' (1970: 174). Whether explicitly or implicitly, several points might be said to act as structuring elements in the reviews under consideration: the politics of production, the institution of censorship, the generic choice (as part of a wider debate on the cultural status of the film), and the figure of the director. Symptomatic of such readings is Antonio Pelayo's review in *Cinestudio*. Before a brief textual analysis of the film, Pelayo draws attention to the unprecedented financial and institutional support at the service of the film, a 'Trojan horse' in the Euroamerican film market since, to quote the press-book, 'the production values and the censors' decisions have reached an enviable European "standard"' (1970: 39). Pelayo questions the need for such an exorbitant budget at such a critical moment in the Spanish film industry; other Spanish film-makers – no names given – could have produced 'at least two films of the same technical standard' (1970: 40). As for the censors, he expresses his dissatisfaction with double standards: 'a censor should be able to discriminate between pornography, box-office appeal and expressive needs' (1970: 39). On a more positive note, Pérez Gómez in *Reseña* considers the significance of *La residencia* in the context of contemporary Spanish cinema: valuing the uniqueness of Ibáñez Serrador's project in the country's cinematic production, his ability to draw audiences, Pérez Gómez describes the film as 'respectable commercial cinema' (1970: 175) and concludes that the film is 'an example of what can be achieved at the level of production, but not an example of an artistic formula or as the way forward for a cinematography' (1970: 170). Interestingly, this same issue of *Reseña* in its editorial statement addresses the crisis in Spanish cinema, demanding a 'complete restructuring of the Spanish Film Industry' (1970: 171) in all sectors, in particular those involved in the economic infrastructure – producers and exhibitors, and the end – or at least the 'democratization' – of censorship.

Watching over the 'interests' of Spanish cinema as well as those of Spanish audiences were Miguel Marías, contributor to *Nuestro Cine*, and José María Latorre, writing for *Film Ideal*. For Marías,

Ibáñez Serrador's film is disrespectful to both the institution of cinema and to audiences; the latter's financial support for films that 'insult her/him and consider her/him a retard whose bad taste and subnormality needs to be fed' (1970: 73) is inexplicable. Marías, as well as Latorre, sets himself up as a custodian of taste, protecting a retarded industry (and a retarded viewer) from the perils of *La residencia*; he even calls into question the value judgements of the 'crítica rutinaria' [mainstream film critics] who have approved the film. Thus cultural distinctions are at stake not only between the critic and the filmgoer but also between a critical élite and mainstream journalism, reproducing thereby a hierarchy of taste in film criticism. Marías' position seems to be indicative of mass-culture theories which warned against the negative media effects of mass culture on the viewer and pathologized mass taste by presenting it as aesthetically and politically dangerous.

On a formal and stylistic level, specialist film journal reviewers refuse to engage with the horror genre by displaying a series of conventional arguments against it. Firstly, their approach to this generic form as a 'formula' film responds to mass-culture and auteurist theories on popular cinema; secondly, this type of criticism rejects popular forms on aesthetic grounds. As Mark Jancovich has argued in his introduction to *Horror, the Film Reader* (2002), some critical approaches to popular film, in particular mass-culture theory and auteurism, 'shared the common claim that popular film was dominated by generic formulas' (2002: 10). Should one read closely the critical discourse underlying these reviews, one cannot fail to notice an ideological allegiance to mass-culture and auteurist theorists for whom genre is 'a procedure (rather than a process) in which certain elements are put together in a particular order to produce a particular predetermined and invariable result' (2002: 10). *La residencia* is formulaic and predictable: 'a purely formulaic film' which features 'a panoply of commonplaces' (Latorre, 1970: 72), nothing more than 'a collection of typical generic effects' (Pelayo, 1970: 40); here, for instance, is Marías' sarcastic note on the potential interchangeability of plots between Ibáñez Serrador's film and Franco's *99 mujeres*: 'we are introduced to an enclosed space (prison, residence) where several women (some of whom have not lead exemplary lives, and all to the good if they have not) live together under the vigilance of a sadist (preferably lesbian) and a triangle of "favourites" (preferably lesbian too), who are equally cruel' (1970: 72).

The ideological underpinnings of auteurism seep through to their treatment of the figure of Chicho Ibáñez Serrador, and once again through the name of Hitchcock. Whereas a horror and science fiction publication like *Terror Fantastic* is willing to note the Hitchcockian association in positive terms, defining *La residencia* as 'that difficult *género de director* [the director as author of the film] (specialism of which "don Alfredo" is the indisputable master), or in other words, making the director into the commercial magnet which attracts the masses' (Montaner, 1972: 19, my italics), Marías and the others show their discursive bias – limitation? References to Hitchcock are not wanting: Latorre and Marías accuse Ibáñez Serrador of being merely derivative of Hitchcock, while Pelayo sums up the film as a 'badly assimilated Hitchcock [sic]' (1970: 40), attributing the final product to a group of 'especialistas' [*metteurs-en-scène*, craftsmen]. The conclusion of these claims is to deny Ibáñez Serrador the category of 'auteur' even before a filmography is established.

> A true auteur . . . was distinguished by the presence in each film, above and beyond generic variations, of a distinctive personality, expressed as a world-view or vision. (Stoddart, 1995: 40)

'There is not a "world-view", one cannot even trace a particular personal vision' (1970: 173) in *La residencia*, writes Pérez Gómez in *Reseña*. The film is a flight from reality and, by extension, lacks any contemporary socio-political significance – 'the world begins and ends behind the walls of "la residencia"' (Latorre, 1970: 483) – or any definable moral stance – 'the panorama of values is bleak' (Pérez Gómez, 1970: 173). Lacking realism, moral fibre and devoid of any political intentions, *La residencia* does not offer one of the major appeals of 'new Spanish Cinema', that is, an ideological stand. This invocation of realist standards against the genre presupposes simplicity and a straightforward reading. Savater gives us his personal view on the critical élite's characteristic attitude towards popular film: 'I have never suffered the liberal syndrome [síndrome progresista] which some decades ago (and perhaps to a certain extent nowadays) automatically rejected fictions of "mere" entertainment, as if to entertain was that easy' (1999: 194).

Contemporary Spanish horror is enjoying something of a revival in cinemas throughout Spain, receiving critical acclaim in national and international circles – an important factor for exportability – and, in terms of conventions, is prompting original takes on the genre. Directors such as Alejandro Amenábar and Alex de la Iglesia have produced commercially successful films which have shared box-office success with Hollywood superproductions, even surpassed them; the reputation of others like Álvaro Fernández Armero and Jaume Balagueró has grown among horror fans.[16] These directors have acknowledged their admiration for and debt to Chicho; the impact their films have had on the Spanish film industry, the popular response they have elicited from (mainly young) audiences, their engagement with popular texts, their recuperation of overlooked genres, their use of generic conventions and their relationship with television culture – as well as other cultural and sub-cultural artifacts – needs to be examined in the context of a Spanish horror tradition of which *Historias para no dormir* and *La residencia* represent significant interventions in Spanish popular culture.

By focusing on the horror ventures of Narciso Ibáñez Serrador, this chapter has illustrated the struggle over the meaning of film at a crucial time within the Spanish film industry. Popular cultural forms like the horror genre are important critical sites for interrogating the politics of taste and the marginalization of aesthetic forms in film and cultural studies, as well as for problematizing and challenging the Spanish cinematic canon. In the words of Jo Labanyi, working with popular culture entails on the one hand an explanation of 'the histor-ical-contingent processes by which different cultural products are classified as constituting "good" or "bad" taste' (2002: 15), and, on the other, an understanding of 'how cultural legitimacy is conferred with regard to canonical as well as non-canonical texts' (2002: 15). Despite performing solidly at the box-office and proving popular with audiences – or even because of it – *La residencia* experiences a corre-sponding loss of credibility among 'serious' critics, and not always for reasons of artistic merit. The consensus among audiences was that *La residencia* looked nothing like a Spanish film, breaking stylistically and qualitatively with cinematic forms of the period;[17] however, its critical consignment to the category of generic or sub-generic cinema effectively quashed the opportunity of developing a 'new Spanish cinema' with popular appeal.

Notes

1 The author would like to thank Pepa Ibáñez for arranging an interview with Narciso Ibáñez Serrador. The interview took place in the Teatro

Infanta Isabel (Madrid) in November 2001, where a charismatic Narciso Ibáñez Serrador was directing and acting in *Aprobado en castidad*.
2 For further reading on Ibáñez Menta and Ibáñez Serrador, see *Diccionario del cine español* (1998) and Torres (1999).
3 The three-part episode 'Los bulbos', 'El marciano', 'La tercera expedi-
ción', 'El hombre que perdió su risa', 'N.N. 23' or 'El cohete' are the
titles that were broadcast during that year.
4 Jaime de Armiñán was the other director and scriptwriter of these 'historias' (Baget Herms, 1993: 85).
5 See García Serrano (1996: 78) for a list of Ibáñez Serrador's TV awards
in international festivals.
6 *Un, dos, tres* ran almost intermittently for a period of twenty years, all
together nine stints: 1972–74, 1976–78, 1982–84, 1984–85, 1985–86,
1987–88, 1991–92, 1992–93, 1993–94.
7 The first series included the following titles: "La bodega', 'El tonel', 'El
pacto', 'El muñeco', 'El cohete', 'La cabaña', 'La espera', 'La alarma',
'La sonrisa', 'La oferta', . . . and 'El asfalto' as the last episode' (Baget
Herms, 1993: 159); whilst the second series featured 'El extraño caso
del señor Valdemar', 'El trapero', 'El fin empezó ayer', and 'Freddy'.
Unfortunately, there are no copies available of the 1966–68 series since
at that time the recording of programmes was not a common practice in
Spanish television.
8 According to Ibáñez Serrador in the introduction to the first episode
('Freddy') of the second series and as he reiterated in the interview with
the author, the 1980s remake was of a experimenting nature. At the suggestion of the director of TVE Enrique de las Casas, the idea was to
experiment and explore the possibilities of the medium of video in
order to reduce costs and maximize production. The original plan was
to produce thirteen programmes although finally only four were made
due to the lack of resources in TVE, mainly post-production equipment.
9 Kapsis argues that Hitchcock 'had to renegotiate the aesthetic contract
with his audience and with the critics' (1992: 42) in his filmic production after the *Alfred Hitchcock Presents* programme.
10 Interview with the author.
11 As Michael Orlando Yaccarino points out in the horror magazine *Filmfax*, there are a number of factors for its lack of success in the United
States, among them the re-titling as *The House That Screamed* 'in an
edited dubbed version, as the drive-in second feature to schlock opus
The Incredible Two-Headed Transplant (1971)' (2000: 46). Like many
other Spanish horror movies of the period, *La residencia* is now a cult
movie in international horror circuits.
12 These films were very important to the first wave of academic writing on
horror (Ivan Butler's *The Horror Film* (1967) and Carlos Clarens's *Horror
Movies: An Illustrated Survey* (1967)). On *The Innocents*, for instance,

Carlos Clarens wrote: 'not often will a prestige picture attempt to lead the horror genre from the beaten path and raise from the level of the penny dreadful to that of the distinguished literary work' (1967: 179).

13 Although this is not the place to undertake an analysis of the formal qualities of the film, it could be argued that beside the films of Jack Clayton and Robert Wise the period settings of Hammer horror productions of the mid-1960s influenced the 'look' of the film.

14 For a historical reading on Spanish 'low' horror directors see Vanaclocha et al. (1974), Tohill and Tombs (1995) and Aguilar (1999). For a critical discussion of Spanish exploitation cinema see, Hawkins (2000: 87–113) and Lázaro-Reboll (2002: 83–95).

15 This information, together with other technical and censorship details, appeared in the February issue of *Cineinforme* (1970: 7).

16 See chapter 14 by Andy Willis in this volume.

17 Although Ibáñez Serrador would direct one other movie, in 1976, *¿Quién puede matar a un niño?* / *Who Can Kill A Child?*, he continued to be the TV icon of horror during the 1980s with a second series of *Historias para no dormir* and during the 1990s in a programme entitled *Mis terrores favoritos* (My Favourite Horrors) in which he introduced classic horror films.

Bibliography

Aguilar, Carlos (1999) *Cine fantástico y de terror español, 1900–1983*, San Sebastián: Donostia Kultura.

anon. (1970) 'Panorámica', in *Reseña*, 33, March, 171–2.

anon. (1970) '*La residencia*: ¿un nuevo cine español?', in *Cineinforme*, 112–13, October, 31–2.

Aranda, Joaquín (1970) 'La residencia', in *Heraldo de Aragón*, 20 January 1970.

Baget Herms, Josep María (1993) *Historia de la televisión española, 1956–1975*, Barcelona: Freed Back Ediciones.

Butler, Ivan (1979) *Horror in the Cinema*, London: Thomas Yoseloff.

Cineinforme (1970), 96, February.

— (1970), 106–7, July.

— (1970), 112–13, October.

Clarens, Carlos (1967) *Horror Movies. An Illustrated Survey*, London: Secker & Warburg.

Company, Juan M. (1974) 'El rito y la sangre. Aproximaciones al subterror hispánico', in José Vanaclocha et al. (1974) *Cine español, cine de subgéneros*, Valencia: Fernando Torres, 23–76.

Diccionario de cine español. Academia de las Artes y las Ciencias Cinematográficas de España (1998), Madrid: Alianza Editorial.

García Serrano, Federico (1996) 'La ficción televisiva en España: del retrato teatral a la domesticación del lenguaje cinematográfico', in *Archivos de la Filmoteca*, 23/24, June–October, 71–89.

Hawkins, Joan (2000) *Cutting Edge: Art Horror and the Horrific Avant-garde*, London and Minneapolis: University of Minnesota Press.

Hopewell, John (1986) *Out of the Past: Spanish Cinema After Franco*, London: British Film Institute.

Hutchings, Peter (1993) *Hammer and Beyond: The British Horror Film*, Manchester: Manchester University Press.

Jancovich, Mark (2002) *Horror, the Film Reader*, London: Routledge.

Kapsis, Robert E. (1992) *Hitchcock: The Making of a Reputation*, Chicago and London: The University of Chicago Press.

Labanyi, Jo (2002) 'Matters of Taste: Working with Popular Culture', in Shelley Godsland and Anne M. White (eds.) *Cultura Popular: Studies in Spanish and Latin American Popular Culture*, Bern: Peter Lang, 13–26.

Latorre, José María (1970) 'La residencia', in *Film Ideal*, 217/218/219, 482–85.

Lázaro-Reboll, Antonio (2002) 'Exploitation in the Cinema of Klimovsky and Franco', in Shelley Godsland and Anne M. White (eds.) *Cultura Popular: Studies in Spanish and Latin American Popular Culture*, Bern: Peter Lang, 83–95.

Marías, Miguel (1970) 'La residencia', *Nuestro Cine*, 95, March, 72–3.

Montaner, Francisco (1972) 'La residencia', *Terror Fantastic*, 11, August, 19.

Palacio, Manuel (2001) *Historia de la televisión en España*, Barcelona: Gedisa.

Pelayo, Antonio (1970) 'La residencia', *Cinestudio*, 82, February, 39–40.

Pérez Gómez, Angel A. (1970) 'La residencia', *Reseña*, 33, March, 172–75.

Savater, Fernando (1999) 'Bendita familia', in Carlos Aguilar (ed.) *Cine fantástico y de terror español, 1900–1983*, San Sebastián: Donostia Kultura, 193–6.

Stoddart, Helen (1995) 'Auteurism and Film Authorship', in Joanne Hollows and Mark Jancovich (eds.) *Approaches to Popular Film*, Manchester: Manchester University Press.

Tohill, Cathall and Pete Tombs (1995) *Immoral Tales. Sex and Horror in Europe 1956–1984*, London: Titan.

Torres, Ana (1999) 'Narciso Ibáñez Serrador. Entrevista', in Carlos Aguilar (ed.) *Cine fantástico y de terror español, 1900–1983*, San Sebastián: Donostia Kultura, 223–56.

Vanaclocha, José et al. (1974) *Cine español, cine de subgéneros*, Valencia: Fernando Torees.

Yaccarino, Michael Orlando (2000) '*La Residencia*: A Classic of Spanish Horror Cinema Revisited', *Filmfax*, 75/76, October–January, 46–53.

10

Re-appraising Antonio Mercero:
film authorship and *intuición popular*

Philip Mitchell

Antonio Mercero's long career as director and screenwriter has
brought him a position of notable respect within the TV and cinema
industries, ratified by his role in recent years as President of the
Academia de las Ciencias y las Artes de Televisión. Needless to say, he
has also met with significant success in terms of box-office receipts
and TV viewing figures. In fact, his work's consistent popularity – in
various senses – might be taken as its defining characteristic. As
Mercero remarked in a mid-1990s interview, 'creo que tengo intui-
ción popular y lo que hago es aplicarla' ('I think I have "popular
intuition" and what I do is apply it') (Prades and Álvarez, 1995: 55).

Mercero's critical standing is an equivocal and intriguing one,
however. Taken overall, his work is less readily categorized, in terms
of both genre and authorship, than may seem apparent at first
glance. Best known for comedy-drama, Mercero also shows a preference for historical reconstruction and socio-psychological study.
Partly as a result of this diversity, there is a danger that Mercero's
contribution to Spanish cinema may be glossed over too easily. This
chapter uses an analysis of key elements of three of his most 'popular' films – *La guerra de papá* (1977), *Espérame en el cielo* (1987)
and *La hora de los valientes* (1998) – to develop two related claims.
One is that his best work is more deserving of close critical attention
than has previously been recognized, and that there is room for an
appraisal of his cinematic style which goes beyond the standard
acknowledgement of its technical accomplishment, while also seeking to account for its popular appeal. A second, related claim of this
study is that Mercero's work points up the need to avoid, from an
academic perspective, too fixed a polarity between an auteurist
directorial tradition and a more populist one, the latter implicitly

associated with formulaic commercialism and a purely functional directorial style.

Mercero's cinematic career and the 'third way'

An early 1960s graduate of Madrid's *Escuela Oficial de Cinematografía*, where the requisite pair of publicly exhibited short films immediately established a solid critical reputation,[1] Mercero made his feature-length debut with a Spanish-Italian co-production of his own comic screenplay *Se necesita chico* (1963). Though by no means a box-office success, this saw Mercero bracketed with other emerging directors seen as emblematic of a 'new Spanish cinema',[2] such as Camus, Borau and Saura, who were also recent graduates of either the *Escuela Oficial* or of its forerunner, the *Instituto de Investigaciones y Experiencias Cinematográficas*.

Perhaps due to a lack of immediate commercial success, most of Mercero's work over the following ten years was in the form of documentaries and television drama, Mercero only returning to the cinema in 1974 with *Manchas de sangre en un coche nuevo*, where a plot which borrows heavily from Bardem's *Muerte de un ciclista* (1955) is fleshed out with Mercero's growing taste, developed in his television work, for a markedly Hitchcockian blending of elements of suspense and humour. Since then, his cinema projects have veered in two fairly distinct directions: either somewhat theatrical comedies such as *Las delicias de los verdes años* (1976) and *Don Juan, mi querido fantasma* (1990); or domestic dramas, centring on inter-generational conflict, such as *La guerra de papá* (1977) and *La próxima estación* (1981). It is the latter type that, at the time, led to him being associated with the *cine de la reforma* tendency (that is, one seen as in tune with the spirit of the contemporaneous political reforms which sought to make the post-Franco transition process as smooth and inclusive as possible) in that some critics have read the socio-political ideology underlying such films as broadly conciliatory.

It will also already be clear that there are reasons to invoke what has become known as the *tercera vía* ('third way') debate when discussing Mercero's work.[3] This term has conventionally come to designate a trend in 1970s Spanish cinema (centring on the work of Dibildos, as producer and screenwriter, and of Armiñán, Bodegas and Garci, as directors) which sought to steer a mid course between two supposed extremes, defined by Monterde (1993: 54) as the '*zafiedad*' ('coarseness') of lowbrow sub-genres such as the *destape* sex come-dies which flourished in the years immediately following Franco's death, on the one hand, and the '*exquisitez minoritaria*' ('minority-interest sophistication') of the art-house films, on the other. The argument was therefore that there was a need for a 'third way' which sought to cater for popular mainstream tastes without sacrificing pro-duction values and artistic integrity. Mercero's work in fact shares considerable common ground, both stylistically and thematically, with that of acknowledged *tercera vía* directors such as Garci. To some degree this 1970s debate survives in distinctions drawn between auteurist and popular traditions, drawn either explicitly (via dichotomies such as those established by, for example, Monterde (1993), Borau (1999) and Evans (1999)) or implicitly (via the cumu-lative canon of Spanish films accorded serious academic scrutiny).

Notwithstanding a range of possible theoretical objections,[4] examples could be found fairly readily of directors representative of each side of this dichotomy. We might cite, say, Érice, Saura, Bigas Luna, Medem, Miró or Borau as examples of the auteurist tradition (though Borau's early career would have placed him in the opposite camp) and Ozores, Larraz, Sáenz de Heredia or the latter part of Summers' career as illustrations of the other. More problematic are directors such as Trueba, Colomo, Garci or Camus, all of whose work has merits lifting it well above the more populist end of the mainstream cinema, yet all of whom have had their films critically questioned on at least some of the commonly applied auteurist cri-teria[5] (for example, whether the work is expressive of a sustained personal vision relatively free of non-cinematic constraints). While there are strong grounds for positioning Mercero in this third group, the analysis in the sections below will also consider whether the dichotomy itself needs reconsideration.

Mercero's television work

Although many of the best-known Spanish film directors have made television series,[6] it is probably true to say that Mercero's sustained combination of work in both media is unique. Another reason for briefly considering his television output is that he himself has stressed the similarities of the writing and directing processes in the two media (see, for example, Mercero (1997)). It was with the 35-minute, Emmy-winning *La cabina* (1970), a darkly comic fable about a bemused everyman trapped inside a telephone booth, that Mercero's television work began to receive acclaim. From a screenplay by Garci, *La cabina* takes Mercero's liking for whimsy towards a darker, surrealist direction to which he has only recently returned (in *La habitación blanca* (2000)) and displays, above all, his visual narrative flair (there is no dialogue): the most impressive sequences in his later cinematic work are also frequently those without speech. *Verano azul* (1981), a 12-part serial depicting the rites-of-passage adventures of a group of youngsters on the Andalusian coast, cemented Mercero's popular reputation. Critically disparaged, at times, on account of its melodramatic and rather contrived incorporation of 'socially relevant' themes (juvenile delinquency, sex education, etc), Mercero's coaxing of plausible performances from a cast composed mainly of children and adolescents remains nonetheless impressive. His mid-1980s drama series *Turno de oficio*, concerning a group of Madrid lawyers, manages to juggle a concern for procedural realism and even social denunciation (the lawyers' clients mostly being drawn from marginalized groups) with a distinctly US-influenced multiple-strand storylining. The series was to some degree ground-breaking in that mainstream, adult-oriented Spanish television drama had hitherto tended to centre on literary adaptations or costume drama.

Mercero has also been instrumental, via his directing of *Farmacia de guardia* (1993), in establishing a distinctly Spanish strain of the situation-comedy genre. He himself has cited US sitcoms such as *Cheers* and *The Golden Girls* as his model (Prades and Álvarez, 1995). Nonetheless, he has also claimed that the success of *Farmacia* has helped to put an end to what he calls 'a certain North American colonization' of Spanish television culture (López and De la Calle (1995)). Certainly, it spawned a whole crop of 1990s Spanish sitcoms, typified by an adherence to *Farmacia*'s blend of US-influenced characterization and episodic structure and, on the other hand, by nods to a more theatrical Spanish comedic tradition, with notably longer dialogues than in the Anglo-American genre, together with a willingness to embrace moments of non-ironic melodrama. The resultant hybrid also spawned elements, conversely, of a certain Americanization of Spanish TV culture, with high-profile marketing of video collections of the most popular sitcoms and even, in *Farmacia*'s case, the logo-ization and franchising of the series' title.

Although Mercero's television directing lacks the visual and narrative richness of his best cinematic work, with the notable exceptions of *La cabina* and *La habitación blanca*, it is nonetheless worth emphasizing its range (over discrete genres and sub-genres), its originality (in its adaptation of formats previously neglected in Spanish television) and its influence (both in leading others to work in similar genres and also in its potentially positive contribution to public debate, notably via his willingness to confront racial discrimination and social exclusion).[7]

La guerra de papá (1977)

Mercero's 1977 film adaptation of Delibes' novel *El príncipe destronado*[8] became one of the largest box-office successes of the transition period. Set in the mid 1960s, the film depicts a day in the life of Quico, a four-year-old whose father had fought on the nationalist side in the Civil War yet whose mother's family had been Republicans. Similar domestic polarizations will later affect the protagonists of both *Espérame en el cielo* and *La hora de los valientes*. The psychological effects of the aftermath of this conflict, in particular as they are played out in inter-generational relationships, had of course been the keynote of Érice's *El espíritu de la colmena / The Spirit of the Beehive* four years earlier, but they also constitute a favourite theme of the *cine de la reforma* (see Arocena (1997: 771)). The film's commercial success has been seen as closely linked to the exploitation of this theme. Deveny argues, for example, that 'the incredible box-office success of the film can only be attributed to the empathy that Spaniards felt towards the socio-political theme of the movie' (1993: 231). It has been pointed out that the treatment of the military would not have been authorized under Franco (see Caparrós Lera (1992: 141–2)) and that even in 1977, when the film was made, Mercero had to give assurances to the authorities not only that he would not involve the army, even in an off-screen capacity (ten years later he would be allowed to use them as historical advisers for *Espérame en el cielo*) but also that there would not be a single scene in which an actor would wear a recognizable Spanish uniform. There is a sense, therefore, in which Mercero was making a virtue of necessity in constructing a drama whose relationship to the Civil War legacy is diffuse and conciliatory in tone (rather than denunciatory), and whose thematic focus is introspective and familial as much as socio-political.

The film is grounded, therefore, in a search for psychological truth, one centring on inter-generational conflict; although one of its strengths, as Deveny has observed (in a comparison he develops between this film and work by Aranda and Saura), is that 'the ideological division is underscored by a generational division that augments the rift among family members' (1993: 293).

Despite the perceived conciliatory tone, the film retains a certain harshness: the young boy whose gaze we identify with and through which we see events unfold has clearly been deeply affected by this familial conflict; his chronic bedwetting is foregrounded via its link to the maid's singing of 'El puñal de dos filos' ('the double-edged blade') as a manifestation of this. As in *El espíritu de la colmena*, the opening stills are of a child's drawings, in this case representing a tank and a pistol. Our first sight is thus both the object of the boy's gaze and a vision of the reality that he himself has construed from his semi-understanding of the stories told to him by the adults. Whereas Érice's film links the child's act of viewing very explicitly to the spectator's perspective via the incorporation of the screen-viewing experience into the plot itself (through the itinerant film show which brings James Whales' *Frankenstein* to the young girl's village) and rigorously pursues this link, yielding much greater resonance and psychological depth, Mercero's treatment is both more diffuse and more conventional, including some lachrymose moments decried even by critics broadly sympathetic to the film (see, for example, Caparrós Lera (1992: 142)). This recourse to an over-conventional scene resolution has generally left Mercero open to the charge that his populist inclinations subvert his attempts to imbue his cinema with a less compromising, more forceful impact, though the tendency is notably less evident in a much more substantial later work such as *La hora de los valientes*.

Espérame en el cielo (1988)

One of the highest-grossing domestically produced films of 1988, this is a relatively isolated instance of the Spanish cinema depicting the figure of Franco himself (albeit obliquely), in addition to the socio-cultural and socio-psychological effects of his régime or the aftermath of the conflict whose resolution gave birth to it. Mercero had first conceived the idea for a film based on Franco's putative double when he was still at the *Escuela Oficial de Cinematografía* in the early 1960s, a time when rumours about this double's existence had been rife for some years. A deceptively undemanding comedy is constructed from the project supposedly undertaken by the régime's secret service to kidnap Paulino Alonso (played by the Argentine actor Pepe Soriano), an anonymous salesman of orthopaedic products, on account of his close resemblance to the *caudillo*, and to train him to imitate the leader's speech, gait and personal habits so as to pass him off as Franco on certain public occasions at which the head of state's actual presence might be considered dangerous or otherwise ill-advised.

The treatment given to this premise has often been seen as lacking in any political depth.[9] Much of the comedy, certainly, derives from caricature and comic exaggeration: Paulino's arm is at one point attached to a pulley so as to facilitate a regularly-timed salute when on official engagements; upon seeing Paulino as 'Franco', characters faint, take to the bottle or hurl themselves through windows; bromide is mixed in with the captive Paulino's food in a bid to curb his libido ('Franco does not have erotic obsessions'). Much theatrical humour is milked from the mistaken identities which ensue from Paulino's escape into Franco's cabinet room and private chambers. Such knockabout elements no doubt helped cement the film's wide popular appeal, however conducive they also are to an overall unevenness of tone, an enduring shortcoming of Mercero's cinema.

A richer and more subtle source of the film's humour, however, lies in its satirizing of the régime's public discourse, notably as constructed in the *Noticiario Documental* cinema newsreels, the *No-Do*. Indeed, this is a film most fruitfully read as a sustained satire of the régime's language and its techniques of news management. Parodies of Francoist officialese abound. The letter sent to Paulino's wife, following his kidnapping, informing her of his 'death' is signed by the 'Chief of Propaganda' and apportions blame to 'agents of the Jewish-Masonic conspiracy'.[10] A running joke is the repeated reference to the *pertinaz sequía* ('persistent drought'), one of the régime's stock phrases, undercut by the lament from the government's priest that their prayers for rain have not been answered. The church's role in disseminating the régime's ideology is a related target of this satire: we see Paulino and his wife Emilia hearing the view from the pulpit that a woman's place is in the home or the temple, and that the chief sources of moral danger are dances, beaches and the cinema, in particular 'that film whose title is a women's name', a reference to *Gilda* which locates the film's initial action within the late 1940s. The subsequent reference to the eagerness of Paulino and his friends to attend that night's *adoración nocturna* momentarily misleads us regarding their attitude to such pieties, until a brisk time-cut to the next scene visually confounds our expectation, a trade-mark Mercero device, by placing the men in a Madrid bordello.

The heart of the film, however, lies in the use made of the *No-Do* and its place in the collective memory. Having himself been an avid cinema-goer through the 1940s and 1950s, when these newsreels' influence was arguably at its height,[11] and having a background as a documentary film-maker, Mercero was well placed not only to reproduce their visual and verbal mode of address but also to exploit and satirize their socio-psychological impact. Thus we see recre-ations of the *No-Do*'s unmistakable monochrome images, stentorian narration and martial music as the *Caudillo* receives by turns tumul-tuous applause while inaugurating a new reservoir and international acclaim while accepting a new ambassador's credentials. We see, in turn, recreations of the 1950s cinema audience watching these images, their chief source of news events. The *No-Do* inserts are framed, however, by colour sequences which reveal the stage man-agement of the events in question: how the *¡Viva Franco!* banners are handed out beforehand by the secret service (and subsequently stored in the same basement rooms of Franco's residence where Paulino is held captive); how the journalists and photographers are shepherded and dragooned; how the chants of enthusiasm are rehearsed and standardized. Another characteristic Mercero touch here sees one free-spirited child refusing to join in and eventually fleeing the scene. Thus the already bizarre *No-Do* sight of the Bishop of Asturias blessing a statue at the bottom of a coal mine has its authority further undermined by the colour sequences which pre-cede and follow it, unmasking the blatant 'photo-opportunity' orchestration of such events.

This switching to and from the *No-Do* newsreel is a key strategy of Mercero's. The film itself begins with a black-and-white *No-Do* sequence over the main credits which, the viewer later realizes, is a blend of real and recreated footage. The sequence ends on a shot of a Madrid street; the shot is held and then slowly turns to colour, coinciding with the arrival of the diegetic street sounds. The effect is almost that of a picture coming to life,[12] one which neatly captures the film's whimsical air, set up as a counterpoint to the documentary elements. This technique is later reprised by means of further colour-switches from *No-Do* to the film 'proper'.

The *No-Do* sequences thus have an ambivalent diegetic status. They are both part of the 'story-world' (since the viewer recognizes, in the sequences following Paulino's kidnapping and training, that 'Franco' is Paulino – and also retrospectively recognizes that in the opening *No-Do* sequences 'Franco' must be the actor Pepe Soriano)[13] and simultaneously outside it, in that they function as quasi-documentary testimony to the era's mediated reality. The playfulness of this tension culminates in the pact between Paulino and his wife: though they will never be able to see each other again he will send her a secret token of affection in his *No-Do* appearances by scratching his right ear on camera. The subsequent ear-scratching at opportune moments in the *No-Do*, for all its comic effect, also registers a genuine *frisson* in the audience; it is as though Mercero's protagonist has jumped between the diegetic and non-diegetic worlds.[14] Parallel to this running contrast between the monochrome 'official' representation of reality and the film world's own, deflating version of it, there is in fact a whole set of 'doubles' in the film: for example, a Carrero Blanco look-alike intervenes in several key scenes, as does an actor clearly chosen for his close resemblance to Matías Prats, the celebrated radio journalist whose 'real' voice is heard in the *No-Do* recreations. As a consequence, when we see a large yacht looking very plausibly like Franco's *Azor* we are left reflecting on its status as 'real' or 're-creation', just as with the cabinet office and private rooms of the Pardo residence.[15] The fact that Paulino deals in false limbs, orthopaedic 'doubles', is presumably part of this running joke.

It bears reiterating, of course, that the immediate effect of all these devices is largely whimsical and comic; a film with a less populist sense of its target audience, of course, might have developed such features to a sharper political point. At the same time, these considerations do emphasize how easily the multi-layered characteristics of Mercero's cinematic style can be neglected. As the historian Tamames (2001) has argued, this film is in fact best read as a political parable; Mercero's achievement thus lies in reconciling the appropriately playful handling of the storyline's probably apocryphal premise with an ironic treatment – functioning at various levels of sophistication – of both the régime itself and of its media representation.

La hora de los valientes (1998)

This 1998 return to the cinema has won high praise even from critics previously dismissive of Mercero's work.[16] It continues his well-established interest in the Civil War-related past, although this is the first time he has set the action during the conflict itself. As with *Espérame en el cielo*, the starting point is a plausible 'urban myth': in this case, that in the process of evacuating the Prado's treasures to Valencia, while Madrid was under siege, at least one of the gallery's masterpieces was kept safe in private hands until the war's end. Thus, young Manuel, one of the gallery's curators, finds himself hiding a Goya self-portrait in various ingenious places in his aunt's boarding-house.

In a prolongation of the *cine de la reforma* emphases which pervade *La guerra de papá*, the focus is on the psychological and familial effects of the war rather than the conflict itself. The military operations themselves are scarcely represented. What *is* shown is their aftermath, both immediate, in several impressively staged scenes following the impact of a missile, and cumulative, via the film's sustained exploration of the conflict's psychological effects. The film's opening five minutes establish these themes with admirable concision. We look over an interior patio onto a balcony where a quintessential Mercero domestic scene is being played out: harassed parents alongside brazen, insightful young child, whose hair is playfully tousled by an amused young adult sister. The requisite narrative disruption, however, is boldly and starkly achieved: as the sister, Carmen, leaves the building the camera's slow track-out is interrupted by a jump cut to a shot of the same building from a slightly more oblique angle. The viewer's momentary disorientation is in turn disrupted by a sudden and huge explosion. As a place and time caption comes into view, we realize that the family scene has taken place during the siege of Madrid, and that we have just witnessed the impact of a nationalist missile. In narrative terms, this disruption is never truly resolved. In fact, accusations that Mercero's cinema is hackneyed in its story structure neglect the fact that his narrative resolutions tend to be bittersweet, at best. In *La guerra de papá* the family's communication problems remain unresolved; in *Espérame en el cielo* the closing images show Emilia (Franco's double's wife) visibly aging alone in front of the *No-Do*, as Mercero uses a series of lap dissolves to fast-forward to 1975. In *La hora de los valientes*, the death of Carmen's family in this explosion will be substituted later by the surrogate family of the boarding-house where she stays, and eventually by her marriage to Manuel, but the film's final images leave her widowed. Recurrently the various physical settings are presented as places of calm, order or respite, only for the conflict to disrupt this: the UGT union headquarters, for example, is struck by a bomb; the Prado itself; the boarding-house and even the rural restaurant where Manuel and Carmen's wedding reception is being held.

The insistence with which the Goya self-portrait is deployed as a recurring motif has no counterpart elsewhere in Mercero's cinema. The early scene, based on the description in Azaña's memoirs, in which the Prado's treasures are packed up and evacuated ends on a lingering close-up of Goya's eyes. This same effect is reprised at regular intervals through the film: notably, for example, after the failed attempt by the local militia to confiscate the painting. This latter scene also shows Mercero at his succinct, visually-reliant best: when the boarding-house is being searched we have not been privy to the occupants' discussion about where to hide the painting. As the militiamen search the room we are left to pick out for ourselves, in long shot, the fact that the portrait has ingeniously been 'hidden' by being hung on the wall, alongside other household decorations, Manuel having correctly surmised that it will not be recognized (he had earlier bemoaned the *madrileños*' lack of interest in the Prado's riches).[17] This insistence culminates at the film's closing scene, when the portrait has been restored to the Prado. We gather that a few years have passed since the end of the war, as Goya's close-up gaze first scrutinizes a group of nuns in 1940s headgear, in sharp contrast to the earlier street scene where, as religious icons languish in flames, a priest is led away to be shot, and then sees Carmen's school-age son hearing how the new régime has honoured the nationalist official, his father's killer, who claimed to have rescued the portrait. The viewer senses a keenly-felt directorial sentiment in this insistence. It is as though the portrait not only represents the artist looking on at the suffering and injustice before his gaze just as (we are told in one of the opening scenes) he had observed the aftermath of the 3rd May shootings in detail before re-creating the last moments of the victims, but that it also stands in for the director's own gaze, as, in his sixties, just like the Goya of the self-portrait, he looks back at his childhood self (Mercero was born just before the start of the Civil War).

Relatedly, this film also serves as a perspicuous example of Mercero's acknowledged trump card: his portrayal of childhood disrupted by a precocious exposure to adult sadness. Like Quico in *La guerra de papá*, Pepito is struggling to understand the images and sounds he is exposed to. Mercero is very attentive here to the expressive power of speech and its paradoxical opacity to the child's ear. Just as Quico had relayed to his mother his father's wish that she should go and 'freír puñetas' (literally the nonsensical 'to fry wristbands'), without registering the insulting colloquial meaning ('to go to hell'), so Pepito and his friends reproduce military phrases without fully grasping their import. In inter-generational dialogues Mercero deploys his characteristic loaded cutting, with standard 'shot–reverse shot' for the adult speakers interrupted by a sudden cut to the child's eyes, cued by a key lexical item and followed by a further cut to the object of the child's gaze. A textbook example occurs with the distraught, recently bereaved Carmen's first arrival at the boarding-house. The building's caretaker, following a tip-off, accuses her of being a prostitute, first indirectly and then with 'es una puta, vamos' ('let's face it, she's a whore'). On the word 'whore' Mercero cuts to Pepito's face, his eyes first registering shock and then shifting as he becomes the first to notice something; there follows a point of view shot revealing Carmen's appearance and collapse at the doorway. This will be echoed in the later scene where Carmen is giving birth: there is a cut from the bed to the child's gaze.

Just as Quico and his friends, in *La guerra de papá*, had stained themselves with Mercurochrome so as to better imitate the battle scenes they had heard his father describe, so Pepito and his gang act out a firing squad execution in a burnt-out building, urging each other to 'die' as realistically as possible.[18] There is a double-layered irony here. In a later scene in the same setting, these friends will indeed see Pepito die realistically, as he is blown to pieces by a bomb; moreover, Mercero depicts their games with an almost exaggerated cinematic intensity, precisely as if they stand in for the real adult horrors happening off-screen: the film's opening music, a thunderous pastiche of military marches, is reprised at this point and we see a characteristic Mercero delayed revelation, via a track-back, to show us the 'firing squad'. Pepito spends much of his time searching for shrapnel or rocks from ruined buildings, etc,[19] as if his struggle to interpret the cruelty and chaos around him is aided by this highly tangible evidence of its effects; it is this search, however, that will eventually kill him, as he fatally touches the unexploded bomb.

As in *Espérame en el cielo*, Mercero problematizes the media's role in representing this reality. This tension is signalled from the start: the jump cut to the exploding Madrid dwellings dissolves to black-and-white footage of the same event; the camera then tracks back to reveal two government officials viewing a Republican newsreel. The radio, similarly, provides a constant backdrop to and commentary on the plot development: the film title itself comes from one of the slogans broadcast from the Republican transmitters; the characters, moreover, continually relay information to each other ('comrade Durruti has reached Aragon') gleaned from these broadcasts. This is used partly for ironic effect: the viewer realizes this broadcast optimism will be deflated. It is also used as a concise means of switching focus: our first realization that we will also see a depiction of nationalist sympathies is triggered by an aural scene transition as we hear a snatch of Radio Sevilla, the main Francoist station transmitting towards Madrid. In a similar way, our realization in the final reel that the war is over comes when the boarding-house radio is switched on and we hear not the customary '¡viva la república!' but Franco's famous 1st April broadcast from Burgos. This tension which surrounds the credibility of these external sources is neatly encapsulated when Pepito arrives with some fresh loaves of bread dropped by nationalist planes, wrapped in propaganda leaflets: he and Carmen wrestle with their hunger and the radio's warnings that the bread is poisoned, their eventual consumption of the bread neatly indicating the unspoken scepticism.

The film has a number of effective sequences which are completely wordless: the re-creation of the use of the Madrid underground as an air-raid shelter, for example, or the evacuation of the paintings from the Prado; an especially felicitous moment here occurs when Velázquez's *Las meninas* is slowly brought into view on its way to being boxed up, momentarily forming a perfect frame-within-a-frame on the screen and causing the removal workers, whose physical point of view we share, to stand transfixed.

At the film's climax, with the war now over, Manuel returns the Goya to the Prado, only to be ambushed and shot in front of the painting by nationalist troops, as he cries '¡viva la libertad!'. This scene is shot so as to replicate Goya's '3rd of May' painting (*Los fusilamientos de la montaña de Príncipe Pío*), with the white-shirted

Manuel splaying his arms wide in imitation of the central figure in the painting. This provides an illustration of Kinder's observation (1993: 138) regarding Goya's position as a reference point for representations of violence in Spanish film. The scene might usefully be contrasted with the widely discussed closing moments of Bigas Luna's *Jamón jamón* (1992), where the two male protagonists enact a tragicomic fight to the death with a pair of hams as cudgels, in a clearly deliberate echo of Goya's *Riña a garrotazos*.[20] Evidently, both scenes re-present and quote from one of the paintings in question. The scene constructed by Bigas Luna, however, functions as an implicit, external reference: the Goya 'text' being quoted is outside the film world. Indeed, any viewer unfamiliar with the painting would not infer the scene's intertextual status at all. Mercero's scene, in contrast, functions as an intra-textual reference: the painting quoted is one we have seen in sustained close-up in the first reel of the film. Bigas Lunas' scene, moreover, functions as one of a set of inter-textual references within the film to Spanish cinema, theatre and painting (see Deleyto (1999)). We may contrast, then, an allusive approach which makes certain assumptions about the film's audience's inter-textual knowledge if the scene's full range of allusive meanings is to be triggered, with Mercero's more direct quotative style, one which makes no such demands on the viewer. It is tempting to see these differences as an encapsulation of differential approaches from, on the one hand, an auteurist director, in the case of *Jamón jamón*, and on the other a 'popular' directorial approach embodied by Mercero. It would be misleading to conclude from this that Mercero's achievement in a film like *Valientes* is thereby diminished, however, and the final section of this chapter therefore reconsiders this demarcation in more detail.

The *tercera vía* revisited

This discussion of the work of a director seen as being outside the arthouse tradition allows us to assess how the original *tercera vía* debate might be re-inflected. One starting point is to ask to what extent any director actually achieves popularity 'on their own terms' (Evans, 1999: 3)? The inherent risk-taking implied by such a description is a theoretically difficult phenomenon to identify, even in the case of directors renowned for their uncompromising approach. Returning briefly to Víctor Érice provides a salutary case in point here. Despite the praise lavished on *El espíritu de la colmena*, Érice was in fact perturbed at the apparent minority appeal of his film[21] and had conceived his next project, *El sur* (1983), as a more commercial enterprise, even agreeing to a trimming of its running time by an hour in the hope of gaining a wider audience. The difficulty of separating commercial and aesthetic considerations is not, in other words, the sole concern of more 'popular' directorial approaches.

It is also true, of course, that the deliberate rejection of conventionalized narrative and stylistic features in favour of a relatively hermetic mode of address carries with it an ideological positioning from which much of the potency of key Spanish auteurist films has been derived (see Morgan (1993)). We might further conjecture, however, that one factor in the enhanced commercial appeal of a vein of auteurist Spanish cinema, alongside the sociological reasons often advanced, has been a reduction in its hermeticism; among other factors this change may itself be partly ascribable to the influence of an identifiably postmodern trend towards genre-mixing and multi-level references and ironies, resulting in the increased frequency of occurrence of a more universally approachable 'entry level' to many films whose less accessible forerunners made more demands on the spectators' degree of engagement and cultural baggage. As discussed above, a certain conventionalizing tendency (in particular regarding scene resolution) is a feature of Mercero's work and he is clearly, moreover, among the least hermetic of Spanish directors. It would be unfair to categorize his cinematic style as purely functional, however. The analyses in this chapter have pointed out some of Mercero's characteristic devices of framing, editing, aural accompaniment (or its absence) and multi-level irony which, while less distinctive than the comparable favoured techniques of acknowledged 'auteur' directors[22] may nonetheless be identified as instances of what Jameson (1990: 103) has termed directorial 'encodings' or 'private signifiers'. Also pertinent is Perkins' dictum (1972: 181–2) that a director 'controls a film not just by what he himself [sic] invents, but also by what he allows actors, cameramen, and others to do'. This is particularly relevant, of course, to Mercero's skill with child actors, but it can also be applied more broadly.

What may be elucidated, then, by consideration of the work of a director like Mercero, is the possible need for the compartmentalizing tendency in academic approaches to Spanish cinema to be loosened. If it is true, as Borau argues (1999: xxii), that the box-office success of auteurist cinema means that 'the inmates . . . have ended up by taking over the asylum', then perhaps it is only fitting that critical perspectives should be renewed as well, at least in recognizing that Mercero's sustained popular appeal derives from his following a *tercera vía* of his own, in the sense that his films demonstrably seek to bridge the gap between the auteurist and populist traditions.

Notes

1 The first of these shorts, *Lección de arte* (1961), won prizes at the San Sebastián and Cork film festivals, while the second, *Trotín Troteras* (1962), won the Parisian *Prix de la Biennale des Arts*.

2 For further discussion of this, see Besas (1985: 74) and Torreiro (1995: 308–11).

3 For more on the *tercera vía* debate see Rodríguez Lafuente (1991: 256) and Jordan and Morgan-Tamosunas (1998: 66–8).

4 In particular, there is insufficient space here for a thorough discussion of the relevant aspects of auteur theory or competing definitions of 'the popular'.

5 See, for example, Monterde's strictures on the work of Camus, Colomo and Garci (1993: 180–93).

6 These include forays into TV comedy-drama from Trueba (*La mujer de tu vida*, 1989), Chavarri (*Yo soy el que tú buscas*, 1988) and Colomo (*Dime que me quieres*, 2001); adaptations from literary sources from Camus (*La forja de un rebelde*, 1990), Gutiérrez Aragón (*El Quijote de Miguel de Cervantes*, 1991) and Aranda (*Los jinetes del alba*, 1990); situation comedy from Escrivá (*Lleno por favor*, 1993; *Éste es mi barrio*, 1996); children's drama from Borau (*Celia*, 1993); and suspense from Garci (*Historias del otro lado*, 1990).

7 Without overstating this impact, it is worth bearing in mind that Mercero himself described his intentions in *Farmacia de guardia* as ultimately a form of 'psicoterapia social' ('social psycho-therapy') and that anti-racism organizations have praised his television work (see Prades and Álvarez, 1995).

8 Ten years later Mercero adapted another Delibes novel for the cinema, *El tesoro* (1987), although with less commercial success.

9 For example, Heredero (1989: 21) describes the film's handling of its subject matter as 'cuidadosamente ajena al análisis político' ('carefully avoiding any political analysis').

10 A similar satirical point is made in Alex de la Iglesia's 1992 film *Acción Mutante* (another work rich in parodies of mediated political discourse), when a television newsreader warns viewers that an armed terrorist is also 'a Jew and a freemason'.

11 See Ellwood (1987) and Trenzado (1999).

12 One might compare this opening to the post-credits sequence used by Almodóvar in *Átame* (1989), where a watercolour painting of the institution where the protagonist is being held (a painting we later see on the wall of the Principal's office) slowly turns into a photographic still and then into a moving image, signalling the start of the 'story' proper. A related instance – though one which verges on a Brechtian distanciation effect – is provided by Saura's decision to begin *El amor brujo* (1986) with a pre-credits sequence clearly showing that the shanty town where the film's action is about to take place is in fact a studio set surrounded by lights, cameras, etc.

13 The viewer's diegetic 'awareness' may, in fact, be more complex: we become aware that the 'Franco' in the opening credits sequence must be the actor Pepe Soriano, acting the part of Franco and under the instructions of Antonio Mercero, as opposed to our awareness in the later sequences that 'Franco' is the character Paulino, also acting the part of Franco but under the instructions of the Comrade Sinsoles character, his secret service mentor.

14 Internationally, the best-known example of this effect, of course, occurs in Allen's *The Purple Rose of Cairo*, when Mia Farrow's character literally jumps into the black-and-white footage on the screen; an analogous instance from Spanish cinema occurs in Fernán-Gómez's *El viaje a ninguna parte* (1986), when the viewer is presented with sequences supposedly taken from 'real' (i.e. non-diegetic) films in which the itinerant actors claim to have appeared as extras. All three of these instances, their disparity notwithstanding, yield a comparable effect of poignant humour.

15 In both cases, it so happens, Mercero did in fact use the 'authentic' settings.

16 See, for example, the review in *El País* (20 December 1998) by Torres (and contrast it with the evaluation of Mercero's worth as a director in the same author's *Diccionario del Cine* (1996)).

17 An insouciant note of humour is injected here when Manuel's anarchist grandfather, on being asked by one of the militiamen to identify the figure in the portrait, refers to him as 'my uncle Paco from Zaragoza', a play on Goya's first name and place of birth.

18 This recalls the opening sequence of Chavarri's *Las bicicletas son para el verano* (1984), where the children's acting-out of gun battles is given a sepia tint and slow-motion treatment, at one point deliberately evoking Robert Capa's classic 1936 photograph of a loyalist soldier in the Cordoban Cerro Muriano at the moment of death.

19 The boy's obsessive interest in these objects is depicted as understandable but nonetheless disturbed behaviour, and therefore as the counterpart of Quico's bedwetting in *La guerra de papá*, that is to say as an external indication of a psychological trauma.

20 For a detailed discussion of this sequence from *Jamón jamón* and its
    relationship with the Goya painting, see Holder (1998).
21 Interviewed on BBC 2's *Talking Pictures* (broadcast 23 October 1993).
22 To cite a few random examples: Berlanga's celebrated ensemble-scene
    long takes, Alomódovar's overhead views or disorienting establishing
    shots, or Bigas Luna's studiedly arranged compositions, such as at the
    resolution of the cudgel scene described above.

Bibliography

Arocena, Carmen (1997) 'La guerra de papá', in Julio Pérez Perucha (ed.)
    Antología crítica del cine español 1906–1995: flor en la sombra, Madrid:
    Cátedra, 770–2.
Besas, Peter (1985) *Behind the Spanish Lens: Spanish Cinema under Fascism
    and Democracy*, Colorado: Arden Press.
Borau, José Luis (1999) 'Prologue: The Long March of the Spanish Cinema
    Towards Itself', in Peter William Evans (ed.) *Spanish Cinema: The
    Auteurist Tradition*, Oxford: Oxford University Press, xvii–xxii.
Caparrós Lera, J. M. (1992) *El cine español de la democracia*, Barcelona:
    Anthropos.
Deleyto, Celestino (1999) 'Motherland: Space, Femininity and Spanishness
    in *Jamón jamón*', in Peter William Evans (ed.) *Spanish Cinema: The
    Auteurist Tradition*, Oxford: Oxford University Press, 270–85.
Deveny, Thomas G. (1993) *Cain on Screen*, Metuchen, NJ: Scarecrow Press.
Ellwood, Sheelagh M. (1987) 'Spanish Newsreels 1943–1975: The Image
    of the Franco Régime', *Historical Journal of Film, Radio and Television*,
    7: 3, 225–38.
Evans, Peter William (1999) 'Introduction', in Peter William Evans (ed.) *Span-
    ish Cinema: the Auteurist Tradition*, Oxford: Oxford University Press, 1–7.
Heredero, Carlos F. (1989) 'El reflejo de la evolución social y política en
    el cine español de la transición y de la democracia: historia de un desen-
    cuentro', in José A. Hurtado and Francisco M. Picó (eds.) *Escritos
    sobre el cine español: 1973–1987*, Valencia: Filmoteca de la Generalitat
    Valenciana, 17–32.
Holder, John (1998) 'Pata negra: Goya's Cudgel Motif in Two Contempo-
    rary Spanish Films', *Donaire*, 10, April, 31–6.
Jameson, Fredric (1990) *Signatures of the Visible*, New York: Routledge.
Jordan, Barry and Rikki Morgan-Tamosunas (1998) *Contemporary Spanish
    Cinema*, Manchester: Manchester University Press.
Kinder, Marsha (1993) *Blood Cinema: The Reconstruction of National
    Identity in Spain*, Berkeley, CA: University of California Press.
López, Francisco J. and Pablo De La Calle (1995) 'De los "reality" a las tele-
    comedias', *El Mundo*, 20th January, 41.

Mercero, Antonio (1997) 'La jerga juvenil y sus dificultades en el guión', paper presented to the *Primer Congreso de la Lengua Española*, Zacatecas.

Monterde, José Enrique (1993) *Veinte años de cine español (1973–1992)*, Barcelona: Paidós.

Morgan, Rikki (1993) 'Romper los moldes: implicaciones estéticas e ideológicas de *El espíritu de la colmena*', *Journal of the Association for Contemporary Iberian Studies*, 6: 1, 25–30.

Perkins, V. F. (1972) *Film as Film*, Harmondsworth: Penguin.

Prades, J. and P. Álvarez (1995) 'Lo que nosotros hacemos es terapia social', *El País*, 21st May, 55.

Rodríguez Lafuente, Fernando (1991) 'Cine español: 1939–1990', in Antonio Ramos Gascón (ed.) *España hoy: cultura*, Madrid: Cátedra, 241–80.

Tamames, Ramón (2001) 'El eterno retorno', *El Mundo*, 9th November, 27.

Torreiro, Casimiro (1995) '¿Una dictadura liberal?', in Román Gubern et al. (eds.) *Historia del cine español*, Madrid: Cátedra, 295–340.

Torres, Augusto M. (1996) *Diccionario del cine*, Madrid: Espasa Calpe.

—— (1998) 'Brillante homenaje al Prado', *El País*, 20th December, 23.

Trenzado Romero, Manuel (1999) *Cultura de masas y cambio político: el cine español de la transición*, Madrid: C.I.S.

11

Rated S: softcore pornography and the Spanish transition to democracy, 1977–82

Daniel Kowalsky

The end of the Franco dictatorship in November 1975 set in motion the historical era now known as the *transición*, a seven-year period during which Spain was transformed from an authoritarian Catholic regime to a secular social democracy. Perhaps the most remarkable feature of the *transición* was the lack of a popular consensus over the desired direction of a post-Franco Spain. For some, the death of the dictator signalled an opportunity to break conclusively with the traditionalist values that had characterized the thirty-nine-year Franco reign, and more closely replicate the parliamentary democracies of Spain's Western European neighbours. Meanwhile, the country's conservative élite tended to resist the wholesale abandonment of the entrenched mores of Franco's Spain. Nowhere is the on-going socio-cultural cleavage of the *transición* more in evidence than in the direction of post-Franco Spanish cinema. This chapter will treat in detail one of the unique bi-products of Spain's process of democratization: the highly unusual experiment in adult cinema known as the S film.

Due to internal political indecision and strife among parties vying for power, in the wake of the *generalísimo*'s demise, no prompt decision was taken on the issue of acceptable film and media content. Only with Royal Decree 3071, signed on 11 November 1977, did the newly elected government of Adolfo Suárez formally abolish all media censorship. In place of censorship, the Spanish government instituted a four-tiered rating system for film products: (1) all audiences; (2) over 14 years of age; (3) over 18; and (4) S.[1] The S rating was attached to products that 'due to their theme or content might offend the sensibility of the spectator'.

Between 1977 and 1982, the Spanish Ministry of Culture classified some 424 pictures with the S rating. Just under 300 of these

films were of foreign provenance, while Spanish productions or co-
productions accounted for approximately 130.[2] A small number of
S films had nothing to do with sex but were deemed potentially
offensive on account of extreme violence or incendiary politics – the
most notable example was *El crimen de Cuenca* (Pilar Miró, 1979),
whose subject was the arrest and torture of two peasants for a crime
they did not commit. Some horror and slasher films of foreign
origin, including *Dawn of the Dead* (George Romero, 1978) and
Friday the 13th (Sean Cunningham, 1980) also earned the S. Apart
from these few exceptions, the rating was overwhelmingly associated with softcore pornography.[3] Most significantly, the S film
marked the full development of a domestic softcore film industry,
predominantly produced for local consumption.[4]

The S films can only be understood in the context of Spain's turbulent cinematic history. The dictatorship of General Francisco
Franco, which dated from his victory in the Civil War of 1936–39 to
his death in November 1975, placed major restrictions on cinematic
representations. Film narratives were carefully controlled so as to
perpetuate the *Franquista* vision of a unified, Catholic and national-
istic Spain.[5] Franco's ideology was an anachronism; not looking forward to a new society, but back several centuries, to the early
modern Spain of Velázquez, Don Quixote and *El Escorial*, or back
still further, to the Crusade against Muslim occupation in the late
Middle Ages.

Much of Franco's moral authority was derived from his close
association with the Catholic Church. As a result of this alliance,
Franco made Catholic doctrine state policy; for example, birth control, abortion and sexual education were forbidden, and divorce
severely limited. The Church's heavy influence cast a long shadow
over the arts and popular culture, not least in the cinema. The
Franco régime took film censorship very seriously, and from early
1937 until 1978, approximately sixty thousand films were scruti-
nized by state censors for images or dialogue that mocked or challenged Catholic sensibilities.[6] In short, cinema under Franco sought
to uphold the entrenched values of the *Franquista* system.[7]

A small cluster of scholars have recently attempted to recast
Franco-era film censorship in a more nuanced light.[8] This revisionism
has led to a reconsideration of earlier blanket condemnations
of cinema under the Franco régime. The consensus now emerging
is that even under the dictator, a discreet director could succeed in

presenting a subversive idea or occasional image. Thus in the early 1950s, the predominance of virginal heroines was already being challenged: adultery was taken up in *Muerte de un ciclista* (Juan Antonio Bardem, 1955), while Marisa de Leza was permitted to provocatively smoke a cigarette in *Surcos* (José Antonio Nieves Conde, 1951). In the 1960s, increasing amounts of visible flesh crept into Spanish productions. Predictably perhaps, the first bikini in a Spanish film was worn by a German national – in this case Elke Sommer in *Bahía de Palma* (Juan Bosch, 1962). By the end of the decade, however, it was a Spanish actress, Elisa Ramírez, who flashed the first bare breast on a Spanish screen (*La Celestina*, César Ardavín, 1969).

The early 1970s marked the advent of the Spanish *destape* – the word means 'topless' – an era when the bare-breasted female gradually became a fixture in print media, stage plays and cinema. The development of the *destape* film genre was a strong indication that the *Franquista* moral order was breaking down. Films of the *destape* are best described as light Iberian sex comedies, usually concerned with a middle-aged man afflicted with satyriasis; or, as Rafael Torres has offered, 'scrawny, insincere men obsessed with genitals' (1996: 36–7). Indeed, one actor, Alfredo Landa, was featured in so many of the major products of this genre that one can speak of an era of *landismo*.[9] The *destape* was concerned primarily with displaying naked breasts; nonetheless, after four decades of censorship, the Spanish appetite for this limited variety of visual stimulation could not be contained. Observing the phenomenon of the *destape*, the Nobel prize laureate Camilo José Cela bluntly noted, 'España se ha puesto cachonda' ('Spain has become horny').[10]

Even before the dictator died, it was clear that the locomotive of liberalization could not be slowed, much less stopped. The *destape*, it turned out, was but a preliminary station along the way towards full freedom of expression. In February 1975, the Ministry of Information and Tourism reversed the long-standing and lately unenforced ban on nudity in film. New regulations now permitted images of nudity 'according to the director's needs'.[11] Within months, full frontal nudity was first seen in a Spanish film – Jorge Grau's *La trastienda* (1975); the actress was María José Cantudo.

From late 1975 until the election of the Spanish Socialist Party (PSOE) in 1982, the sexualization of Spanish film diverged in two distinct directions. On the one hand, there emerged the mainstream eroticism of Vicente Aranda, Bigas Luna, Pedro Almodóvar and

Carlos Saura, directors who, while rejecting exhibitionism and explicit sex, were interested in the psychological underpinnings of those forms of sexuality long repressed in Spanish society – homosexuality, transsexuality, incest, fetishes and perversions. At the same time, a second strand of sexual representation carried Spanish film from the *destape* to softcore (and in many cases nearly hardcore) pornography. These pornographic features were rated S.

The anti-censorship decree of 1977 was remarkable for the freedom it afforded both directors and exhibitors. Elsewhere in Europe and the US, the era of mainstream sexploitation had come and gone, and most sexually explicit films were already rated X, their distribution limited to venues licensed to screen these features. This had been the case in the US since as early as 1968 and in France since 1975.[12] Indeed, before the development of the American hardcore industry in the early 1970s, the X stigma was sometimes attached to non-hardcore products, such as *Midnight Cowboy* (John Schlesinger, 1969) and *Last Tango in Paris* (Bernardo Bertolucci, 1972), both of whose X rating severely limited distribution in the American market. Between 1977 and 1982, Spain was the only Western state where potentially offensive or pornographic products were not automatically condemned to the ghetto of X.

While hardcore representations were still banned in Spain, the S rating permitted a wide distribution of softcore pornography. In general, S-rated pictures enjoyed all of the advantages of any other feature film: they could be exhibited in any cinema in the country, their receipts were taxed like other films and their publicity was unrestricted. Most important, S films, like all other Spanish features, were eligible for a 15 per cent matching federal subsidy during the five years following each film's première.[13] Apart from the warning label, the S film was in every way a mainstream film product.

One of the results of the 1977 abolition of cinematic censorship was the return to Spain of a number of film directors who had long preferred to work in the less artistically restrictive states of Western Europe. These included the horror specialist José Larraz and spaghetti western director Alfonso Balcázar (soon to go by the pseudonym Al Bagran), though the most notable returnee was Jess Franco, whose 160 plus feature films make him the most prolific director in the history of Spanish film, if not world cinema in general.[14]

Jess Franco initially waited for the waters of Spanish media permissiveness to be tested out by others. From 1977 to 1979, only

three of Franco's eighteen films were produced in Spain. Within a
few years of the 1977 decree, however, Franco, like many other producers and directors on the fringe of European cinema, was well
aware that Spain had become a haven for explicit film-making, now
more liberal than the previously preferred Switzerland, Germany
and France. In 1980, Franco accelerated his breakneck production
pace, churning out six S-rated Spanish titles. In 1981, he directed
another seven, and in 1982, the last year for the S film, his output
was no fewer than nine.

In addition to the returning exiles, several directors who had been
key figures in Spanish film since the early days of the Franco régime
now turned their attention to long-taboo erotic cinema. Consider,
for example, Ignacio F. Iquino, whose directorial career dated to pre-
Civil War Spain, and whose 1946 *Aquel viejo molino* / *That Old
Windmill* had garnered the top prize of the Spanish national film syn-
dicate. Born in 1910, Iquino's output had run the gamut of fiction
films, including melodramas, comedies, crime pictures and westerns.
With the coming of S, however, the septuagenarian Iquino jettisoned
all mainstream genre pictures in favour of the most brazenly sex-
ploitative fare. Among his many S titles are *¿Podrías con cinco chicas
a la vez?* / *Can You Do It With Five Girls at a Time?*, *Los sueños
húmedos de Patrizia* / *Patrizia's Wet Dreams*, *Inclinación sexual al
desnudo* / *Sexually Inclined to be Nude*, and the popular *La caliente
niña Julieta* / *The Hot Girl Julieta*, discussed below. Other Franco-era
directors who went on to dabble in softcore S included Carlos Aured,
Francisco Lara and a director who had made comedies and musicals
as far back as the 1950s and 1960s, José Maria Zabalza. Indeed, one
of the most striking aspects of the S experiment was that it attracted
primarily older, established Spanish film-makers who had laboured
for years under *Franquista* restrictions and now, in old age, sought to
engage with the new media permissiveness.

The six-year existence of the S film is best appreciated as two
distinct, if imprecisely demarcated, cycles. The first, from 1977 to
1979, was characterized by tentative experimentation, increasing
sexualization and social introspection. The second, from 1980 to
1982, witnessed an explosion of low-budget projects, many of which
were devoted exclusively to wall-to-wall softcore porn.

The first S films marked a significant departure from their racy
forbears, the *Landismo* sex comedies of the *destape*. First, the representation of sexuality in S films was far more explicit. Second, and

more important, the protagonist of the earlier sex comedies, the oversexed, dirty old man – à la Alfredo Landa – was now more often a sexually vivacious, bi-curious Catholic schoolgirl. Moreover, the escapades of the S film protagonist were pointedly political in nature; her presence on the screen heralded the arrival of a new generation that was savvy, continental and rebellious, a Spanish youth that questioned the mores of their elders. Thus the sexual frankness of the S-film heroine was tied to the reactionary spirit of a new era.

The Spanish film which inaugurated the new S rating was Enrique Guevara's *Una loca extravagancia sexy / A Wacky, Sexy Extravaganza*, which premiered in Madrid on 26 June 1978. As the titillating title suggests, this odd, musical/sex-comedy hybrid, follows the adventures of three schoolgirls as they experiment with masturbation and bisexuality. Just by virtue of the age and gender of our protagonists, it is clear that the *destape* mould had been broken. A far more significant film was the next major S release, *Las eróticas vacaciones de Stela / Stela's Erotic Holiday* (Zacarías Urbiola, 1978). Far from a one-day wonder, low-budget sex film, *Stela* possesses all of the principal attributes of a mainstream picture: the film features a large, attractive cast, including the veteran screen actress Teresa Gimpera, and the popular newcomer Azucena Hernández. The cinematography is varied and interesting, and boasts an abundance of location settings in and around the Spanish capital, and in the photogenic Castilian villages of Torrelodones and Lupiana.

As its title suggests, the plot of *Las eróticas vacaciones de Stela* concerns the sexual adventures of Stela, a mischievous teenage girl who is on vacation from an urban boarding-school at her mother's country home. This liberated girl soon turns the sleepy provincial town on its head. She taunts a young priest, then her maid, and finally her stepfather. She flashes and arouses her own mother, and discovers her stepfather's elaborate sex chamber. In quick succession, the sanctity of the Church, the male–female union and the integrity of the family are suddenly vulnerable to the sexual whims of a schoolgirl. That the part of Stela was played by Hernández, a respected and widely-adored teen model who had been recently crowned Miss Catalonia, gave the character an added ironic punch.

It is no stretch to see in Stela the post-*Franquista* ingenue, who through her sexual wiles overturns and updates the entrenched morals of old Spain. Stela embodies the myriad ironies of the transition to democracy, for she does not merely awaken the village sexually, but reveals what was always simmering below the surface of *Franquista* repression. As the film suggests, the priests had always been sexually inclined, her mother was never a prude, and her stepfather built the sex chamber years ago.

One of the most striking aspects of *Stela* is that the film gives expression to female sexual empowerment, while also celebrating the subversiveness of the protagonist's sexual imagination. Throughout the film, Stela transforms objects, rooms, people and situations into sexual opportunities. In one scene, we see Stela climbing the grand staircase in her mother's home. At the top, her attention is caught by the curved and smooth banister. Raising her skirt, Stela mounts the wooden slide and propels herself into a moment of arousing self-discovery. The director's penchant for exhibitionist indulgence is on display in all of its unabashed glory. In a sequence with few parallels in mainstream cinema, Urbiola proceeds to show us multiple succession shots of Stela's progress down the slide. Intercutting slow-motion views of her splayed legs gripping the shining banister with glimpses of the actress's face registering ever higher states of pleasure, the viewer is led to believe that in the single trip to the bottom of the staircase, the heroine has achieved orgasm.

But Stela's sexuality is at times far more subversive and political. In an extended scene that takes place during Sunday mass, we find Stela sitting demurely in a pew next to her mother. The girl's attention soon strays from the prayer book to the young seminary student reciting scripture before the congregation. Stela begins to daydream. The worshipful setting is now shattered by a fantasy sequence in which Stela literally defrocks the pious boy at the alter and, though not shown explicitly, fellates him. In addition, *Stela* also experiments with the lesbianism that would soon become *de rigor* in most S films. In a scene shot as much for laughs as titillation, Stela demonstrates the proper use of an oversized dildo on a willing female servant.

As risqué as many of Stela's encounters are, she remains a virgin until the penultimate scene. Despite the saucy exhibitionism of the film as a whole, it is noteworthy that nearly all of Stela's sexual experiences take place in her imagination. The only non-fantasy sex act she participates in, apart from some enthusiastic petting with the maid and seminary student, is the brutal rape at the hands of her stepfather. In the end, the film's morality is strikingly illiberal: in the case of our teenage protagonist, precocious sexual teasing can have real and unsavoury consequences. By the time her vacation is over, Stela has not so much liberated her small town as become victim of the sexually rapacious characters lurking beneath its repressed surface.

Stela's adventures continued in *Bacanal en directo / Live Bacchanalia* (Miguel Madrid Ortega, 1979), perhaps the most insightful film of the entire S genre. A product of the same firm (Góndola, PC) that created *Stela*, *Bacanal* retained several of the cast members of the first picture, most notably the lead character, portrayed by Azucena Hernández. In the update, Stela has completed her schooling and is now living in Madrid. Whereas in the provinces she was comparatively savvy, in the capital Stela meets people whose liberalization has gone far beyond her own. The permissiveness of post-Franco urban life scares her, and in an early scene she voices protest over the pace of Spain's liberalization by refusing sex with her boyfriend Fermín (the seminary student we met in *Stela*), and condemns his promiscuous circle of friends. Exasperated, Fermín storms out, though not before informing Stela that a film director has invited him to a special event: a group of young people will be taking part in an orgy that the director will be filming. Later, to make Fermín jealous, Stela decides to attend the orgy.

With both Stela and Fermín in attendance, the orgy depicted in *Bacanal* is at the outset erotic and stylish; the participants openly associate their sexual freedom with the end of the dictatorship; one participant even announces that Spain is now 'like a little version of Europe'. In part to infuriate her boyfriend, though also to arouse herself, Stela engages in extended foreplay with another woman in the crowd. While the two women caress one another, the onlookers question them about their sexual experiences. 'Are you liberated?' they ask Stela. 'I am now', comes the response. 'How many abortions have you had?' they query. 'None', she answers, 'I know how to be careful'. Finally: 'How would you describe your orgasms?'. 'My orgasms', Stela tells them, 'cannot be described, only experienced'.

But the mood of this party steadily degenerates to baser manifestations of liberty and open sexuality. Alcohol begins to flow liberally, then drugs are brought out and consumed; a farm animal appears; and a group of the participants don Nazi attire and act out a bizarre and sadistic stage play. Finally, the group turns on Stela and encourages Fermín to rape her. In the end, the film's message is one of dire warning: the perversity and excesses of Spanish society will destroy youthful romanticism and result in total chaos. Characters in

Bacanal reflect on the consequences of their sexual abandon on the moral order of Spanish society. The medium is explicit, but the moral of the film rejects the same phenomenon that allows the story to be told. As a critique of the *transición, Bacanal* succeeds in questioning the direction a secularized Spain is heading; like many of the S films, it is ultimately conservative.

Bacanal was certainly not the only S-rated feature to combine highly-charged eroticism with 'shot-over-the-bow' admonitions that excessive freedom carries a high price. A similar, if less trenchant product, was the wild sexploitation romp *Viciosas al desnudo / Depraved and Naked* (Manuel Esteba, 1980). In this film, two teenage girls appear at the doorstep of a well-off, middle-aged businessman whose family is away for the weekend. The pair seduces the older man, but then refuse to leave. For kicks, they decide to tie up their host and torture him. To this unpalatable mix is added copious amounts of explicit sex and drug use. Unlike *Bacanal,* where the characters are left wondering why their new freedoms have imprisoned them in nightmare, the girls in *Viciosas* receive a more severe karmic punishment: death in a fiery auto crash – a scene that ends the film.[15]

Viciosas shares a key thematic similarity with both of the films featuring Stela: the sexual experimentation of the female protagonists are punished as sexual transgressions. But what makes these films even more pessimistic is that they seem unable to find any redeeming qualities in the post-Franco era; they overturn the institutional repressions of the *Caudillo*'s Spain, while offering no positive moral order to fill the void.

Some of the Spanish productions under the S rating were surprisingly innovative, even if they ignored the contemporary social issues taken up in the two *Stela* pictures and *Viciosas al desnudo*. Perhaps the most striking picture of the first several years of S production was *La visita del vicio / The Visit of the Depraved* (José Larraz, 1978). In the two decades following his 1969 debut, the Catalan-born Larraz was considered among the most idiosyncratic directors of the horror / sexploitation hybrid sub-genre. Though most of his earlier work was produced in the UK, the post-Franco abolition of media censorship allowed Larraz to create his unique products in Spain. Between 1977 and 1982, Larraz directed five S-rated features, though the first, *La visita del vicio,* is certainly the most interesting. The film was shot on a shoestring budget, without professional actors, very little dialogue and entirely on location.

The story revolves around the visit of a beautiful young gypsy woman to the country home of a frustrated housewife. The action moves slowly and is interrupted by multiple fantasy sequences, some violent and disturbing, others highly erotic. While the picture lacks a coherent storyline, the overall effect is unusually atmospheric; it nearly qualifies as highbrow avant-garde. Indeed, one astute observer has written of 'an eerie ambiance that's different from any other European sexploitation film' (Tohill and Tombs, 1995: 207).

After only two years of S-rated releases, it was clear that directors and audiences in Spain were enthusiastically embracing softcore pornography as a distinctly Spanish film genre. Of the 107 feature-length films produced (or co-produced) in Spain in 1978, some 15 per cent, or 17 pictures, were rated S. In 1979, the figure was comparable: 12 of 89. In its initial period of experimentation, the S-rated Spanish film also witnessed the development of its most conspicuous feature: the predilection of the directors to give their films lewd and graphic titles. Explicit titles often assured a healthy box-office, but they also led critics to reject the entire S experiment as base and exploitative. Nonetheless, it is difficult not to admire the sheer audacity of the S film-makers, who advertised and subsequently screened in thousands of popular venues films with titles such as *Las que empiezan a los quince / Girls Who Start at Fifteen* (Ignacio F. Iquino, 1978), *La chica con las bragas transparentes / The Girl With the See-Through Panties* (Jesús Franco, 1980), *Apocalipsis sexual / Sexual Apocalypse* (Carlos Aured, 1981), *Orgía de ninfómanas / Nymphomaniac Orgy* (Jesús Franco, 1980), *Con las bragas en la mano / With Panties in Her Hand* (Julio Pérez Tabernero, 1981), *Violación inconfesable / Unconfessable Violation* (Miguel Iglesias, 1981), *Jóvenes amiguitas buscan placer / Young Girlfriends Seeking Pleasure* (Ignacio F. Iquino, 1981), *Inclinación sexual al desnudo / Sexually Inclined to be Nude* (Ignacio F. Iquino, 1981), *Mi conejo es lo mejor / My Pussy is the Best* (Ricardo Palacios, 1982), *Sin bragas y a lo loco / Crazy and Pantyless* (Klaus Jurick, 1982), *Sueca bisexual necesita semental / Bisexual Swedish Girl Desires Injection* (Richard Vogue, 1982), *Bragas calientes / Hot Panties* (Jose María Zabalza, 1982), *Las viciosas y la menor / The Depraved and the Minor* (Alfonso Balcazar, 1982) and *Las calientes orgías de una virgen / The Hot Orgies of a Virgin* (Antonio Verdaguer, 1982). It must be admitted, of course, that in this regard S film producers were following the lead of the French soft and hardcore industry, which since the early 1970s had cultivated a similar flair for outrageously crass film titles.[16]

From 1980 to 1982, the number of S titles produced in Spain steadily increased, while at the same time the products of the genre became less concerned with social and political commentary specifically concerning the Spanish *transición,* or even the experimental art films of Larraz, and began to prefer more explicit sex. In terms of absolute numbers, S films were no longer a fringe experiment. In 1981, 33 out of 137 Spanish films were rated S, or nearly one quarter of all Spanish production. A year later, in 1982, the number increased even more, to 41 out of 146 films – close to a third of national output.[17]

More remarkable than the increased market share of the S genre was the generalized tendency of these films to continue pushing the limits of acceptable softcore content. Simulated sex now garnered greater screen time, and extended scenes of female masturbation and lesbian sex became standard in nearly every new release. A telling example of the new direction of the S films was *La frígida y la viciosa / The Frigid and the Depraved* (Carlos Aured, 1980). The plot concerns the frustrations of Paula (Sara Mora), a frigid housewife finally loosened up by her promiscuous, bisexual girlfriend Celia (Andrea Guzon). The film is essentially a low-budget series of softcore set-pieces which culminate in the transformation of the married woman into an enthusiastic sexpot.

Typifying the more overt sexualization of S pictures was the arrival of a new screen actress, Andrea Albani. First appearing in *La caliente niña Julieta / Julieta, The Randy Girl* (Ignacio F. Iquino, 1980), Albani went on to star in at least eight more features, and emerged as the first reliable box-office draw in erotic Spanish films of the *transición.* Her characters may be contrasted with the other popular Catalan ingenue, Azucena Hernández. Unlike the coy and playful Stela, Albani's characters tend to be teenage nymphomaniacs, girls as quick to jump into bed with women as with men.[18]

La caliente niña Julieta, Albani's first vehicle, is essentially a screwball comedy about the millionaire Julieta's sexual exploits with her husband, girlfriends and their husbands. The plot's development, however convoluted, serves mainly to take the characters from one sexual encounter to another; by the end of the film we have witnessed a veritable catalogue of fetishes: spouse swapping, lesbianism, masturbation, voyeurism, group sex, oral sex, sex with food and even zoophilia.

Though at first glance *Julieta* might be dismissed as a wall-to-wall porno, a closer reading suggests that the film has a specific agenda, one not without political and social overtones. An instructive scene in the first part of the picture well illustrates Juliet's world view. She and a girlfriend Rita decide to share a man, whom they have picked up and taken home. In a five minute sequence, the two girls take turns engaging in various sex acts with the stranger. While the man performs oral sex on Julieta, Rita sits opposite, looking at a pornographic magazine. Switching off several more times, Julieta ends up seated upon her male charge while enthusiastically kissing a mirror image of herself. When her partner asks her whom she is thinking about, Julieta declares 'Rita'. 'Liar!' the man retorts. 'You're thinking about the Ayatollah Khomeini'. Julieta laughs this off. Now her partner holds up a brochure emblazoned with the Spanish flag. We are shown a close-up of bold lettering that reads, 'Don't waste electricity!'. 'Look what our leaders are telling us', the man says. Julieta slaps the flyer to the floor, shouting 'Away!' and resumes copulating with renewed vigour.

The suggestion that Julieta might be thinking about the Ayatollah Khomeini or that she has an opinion on the Spanish government's energy policy is revealed in the film as patently absurd. The narcissistic Julieta, who can simultaneously engage in sex with a stranger, kiss herself in the mirror and fantasize about her girlfriend, lives for sex and only for sex. She has as little interest in the Iranian revolution, an event still convulsing Iran when *Julieta* was shot in 1980, as the important issues facing her own country.

Julieta, it seems, is a creature with no apparent political or social consciousness. She does not, like Stela, view sex as an act of rebellion against authority, nor as a key component in transforming a Catholic / authoritarian Spain into a secular democracy. Julieta's world has already been transformed; she is living the fantasies that Stela experienced only in her daydreams. Nor, for that matter, is she punished, as Stela was, for acting out sexually. More importantly, Julieta's sex-making is not part of any social or political transformation, nor is the sex act any longer taboo. Julieta is not a metaphor for democracy or freedom, but a sex-crazed teenager, solely consumed by her own sexual appetite, living in a society that does not bat an eye at an oversexed single woman.

From *Julieta* onwards – that is, the final three years of the S phenomenon – most S-rated products were unabashed exposés of the sex lives of their protagonists, with no greater purpose than creating aesthetically interesting ways to titillate eager Spanish viewers. As softcore and nothing more, the later S films still had undeniable selling points. Many were shot on location in spectacular Spanish settings; more often than not, on the Costa Brava or Costa del Sol. Al Bagran's 1982 *Las colegialas lesbianas y el placer de pervertir / Lesbian Schoolgirls and the Pleasure of Perverting,* for example, featured five separate Catalan locations: Barcelona, Bellaterra, Tossa del Mar, Palamós and Sant Feliu de Guixols. In addition, the cast lists of many S pictures boasted an attractive set of national and even international stars – albeit of the softcore / sexploitation set.

Not all of the late S films possessed the sybaritic, sex-in-the-sun breeziness of the *Julieta*-style pictures. Some of the sex films produced in Spain between 1981 and 1983 were bleak portrayals of the darker side of sexual obsession, jealousy and dysfunction. A singularly disturbing example is *El fontanero, su mujer y otras cosas que meter / The Plumber, His Wife and Other Things to Stick In* (Carlos Aured, 1981), whose title, in a crowded field, remains jarringly crass. The film's plot revolves around an unfaithful plumber and his frustrated wife. In its depiction of simulated sex and multiple fetishes, *El fontanero* has nothing new to offer the genre. What is striking, however, is that the protagonists in this feature are older and more jaded than the curious adolescents who brought a youthful exuberance to many earlier S pictures. However vacuous their existence, one never doubted that Julieta and her friends *enjoyed* sex. This is scarcely the case with Lina Romay, Montserat Prous and the coterie of over-the-hill sexploitation actors who are put through their tired softcore paces in the sad-looking *El fontanero.*[19]

But *El fontanero* was an extreme case of how badly awry the softcore formula could go. A better product, and one that sums up the new objectives of the genre, was *Confesiones íntimas de una exhibicionista / Intimate Confessions of an Exhibitionist* (Lina Romay as Candy Coster, 1982), a picture devoted entirely to its sex-obsessed star and director. The sexually mature and voracious Romay – Jess Franco's leading lady since the early 1970s – is an older, though hardly mellowed version of the characters portrayed by Andrea Albani, but still the antithesis of the comparatively tame creations of Azucena Hernández. Whereas Stela's youthful and tentative sexuality underlined the issue of generational liberation as a key feature of the democratic transition, Romay's characters are the personification of the brazenly confident sexuality of post-transition Spain.[20] Indeed, the title of the 1982 film, 'Intimate confessions . . .', aptly sums up the *raison d'être* of S cinema in its last year of existence.

The gimmick in *Confesiones* – the feature that sets it apart from scores of other Spanish sex films of this period – was Romay's focus on the spectator. The film opens with the Catalan actress masturbating on a bed while addressing the camera. She informs the audience that she will recount her experiences as an exhibitionist, beginning with a formative episode as a youth when she observed her sister having sex with a boyfriend. For the balance of the feature, the film intercuts flashbacks of the star's various sexual adventures with the ongoing masturbatory confession in bed. Not suprisingly, Romay incorporates in her film many of the fetishistic sub-themes that typify the work of the prolific horror and sexploitation schlockmeister, Jess Franco. Thus lesbianism abounds, as does masturbation with food (in this case, milk), group sex, penetration with foreign objects and even necrophilia. Like much of Franco's work, Romay's film moves at a relaxed, lazy pace; slow zooms zero in and linger on the soft curves of the female actresses, and a languorous Pablo Villa soundtrack greatly contributes to the overall effect. Much of the shooting was apparently done under the midday Catalan sun, and the film has the ethereal atmosphere of an afternoon Iberian siesta. In short, *Confesiones* is a unique achievement: a simply-told, compelling and artful pornographic film.

That a film like *Confesiones* could be screened alongside mainstream Spanish and Hollywood products is quite remarkable, but the unapologetically pornographic nature of later S features led rapidly to the demise of the entire softcore genre. Increasingly short on political and social commentary, pushing the envelope of hardcore and hogging the box office, the S pictures were widely seen as possessing no redeeming artistic value and, indeed, threatening the development of a national art cinema. To be sure, the demise of S was also accelerated by external factors, independent of the genre's own qualitative trajectory. By 1982, conservative governments had swept to power on both sides of the Atlantic, most prominently in Germany, Great Britain and the United States. Spain, seeking membership in the European Union and a respectable international profile, needed a national cinema more elevated than S-rated pornography – a cinema suitable for export. Thus in February 1982, the Socialist government of Felipe González issued a decree abolishing the S rating and establishing regulations for X-rated cinema similar to those existing in Europe and the US.

The new standards were codified in Royal Decree 3304 of 28 December 1983, a decision largely authored by Pilar Miró, the PSOE's Minister of Culture. The so-called 'Miró Law' granted generous funding to 'serious', 'quality' and 'artistic' pictures, while ending favourable fiscal subsidies or tax breaks for products considered purely 'commercial'.[21] In this way, the rug was effectively pulled out from under the more popular sub-genres. The clearest and most spectacular victim of the Miró Law was S-rated softcore pornography, which almost immediately disappeared. The same year the decree was issued, production of sex films (soft- and hardcore combined) plummeted to just nine features, a drop of 82% from the previous year.[22] Thus ironically, the culmination of Spain's political and cultural liberalization was marked by the abolition of an enormously popular explicit sub-genre.

In March 1984, the first X-rated cinemas began functioning in Spain and Spanish softcore passed into history. While seeking to protect mainstream cinema and regulate X, the government left S softcore an abandoned orphan, with no legal means of distribution. Softcore was thus forced to become hardcore; for example, Jess Franco had to insert hardcore sequences into his two last S films in order to make them legal (*Furia en el trópico / Fury in the Tropics* and *Lilian, la virgen pervertida / Lilian, the Perverted Virgin*, (both 1983).[23] But Spanish X-rated films enjoyed none of the success of their S-rated predecessors. A hefty tax of 33 per cent was levied on all box-office receipts, advertising was prohibited in public spaces and mainstream print media, and few theatre owners were granted screening licences. Whereas at the height of the S phenomenon some 1500 theatres screened S films, in 1987 Spain had just 85 X-rated venues.[24]

In the nearly two decades since the Miró Law was introduced, the most conspicuous aspect of Spanish film production is not only the disappearance of low-budget, shot-on-film pornography, but the steady contraction and homogenization of the national film industry.[25] All of the sub-genres that flourished in Spain from the late 1960s to the early 1980s: (the western, horror, sex comedies and softcore porn) have either vanished entirely or survive only in a mainstream variation. The successor product to the varied Spanish sub-genres is the new Iberian art film: well-funded, nicely shot projects that have by and large garnered only lukewarm reviews in either the domestic or foreign markets.[26]

Who will mourn the passing of Spain's S-rated experiment? Certainly not the current crop of Spanish film critics and historians, nearly all of whom reject the genre out of hand, without qualification. Consider two major scholarly accounts of the transition cinema, those of Ramiro Gómez de Castro and José Enrique Monterde. In his monograph on Spanish film in the decade of the transition, Gómez de Castro devotes just a page and a half out of nearly 300 to S films. According to the author, 'the very titles of the genre themselves speak for the complete decadence and absence of quality in each and every production' (Gómez de Castro, 1988: 79). This disdain is echoed in the account of Monterde, who is sufficiently embarrassed by S film titles that his review of the genre is a single paragraph long. He writes that 'apart from an interest in a semantic analysis of these titles, obsessed with prefiguring in their explicitness the promise of the film, and permitting some kind of distinction in completely homogeneous territory, we will not dedicate any further attention to this passing fad . . .' (1993: 165). Indeed, in a survey of the literature on Spanish film since the *transición*, I found only one scholar refer to the demise of the S phenomenon with anything approaching serious academic interest. Writing of the effective abolition of the sex film genre, a Spanish political scientist has observed that '[t]ogether with infamous erotic products designed for immediate consumption, [the industry] lost forever the possibility of an experimental erotic cinematography of auteurs like Jess Franco'.[27]

But a passing fad which lasts seven years and accounts for up to 30% of a major national cinema perhaps does merit further attention. The S film may be seen as emblematic of the transition from the Franco era to the stable social democratic state whose values and mission were firmly defined only after 1982. The genre's trajectory marked an important staging period during which Spaniards tested the limits of their new freedoms. Moreover, as this chapter has demonstrated, the S films featured moments of genuine political and artistic revelation. Though many of the S films may be easily dismissed as low-budget, softcore pornography, this pornography played a significant role in the sexual catharsis of a society just released from forty years of dictatorship.[28]

Notes

1 For a solid English-language account of the end of censorship, see Peter Besas (1985), pp. 185–96.

2 It has become virtually impossible to view in any form the majority of S-rated features released in Spain between 1977 and 1982. Though many were issued on videotape in the 1980s, very few remain in circulation today. In 1997, the Valladolid-based Divisa Ediciones released video transfers of ten S-rated films in a series entitled 'Cine Erótico de la Transición'. Curiously, the most reliable sources for out-of-print S titles are web-based, underground genre outlets in the United States, the best of which is Luminous Film and Video Wurks in Medford, NY (accessible at www.lfvw.com).

3 A small number of the S films were shot in two versions, a soft and hard edit. The production of a hardcore version served two purposes: first, it could be exhibited in foreign countries where the X rating had been legalized; or, second, it could be kept on hand in the event that Spanish lawmakers authorized the exhibition of hardcore. Among those S films screened abroad in hardcore versions were *La visita del vicio* (José Larraz, 1978) and *Apocalipsis sexual* (Carlos Aured, 1981). These two examples were exported to Italy, though it is safe to assume that due to the liberal distribution policies for S-rated features in Spain compared to Italian governance of hardcore exhibition, the softcore version enjoyed a far wider audience in the Iberian market.

4 Notwithstanding the export of a handful of hardcore edits, Spanish-produced S films rarely left the domestic market. A recent comprehensive survey of all softcore features screened or released on video in the German market revealed fewer than five by Spanish S-film directors. See Hahn (1993).

5 The most important English-language work on Franco's long dictatorship is Stanley G. Payne, *The Franco Regime, 1936–1975* (Madison: University of Wisconsin Press, 1987).

6 See Mitchell (1998: 110–15). The key study of film censorship under Franco is González Ballesteros (1981).

7 On the Church's role in national, institutional and individual censorship during the Franco era, see Trenzado Romero (1999: 82–3).

8 In addition to the present collection, see Kinder (1993), especially pp. 241–44, as well as two recent edited volumes: Kinder (1997), and Talens and Zunzunegui (1998).

9 For a concise discussion of *landismo*, see Román Gubern et al. (1995: 364). On the origins of the *destape*, see de Mata Mancho et al. (1974: 196–267).

10 Cited in Eslava Galán (1997: 85).

11 See Bassa and Freixas (1996: 113).

12 For a concise overview of the development of the American X rating, see Randall (1985: 510–36). On the same process in France, see Crawley and Jouffa (1989).

13 See Trenzado Romero (1999: 148–60).

14 Arriving at a precise or even close estimate of Franco's oeuvre is complicated by his penchant for directing under pseudonyms; he has signed his work Clifford Brown, Dave Tough, Franco Manera, Charlie Chrisian and James P. Johnson, among many others. The literature on the Franco filmography tends to ignore his softcore S period, concentrating instead on his work in horror during the 1960s and early 1970s. The only volume to treat in detail Franco's S-era output is Tohill and Tombs' *Immoral Tales: European Sex and Horror Movies 1956–1984* (1995). It is the conclusion of Tohill and Tombs – and the present author concurs – that the S films Franco made in Spain did not differ fundamentally from his explicit fare financed and shot elsewhere in Germany and France, though the former are undeniably more *Spanish*, in that they employ Spanish actors and take advantage of Iberian locations.

15 *Viciosas al desnudo* was a remake of an American picture, Peter Traynor's 1977 *Death Game* (aka *The Seducers)*, which featured Sondre Locke and Colleen Camp as the two troublemakers. To be sure, the Spanish S version considerably ups the ante over the earlier version: the sex is far more explicit, the torture scenes more heinous and the finale more violent and shocking.

16 See Rampazzoni (1991 : 112–19).

17 Overall, from 1978 to 1983, S films constituted 16 per cent of Spanish production. See Gubern et al. (1995: 372–3).

18 Among Albani's films were *Perversión en el paraíso* ('Perversion in Paradise') (Jaime Puig, 1981), *El hombre del pito magico* ('The Man With the Magic Touch') (Carlos Aured, 1982), *Las colegialas lesbianas y el placer de pervertir* (Lesbian Schoolgirls and the Pleasure of Perversion') (Al Bagran, 1982), *Las viciosas y la menor* ('The Depraved and the Minor') (Al Bagran, 1982), *El marqués, la menor y el travestí* ('The Marquis, the Minor and the Transvestite') (Al Bagran, 1982), *La ingenua, la lesbiana y el travestí* ('The Ingenue, the Lesbian and the Transvestite') (Al Bagran, 1982) and *Las lesbianas y la caliente niña Julieta* (The Lesbians and the Hot Girl Julieta') (Al Bagran, 1982).

19 In place of depicting genuine pleasure, *El fontanero* falls back on an overkill of tastelessness, as, for example, when Lina Romay penetrates herself with a toilet plunger. This scene, perhaps the single most audacious moment in post-Franco cinema, is an apt metaphor for the crude level to which the S film had fallen since 1977. To be sure, the present author's dim view of *El fontanero* was not shared by Spanish filmgoers in 1981, 399,892 of whom queued up to see the film in its initial

theatrical run. The picture would eventually gross over 70 million pesetas. Moreover, at least one recent film scholar has written of this feature in the most glowing terms, singling out, no less, the toilet plunger sequence. See Barroso (2001: 132–35).

20 Romay once told an interviewer that she would put her clothes on only if the director found it absolutely essential to the artistic integrity of the picture. See 'El Avernáculo', *Kiss*, 1998, no. 81, p. 65.

21 On the Miró Law and its impact, see 'Polémica en torno al Decreto Ley sobre protección al cine español', in *Dirigido por*, no. 109, 1983, p. 4; Peter Besas (1997: 247–59) and Trenzado Romero (1999: 167–77).

22 Trenzado Romero (1999: 169).

23 Bassa and Freixas (1996: 155).

24 Casto Escópico (1996: 158).

25 The statistics on national film production speak for themselves. According to the Ministry of Culture, in 1982, the last year of S-rated releases, national or co-produced Spanish films numbered 146. In 1983, total production shrank to 99 pictures and the number continued to decline almost every year thereafter: 1984, 75; 1985, 77; 1986, 60; 1987, 69; 1988, 63; 1989, 47. Throughout the 1990s production levelled off at approximately 50–60 pictures per year.

26 Scholars seeking to identify subversive or titillating themes in post-Miró Spanish cinema have been forced to endlessly recycle the same superlatives to describe the relatively tame work of Almodóvar, Saura, Trueba and other auteurs deemed sufficiently 'artistic' to receive state subsidies. In light of the recent though now defunct 'S' genre pictures, scholarly validation of the generally unimpressive recent crop of national offerings verges on the hyperbolic or even absurd. For example, a recent anthology contribution is entitled 'Promiscuity, Pleasure, and Girl Power'. The film under consideration? *Belle Epoque* (Trueba, 1992), a bland, Merchant-Ivoryesque feature that seemed designed solely with the American Academy of Motion Pictures in mind. Indeed, *Belle Epoque* won the foreign film Oscar, not least because it took almost no political or social risks – never mind Ariana Gil's much-discussed donning of a moustache, for which she was rewarded with a Goya, the Spanish Oscar. But the superficial 'girl power' of post-Miró Spanish cinema is a far cry from the bold and assertive female characters – the Stelas and Julietas – who appeared regularly in scores of S productions. See Jordan (1999: 286–309).

27 Trenzado Romero (1999: 169–70). Of course, the same barriers to production and distribution that stymied Spanish auteurs after 1982 had already discouraged many film makers working elsewhere in Europe or the United States. One need look no further than the frustrated career

of the often brilliant Walerian Borowczyk to see the institutionalized limitations in the French film industry after 1976.

28 The author wishes to thank the following people for their comments regarding this chapter: Jennifer Fay, Enrique Sanabria, Morgan Hall and Sasha Pack.

Bibliography

Balio, Tino (ed.) (1985) *The American Film Industry*, Madison: University of Wisconsin Press.

Barroso, Miguel Ángel (2001) *Cine erótico en cien jornadas*, Madrid: Ediciones Jaguar.

Bassa, Joan and Ramón Freixas (1996) *Expediente S: softcore, sexploitation, cine S*, Barcelona: Futura Ediciones.

Besas, Peter (1985) *Behind the Spanish Lens: Spanish Cinema under Fascism and Democracy*, Denver: Arden Press.

—— (1997) 'The Financial Structure of Spanish Cinema', in Marsha Kinder (ed.) *Refiguring Spain: Cinema / Media / Representation*, Durham, NC: Duke University Press, 247–59.

Crawley, Tony and Jouffa, François (1989) *Entre deux censures: Le cinéma érotique de 1973 à 1976*, Paris: Editions Ramsay.

Escópico, Casto (1996) *Sólo para adultos: historia del cine X*, Valencia: La Máscara.

Eslava Galán, Juan (1997) *La España de las libertades*, Madrid: Espasa Calpe.

Evans, Peter William (ed.) (1999) *Spanish Cinema: The Auteurist Tradition*, Oxford: Oxford University Press.

Gasca, Luis (1998) *Un siglo de cine español*, Barcelona: Planeta.

Gómez Benítez de Castro, Ramiro (1998) *La producción cinematográfica española de la transición a la democracia (1976–1986)*, Bilbao: Mensajero.

González Ballesteros, Teodoro (1981) *Aspectos jurídicos de la censura cinematográfica en España con especial referencia al período 1936–1977*, Madrid: Editorial de la Universidad Complutense de Madrid.

Gubern, Román, et al. (1995), *Historia del cine español*, Madrid: Catedra.

Hahn, Ronald M. (1993) *Das Heyne Lexikon des Erotischen Films*, Munich: Heyne.

Jordan, Barry (1999) 'Promiscuity, Pleasure, and Girl Power: Fernando Trueba's *Belle Epoque* (1992)', in Peter William Evans (ed.) *Spanish Cinema: The Auteurist Tradition*, Oxford: Oxford University Press, 286–309.

Kinder, Marsha (1993) *Blood Cinema: The Reconstitution of National Identity in Spain*, Berkeley: University of California Press.

—— (ed.) (1997) *Refiguring Spain: Cinema / Media / Representation*, Durham, NC: Duke University Press.

Mancho, Juan de Mata, et al. (1974) *Cine español: cine de subgéneros*, Valencia: F. Torres.

Mitchell, Timothy (1998) *Betrayal of the Innocents: Desire, Power, and the Catholic Church in Spain*, Philadelphia: University of Pennsylvania Press.

Monterde, José Enrique (1993) *Veinte años de cine español (1973–1992)*, Barcelona: Ediciones Paidós.

Pérez Niño, Tomás and Joe Krankol (1996) *España erótica: historia del cine clasificado S*, Madrid: T&B Ediciones.

Rakovsky, Antoine and Daniel Serceau (eds.) (1991) *Les dessous du cinéma porno*, *CinémAction* (special issue).

Rampazzoni, Guido (1991) 'Titres chauds pour frénésies lexicales', in Antoine Rakovsky and Daniel Serceau (eds.), *Les dessous du cinéma porno*, *CinémAction* (special issue), 112–19.

Randall, Richard S. (1985) 'Censorship: From *The Miracle* to *Deep Throat*', in Tino Balio (ed.) *The American Film Industry*, Madison: University of Wisconsin Press, 510–36.

Talens, Jenaro and Santos Zunzunegui (eds.) (1998) *Modes of Representation in Spanish Cinema*, Minnesota: University of Minnesota Press.

Tohill, Cathal and Pete Tombs (1995) *Immoral Tales: European Sex and Horror Movies 1956–1984*, New York: St. Martin's Griffin.

Torres, Rafael (1996) *La vida amorosa en tiempos de Franco*, Madrid: Temas de Hoy.

Trenzado Romero, Manuel (1999) *Cultura de masas y cambio político: el cine español de la transición*, Madrid: Siglo Veintiuno.

12

Alejandro Amenábar's *Abre los ojos* / *Open Your Eyes* (1997)

Chris Perriam

When Alejandro Amenábar's *Abre los ojos* / *Open Your Eyes*,[1] opened in Spain during the Christmas / New Year period of 1997/98 it achieved the biggest first month box-office take in Spanish cinema to that time (700m ptas). Its appeal was addressed to several overlapping audiences. Amenábar's first feature *Tesis* / *Thesis* (1995) – a stark, campus-set psychological thriller with snuff movies its subject matter – had by that stage gained cult status, especially among twenty-something cinema-goers and the link was quickly made (Sartori, 1997). The casting of Penélope Cruz[2] as the virginally erotic Sofía, the film's love interest, was also a hook, with her roles still fresh in audiences' minds as the young Diana in Manuel Gómez Pereira's comedy *El amor perjudica seriamente la salud* / *Love Seriously Damages Your Health* (1996) and as Lucía in Azucena Rodríguez's intense and socially committed prison drama *Entre rojas* (1994). Well judged too – and using two key members of the original *Tesis* team – was the casting of two lesser known young male actors, Eduardo Noriega as the (at first) handsome César and Fele Martínez as Pelayo, César's plain but presentable, normal-laddish best friend, from whom César steals Sofía. In the second half of the 1990s the notion was frequently being put forward that a new wave of young actors (and directors) were becoming established as a necessary challenge to a commercially successful Spanish cinema which had become too restricted to films repeatedly casting just a handful of actors in varying combinations,[3] and Martínez and Noriega keyed effectively into this. Moreover, it was clear in the publicity surrounding the film not only that Noriega's good looks – recalled from *Tesis* – had developed on into seductive, handsome, high masculine glamour (Ponga, 1999), but that there would be a special morbid pleasure to be taken in them precisely because the film is premised on their violent destruction. The sheer intricacy (Sala, 1998) of how this destruction comes about, a persistent question over whether it really has come about and a related web of allusions to other films, classic and popular, are the last of the elements I need to lay out at this stage in explanation of the film's appeal.

César is an orphan in his twenties whose inherited wealth allows him at first to supplement his considerable physical charms, but whose hedonistic lifestyle is disrupted by a car crash (we cannot say whether real or imagined) which smashes up his face, destroys his sanity, leads him (perhaps) to kill the woman he comes to believe is involved in a plot to rob him of his identity, his money and above all Sofía. Antonio (Chete Lera) is a social services psychiatrist assigned to César in the prison where he is being held on the murder charge and who is trying to coax out of César a meaningful therapeutic and justificatory account of what seems to have happened. However, what slides out from under this confessional narrative is a quite different version: in this, through generic and intertextual association, he is aligned not only with the tragic heroes of man-turned-monster narratives but also the tortured superheroes of time paradox and memory-implant sci-fi thrillers. The film had anyway commenced with a wryly derivative apocalyptic sci-fi opening. César emerges tousled and lovely from his bed – wakened by a speaking alarm clock urging him, '¡Abre los ojos!' – admires his semi-naked self in the bathroom mirror, dresses, goes to the garage and starts up his smooth-lifestyle VW Beetle: but the streets of the notoriously traffic-choked centre of Madrid are completely empty, and deep-focus panoramic shots impress that fact, its echoes and the character's fear on the audience. In a second sally from the house César seeks to protect himself from the possible repetition or realization of the dream – one which is a deep threat to his continued enjoyment of his body, his car and his control – with a traditional superstitious gesture and its accompanying conjuration, 'Me toco los huevos' ['I touch my balls']. Deftly – with perhaps a glance back at Javier Bardem's performance of precarious and superstitious hyper-masculinity in Bigas Luna's *Huevos de oro / Golden Balls* (1993) – it is established that for men like César losing your sense of self, your sense of reality and continuity, is palpably connected with losing your virility; losing the plot is connected with losing if not the phallus then its closest friends.

Voices-over in this second awakening scene bring the psychoanalytic implications to the fore and troubles the linearity of the narrative and the coherence of the protagonist in what should be the film's real establishing moments, redressing the balance after the shocking false start. One voice, responding to questions about his lifestyle, is César's; thus he is already severally split between two visual and one auditory presents. The other is Antonio's, apparently drawing out of him the account of a traumatic moment when to the audience this moment seems only to re-establish normality. In the next sequence, one which looks like a conventional extended flashback coherent with the main storyline, César seems to be safe. He drives on, through crowded streets, past a film crew (a slightly disturbing touch however) and a street mime actor (another) to pick up Pelayo. They exchange banter about César's latest sexual conquest and Pelayo's lack of luck; playing squash – in a brief reference to Woody Allen's *Annie Hall* (1977) (J. R. 1998) – Pelayo draws attention to the hollowness of César's comforting assurances about his, Pelayo's looks, and César becomes more and more the Tony Roberts to Pelayo's Allen. A missed ball, Pelayo's remark that god is punishing him for being a loudmouth, and further superstitious exclamation from César, waving his racket at the skies and cursing 'I'll get you for that', though, all provide the link to the next scene in which the voice-over we have heard is revealed as that of Antonio, who asks as part of his attempt to get an explanatory narrative out of César, '¿Crees en Dios?' ['Do you believe in God?'].

These words also belong prominently in another storyline, that in which César's seductive appeal meets its nemesis in Nuria, who, having followed him to Sofía's house after his birthday party, picks him up in her red car, in her red dress and drives him faster and faster through the city, asking '¿Crees en Dios?' just before sending the car hurtling through a wall on a high bend in the outskirts. But Nuria, who dies in the accident, keeps on reappearing, maddeningly replacing Sofía; César suspects – or recounts suspecting – some intricate plot against him, perhaps by the wronged Pelayo, perhaps by associates after his money. Moreover, the crash, the disfigurement and César's finally remembered and consequential suicide attempt are all revealed to be false crises by the intervention of a David Lynch-style demon or *deus ex machina* at the end of the film, one Dr Duvernois. Once César has broken through to the apparent memory of his suicide attempt he is able also to recall a visit to the offices of a company called Life Extension specializing principally in cryogenic storage for human beings. Antonio obtains a day release for him and accompanies him there and they discover that César may not be a living, semi-amnesiac psychotic at all but rather a dead or inert body whose mind is at large in a virtual reality. The company – run by Duvernois – is test-running a new process whereby the moment of death is erased and sutured over by the implantation of an engineered dream continuation of experience; but in a temporal slippage César seems already to have benefited from this: Duvernois, who had previously appeared in glimpsed snippets of television news bulletins in César's late twentieth-century reality now appears and says he is speaking from a time in the middle of the twenty-second century. César's identity is made up of false images implanted on the time line of his apparently lived experience, and the identity of the other characters is unreal. Thus the rich, flaw-lessly handsome, smooth operator turns into a disturbed alleged criminal trapped in a nightmare from which each time he awakens he opens his eyes to some damaging new perspective on the loss not only of his film star looks but of the coherence of the narrative sup-posed to sustain his sense of self. His apparent amnesia and the recounted or relived experiences of déjà vu with which the film is punctuated mean that the 'explanation' elicited from him by Anto-nio is an invitation to confront and overcome the gaps and disconti-nuities. But, perhaps for reasons explained by Slavoj Žižek, to whom I shall be returning at the end, César is as unable as his doctor and confessor to recognize an effective route towards the reinstatement of control, wholeness, good looks, the way things were, mainly because all this is as much an illusion as was his lifestyle. Although frequently called upon to open his eyes, he misrecognizes the call and misdirects his gaze.

The film's title heavily implies that we are to be attentive to the play of appearances, alert to the risks of poor vision, false images and lack of insight. The title words also occupy diegetic space, are implicated strongly in a generic and intertextual exchange to which I have begun to allude and act as pointers to virtuoso narrative com-plexities. The words of the film's title are heard at key moments of transition from one state of consciousness to another in the film. And I phrase it this way, rather than returning to my reference just now to awakening, since the *mise en abîme* has no clear original points of reference or return: we link up with César's drama while he and it are already in free fall; we all end up learning, like the near-feral, sequestered Prince Segismundo did three centuries ago in Calderón de la Barca's famed *La vida es sueño / Life is a Dream* that

'Toda la vida es sueño, y los sueños, sueños son' ['All life is but a dream, and dreams, all dreams']. The title words are also words which even before the audience sits down are already rich with admonishment, like Carlos Saura's uncompleted proverb in the title of another major national classic of performance, *Cría cuervos / Raise ravens* (1976) – '. . . y te sacarán los ojos' ['and they will peck out your eyes'], it should go on; and the vertiginous point-of-view shots in the rooftop finale of Amenábar's film out across the void of air, high above trees and street clearly echo a key fantasy sequence in Saura's film where the young Ana imagines she is flying off and away from herself.[4]

Let us now turn to the film's finale on top of the Picasso Tower – itself a symbol of an improbable, futuristic Madrid, and in a way a simulacrum of eternal corporate life. When César is confronted by radical challenges in Duvernois's revelations to the quality of his existence and the reality of that of those around him, he is plunged into a (relatively) subtle self-questioning and opening-up to emotional and existential pain, in contradistinction to the macho bravado of Quaid in *Total Recall* (Paul Verhöeven, 1990) who at a similarly crucial moment is urged by the mutant rebel leader Kuato to 'Open you mind, open your mind' and discover / remember his true life story. César's reaction is not Quaid / Arnie's blunt 'No shit!' but a complex and empathetic recalibration of his self-perception and analysis of his relationships performed with a thoughtfulness which outwits the expensive paraphernalia and melodramatic intensity of the film's finale. In acute mental and emotional pain he not only reviews the fragmentation of himself but grieves for Sofía, Pelayo and Antonio who are, or may be, only themselves as dreamed by César in the expensively purchased space-time continuum which is cryostasis and artificially sustained consciousness. Noriega's performance of César's realization of his own weakness and insubstantiality, of his susceptibility to vertigo in a number of senses and his embodiment of the film's concerns with guilt and personal demons (Moreno, 1998), all layer with genuine seriousness what is very much a translated and updated *cinéma du look* and a glittering homage to the towering technological advances in image production which audiences associate with the new Hollywood. Thus to the other pleasures (of recognition, looking, unravelling, emoting) for the audience is added that of the recognition of the interplay of issues of high seriousness with virtuoso image-making and the satisfaction of being considered connoisseurs of both.

The narrative alternative represented in these last ten minutes has a powerful hold over the audience in their visual memory after the show; and it is this version of the story which offers an explanatory closure coherent enough to any audience familiar with *Total Recall* (and its television spin-off series), *The Matrix* (anachronistically), episodes of *Star Trek Voyager*, with David Lynch, with *The Game* (which was playing in dubbed version in Madrid theatres at the same time as *Abre los ojos* in its first run); or Borges or Calderón (Bou and Pérez (1997) make the connection briefly between the classical dramatist and the film's moral seriousness and self-reflexivity). The final scene links, then, with a high-art tradition, with questions of definition of self and desire (again, Bou and Pérez, 1997), with the apocalyptic mode of science fiction fantasy, and those mind-game fictions I have just mentioned which themselves call into question (while often also nostalgically elevating) fond notions of the subject's autonomy and sense of social belonging. As all this hurtles into the void (or into a futuristic alternative where, as Dr Duvernois says, 'people aren't needed any more'), and as Antonio weeps his genuine but unreal tears, anarchy is let loose upon the patriarchally constructed worlds of the law, psychiatric therapy, the professional classes (all of which he rather obviously represents), and family (over which he is now grieving for a second time, having already intimated to César his pain at his failures as a father and a husband). Antonio's identity is pathetically deconstructed as its signifying roles and sentiments fly free of any signifieds: his crisis is nicely, chillingly, mirrored back onto César as both men are riven in the most fundamental way as it is revealed to them that they are but the dreamed one and the dreamer.

But César's crisis reaches even further; his desire for the restoration to him of his looks, of Sofía, of love and sex; his desire for a thrusting and satisfying narrative, for a return to his status as young man about town: this spirals about and is pulled into a black hole the entire point of his reconstruction it is to deny. For one thing, this plunge into the dark might be just another repetition: a prospect terrifying enough, and one which is meant to leave the audience thrilled and chastened. But, and here we return to Žižek, and Hitchcock and Lacan:

> what the fact of 'repression' ultimately amounts to is that *the space of 'what can be said', the subject's universe of meaning, is always 'curved'* [or conformed] *by traumatic blanks* organized around what must

> remain unsaid if this universe is to retain its consistency . . . and the
> irrepresentable X which curves the narrative space . . . is ultimately
> the subject's birth and / or death . . . the being of the subject is . . .
> structured in relationship to a traumatic X, a point of simultaneous
> attraction and repulsion, a point whose overproximity causes the
> eclipse of the subject. (Žižek, 1992: 242–3)

In order to look at this dynamic at work I would like in this final section to turn, predictably enough now Hitchcock is back with us, to
the scene of the crime, to the symbols of motivation and to premo-
nitions of that 'eclipse of the subject'. When César, in one of the conflicting storylines, first goes to Sofía's flat and tries to seduce this, the
film's virginally coded woman, their night together involves four high
profile allusions to appearances, performance and representation: the
discovery that she makes money as a street-performing mime artist;
an exchange about actors, whom the two agree are 'dishonest people
. . . you can't tell what they're thinking'; a snatch of a cartoon on the
television, in which the characters teeter on the edge of a cliff affirming 'It's OK, it's solid ground', then plummeting; and, fourth, a
pencil sketch each makes of the other – Sofía drawing a caricature of
César with big head, flash clothes, money bags and car; César making
a realistic portrait of the beautiful Sofía which strikingly captures her.
And yet it is precisely this portrait, along with a photograph of César
and Sofía later taken by Pelayo on a café terrace, which is the sign of
discontinuity, split identity, uncertainty, loss, and a sense of betrayal.
It is already half clear to the audience at this stage that the encounter
between César and Sofía is a narrative poised between flashback and
fantasy, since the sequence of matching length which precedes this is
one whose start we saw, in which Antonio urges César in his cell to
piece together an 'explanation': César and Sofía together in the flat
is a conventionally signalled flashback, but its reliability is already
fragile.

In a later and critical sequence that takes place in the prison cell,
César remembers coming back to the flat in a state of considerable
perturbation. He has been confronted by Pelayo with the photograph clearly showing the other woman, Nuria, at the café terrace
table in Sofía's place. In the flat he finds that all the photographs
on the wall show Nuria not Sofía and the drawing he had earlier
made has far from captured Sofía since her image has migrated to
make way for Nuria's. The unreliability of the photographic image

has a clear enough general import which is sharpened through another of the film's connections to classic science fiction, in this case to Ridley Scott's *Blade Runner* (1982) and its replicants, empty and desirous of human feeling. As Giulana Bruno (1993: 245) observes of that film, as part of her discussion of Baudrillard and schizophrenic vertigo (in *Simulations*) and Jameson on schizophrenia and the material present in 'Postmodernism and Consumer Society', 'if the replicants are to survive, the signifiers of their existence have to be put in order', they have to acquire a past, in other words, 'some semblance of a symbolic dimension has to be put together to release them from the trap of the present [in an] attempt at establishing a temporally persistent identity': to this end, photographs are enabling for the replicants (1991: 246). In the same way, of course (and for *Star Trek*'s Data) part of César's problem is a lack within, a cold heart, no humanity. His attempt to piece together a story is disrupted both by the possibility of the coexistence of multiple and dissonant stories and by the traits of unreconstructed masculinity qua *machismo*. His male pride in his appearance, wealth and pulling power; his cocksure competitive streak; and then his interestingly counter-orthodox disempowerment by his fetishisation of Sofía; these all thwart therapeutic mending and the finding of identity. His 'amnesia' and the flashes of déjà vu are symptoms of his picking through what Jameson, in his account of the Lacanian take on schizophrenia (1991), calls 'a rubble of distinct and unrelated signifiers' (1991: 26); associated with César's relationship to Sofía, these experiences of repetition both insist on a continuity – a pre-existing self who lived this once before – and threaten to render César's story as, in Jameson's words, a 'series of pure and unrelated presents in time' (1991: 27). As Jameson puts one of the Lacanian propositions, 'personal identity is itself the effect of a certain temporal unification of past and future with one's present' (1991: 26); the twin proposition to this is 'that such temporal unification is itself a function of language, or better still, of the sentence, as it moves along its hermeneutic circle through time' (1991: 27). What breaks the circle and fractures the male identity is – in a replay of an old film favourite – a woman who refuses to remain identical to herself; an erotic obsession which refuses rationalization and control.

Just as Buñuel's Mateo / Matthieu, in *Cet obscur objet du désir* / *That Obscure Object of Desire* (1977) is emasculated and eventually disempowered as the teller of his own story by the split between Conchitas, which he narrates from the enclosure of the railway carriage, so too for César there is an obscure and sanity-obscuring split object of desire in the dyad Sofía / Nuria. It is precisely this reiterated instance of the treacherousness of appearances which provokes the crime for which César has been imprisoned. Once he has smashed up the flat, and been knocked out from behind by Nuria (thinking him a burglar), Sofía magically appears in Nuria's place (as we shall see), the two make love, but suddenly she is Nuria once again in his embrace, in a repetition of two previous moments of shock substitution. He moves from horror to gratified perverse acceptance (he continues with the sex), to penetration, and finally to suffocating her with a pillow while still violently fucking her.

High on the roof and teetering on the edge at the end of the film, César turns to Duvernois hesitantly and comments that he suffers from vertigo, 'se me olvidó' ['I forgot']. What this, of course recalls – along with a frequently commented upon scene between Noriega and Cruz on the rooftop, with the camera circling them as they embrace and shift identifications – is Hitchcock, and *Vertigo*, the debts or homages to which are noted by nearly all commentators, not least because Amenábar himself, from the press night on, made much of this (see, for example, GuíaActiv: 1998). What it ushers in, and what people have not yet made time to say,[5] is the whole debate around the Scottie, Judy, Madeleine affair: not only is César in relation to his don Juanesque attraction to the self-destructive Nuria caught up in a male fascination whose source, as Tania Modlewski puts it (1988: 5), 'is [the woman's] own fascination with death, with the gaping abyss', but also for him as for Scottie, 'if woman, who is posited as she whom man must know and possess in order to guarantee his truth and his identity, does not exist, then in some important sense he does not exist either, but rather is faced with the possibility of his own nothingness' (1988: 5).

When César's fantasized and highly mediatized moment of the restoration to him of the pure Sofía is destroyed by passionate sexual congress he, like Scottie, is disempowered (again in Modlewski's words on this in *Vertigo*) 'just when [he] had thought himself to be most in control of the woman, to have achieved the "freedom" and the "power" that he has been longing for and that the film associates with masculinity, he discovers that he is caught up in a repetition'. César's case is in detail different but in psychological and scenic paraphernalia very similar. Although there is a sense, as two Catalan critics pointed out soon after the film's release, that it is more an anti-*Vertigo*, in that it is about the fear of substitution, not fascination for it (Bou and Pérez, 1997), the score in the bars we have just heard and elsewhere in the film, the motifs of vertigo, mirrors, déjà vu, psychiatric illness, crime, and the presence of what Žižek highlights (1992: 242) – the performance of simultaneous denial of and fantasy about one's own death – all point to César as a man caught up in and carrying forward to new complexities a crisis of masculine identity of a Hitchcockian nature but overlaid with postmodern subtleties.

The moral and psychological dimension of *Abre los ojos* is sharpened by conventional recourse not only to dreams but to the motif of looking into mirrors which is established as soon as we have heard the fatal words – significantly as a taped or digitalized reproduction – for the first time (as explained early in this essay). When César flees down the stairs after the murder, he is brought up short by catching sight of himself in a landing mirror that he has raced past; going back up to it he finds that the physically attractive César of the preceding sequence, he who had emerged into our view from the scene of the crime, has been replaced by the disfigured César – that there has in effect been an overlap of Hyde and Jekyll, a reversal of the time line and a further folding in on one another of reality, memory and dream. He smashes the mirror image with his foot as he staggers back from the moment of the loss of sanity, Sofía and himself (the image became subsequently, and perhaps predictably, a key one in the promotion of the film).

As in Cocteau's *La Belle et La Bête* and in Lacan's classic scenario (a connection already made by Susan Hayward (1990)), the mirror reveals in the subject César qua monster the shock of sameness and utter difference overlayed; and later, in César qua contemporary Don Juan, and in line now with Disney and the character of Gaston, it reveals in him a narcissistic satisfaction which is blind to better qualities. Nobody actually says of the handsome César, as the Disney prologue does in explaining the enchantress's transformation of the Prince into the Beast, that 'she had seen that there was no love in his heart' but this lack is very much part of the moral structure of our film; and the transmogrified César does all but ask himself (like Merrick in *The Elephant Man*, like Segismundo), again in the Disney prologue's words, 'for who could ever love a beast?' Not, for sure, himself; and yet there is an extra-textual and ambiguous piquancy to all this, since it is the delicious horror for Noriega's admirers of seeing the flawless new star marked in this way that is one of the film's principal lures. This is, in a way, a star-affirming spectacle of anti-stardom, at once an intelligent and anti-American critique of cinema's marketing of good looks and society's consumption of the body dream or dream body, and yet also a reverse affirmation of the supremacy of the star's physical perfection (Tom Cruise is doing much the same as the pale Lestat in *Interview with the Vampire* and, though through disability rather than facial disfigurement, as Ron Kovic in *Born on the Fourth of July*). Noriega is throughout recognizably Noriega under the elaborate make-up of disfigurement or the prosthetic face, never losing the shining long jet-black hair which is his distinctive sign. His disfigurement is, though not exclusively, the figuring of pathos, a reconfiguring of masculinity and its discontents, and as such it works as a powerful hook for the (young) audience as well as a point of entry into the stream of classic, tragic narrations and playings-out of this (old) drama.

The film has since become a standard epithetic tag for Noriega and the orientation point for most interviews in the substantial popular coverage of his career (now proceeding at the rate of at least one leading or co-starring role per year). The traditional popular film motif exploited there of perversity and psychosis enwrapped in extreme masculine beauty is part of the texture both of *Plata Quemada / Burning Money* (Marcelo Piñeyro, 2000) and *El espinazo del diablo / The Devil's Backbone* (Guillermo del Toro, 2001). Amenábar, like Hitchcock before him, has become transatlantic with the success of the French-Spanish-US co-pro *The Others* (2001), and he has been precociously but insistently positioned in the tradition of the popular auteur.[6] The film has also usefully caught him up in a classic Hollywood tangle of intra- and extra-filmic connections, with Nicole Kidman in the starring role of a film produced by her ex, Tom Cruise, himself now dating the Amenábar favourite Penélope Cruz and playing opposite her in *Vanilla Sky* (Cameron Crowe, 2001; co-produced by Cruise), based closely on *Abre los ojos*, seen by Cruise back at the 1998 Sundance Festival while (coincidentally) working on *Eyes Wide Shut* (Stanley Kubrick, 1999). If César in the film is brought down by inhabiting two realities, Amenábar in the industry (even more than that other Spanish A-director Almodóvar) is so far climbing high on cross-cultural hybridization.

Notes

1 The English-language subtitled version was out on limited release in the USA and UK in April 1999.
2 Cruz's North American career comprises *The Hi Lo Country* (1998), *Woman on Top* (1999), *All the Pretty Horses* (2000) and the UK-France-USA co-pro *Captain Corelli's Mandolin* (2001), and not least Cameron Crowe's version of *Abre los ojos*, *Vanilla Sky*, released in 2001 (and see the concluding paragraph to this chapter).
3 For example, Victoria Abril and Imanol Arias in *A solas contigo* [Alone with You] (1990), Abril and Jorge Sanz in *Amantes / Lovers* (1991), Cruz and Sanz in *Belle Epoque* (1992), Cruz and Javier Bardem in *Jamón, jamón* (1992), Abril and Arias in *Intruso / Intruder* (1993), Cruz and Bardem in *El amor perjudica seriamente la salud / Love Seriously Damages Your Health* (1996), Abril and Sanz in *Libertarias / Freedom Fighters* (1996), Bardem and Cruz in *Carne trémula / Live Flesh* (1997), Cruz and Sanz in *La niña de tus ojos* [The Girl of Your Dreams] (1998), Abril and Bardem in *Entre las piernas / Between Your Legs* (1999).
4 Ana had been played in Saura's film, of course, by Ana Torrent, whom Amenábar had cast as the female lead in *Tesis*.
5 To my knowledge; I am aware that Ryan Prout (Oxford) has been working on the film, but he has so far been unable to alert me to the imminent publication of work which may well already have covered this ground.
6 See reviews, for example, at www.el-mundo.es/especiales/2001/09/cultura/losotros/amenabar.html; www.filmforce.ign.com/articles/302227 p1. html; www.believe-me.com/reviews/others.htm. All accessed 25 November 01.

Bibliography

Bou, Nuria and Xavier Pérez (1997) 'Ulls aberts, boca tancat!', *Avui*, 28 December, 52
Bruno, Giulana (1993) 'Rumble City: Postmodernism and *Blade Runner*', in Christopher Sharrett (ed.) *Crisis Cinema: The Apocalyptic Idea in Postmodern Narrative Film*, Washington, D.C.: Maisonneuve, 237–49.
GuíaActiv (1998) 'Abre los ojos, Alejandro Amenábar: vértigo', section moderated by Hugo Flores, 25 August 1999.
Hayward, Susan (1990) 'Gender Politics – Cocteau's Belle is not that Bête: Jean Cocteau's *La Belle et la Bête*', in Susan Hayward and Ginette Vincendeau (eds.) *French Film: Texts and Contexts*, London: Routledge, 127–36.

J. R. (1998) 'Destruye tu cuerpo, libera tu mente', *El periódico (Dominical)*, 4 January, 107.

Jameson, Fredric (1991) *Postmodernism, or The Cultural Logic of Late Capitalism*, London: Verso.

Modlewski, Tania (1988) *The Women Who Knew Too Much: Hitchcock and Feminism*, New York: Methuen.

Moreno, Francisco (1998) '*Abre los ojos* . . . y dos horas sin pestañear', *Reseña*, 291: 15.

Ponga, Paula (1999) 'Eduardo Noriega: el galán sensato', *Fotogramas*, 1867, 16–22.

Sala, Ángel (1998) '*Abre los ojos*: rizando el rizo', *Imágenes de la actualidad*, February, 119.

Sartori, Beatriz (1997) 'Amenábar mantiene intacta su fijación por las paranoias', *El Mundo* (Madrid), 13 December, 41.

Žižek, Slavoj (1992) *Everything You Always Wanted to Know About Lacan (But Were Afraid To Ask Hitchcock)*, London: Verso.

13

Solas and the unbearable condition of loneliness in the late 1990s

Candyce Leonard

Inspired by a quest for national identity and international commerce, Spain's film industry increased in both stature and productivity in the last decade of the twentieth century. In January of 1990, the Spanish government turned its attention towards the business of making movies for its cultural, industrial and technological potential (Payán, 1993: 43). Three Academy Awards for best foreign language film, two from the 1990s (*Belle Epoque*, 1993 and *Todo sobre mi madre / All About My Mother*, 1999), demonstrate the blossoming of the industry in the democratic period. While the amplification of Spain's film trade illustrates significant gains in capitalist projects, the meaning structured around filmic images points to social changes taking place in the new democracy. For more than a century, cinema has interrogated and interpreted the political, social and cultural biases, aspirations and conflicts that have characterized Spanish society through decades of transition and evolution. Current attention to gender styling, not only as arbitrary prescriptions that cast individuals as characters within the social interface of the community, but also as political acts of ideological confrontation, articulation and assimilation, finds reference points in Spanish cinema of the late 1990s.

In his prologue to the 1999 book-length study by Peter William Evans, *Spanish Cinema: The Auteurist Tradition,* film director José Luis Borau remarks that Spanish cinema is currently at the apex of its creativity. He further argues that the generation of directors that has matured during the post-Franco period has chosen to 'address a real country, avoiding circumlocutions and solemnity at all costs, stressing modernity – in the true sense of the word' (1999: xxi). With a viewing audience largely under the age of thirty, Borau notes, Spanish cinema presents characters in whose 'forms of speech, movement

and dress' the spectators see themselves (1999: xxi). He is not referring to all present directors and movies; rather he addresses directors
of singular distinction and non-commercial enterprise whose films, in
the words of Evans, 'are all characterized by a maturity of approach
in form and content' (1999: 1). Among the recent films that Evans
places in this category are *Cosas que dejé en la Habana* / *Things I
Left in Havana* (Gutiérrez Aragón), *La buena estrella* / *Lucky Star*
(Ricardo Franco), *La mirada del otro* / *The Naked Eye* (Vicente
Aranda), *Abre los ojos* / *Open Your eyes* (Alejandro Amenábar), *Secretos del corazón* / *Secrets of the Heart* (Montxo Armendáriz), *El abuelo*
/ *The Grandfather* (José Luis Garci) and *Solas* / *Alone* (Benito Zambrano) (1999: 1). These titles were all released between 1996 and
1998 and have enjoyed considerable critical and public attention.
Although Evans argues that these directors lean more towards the
auteurist than the commercial posture, he also notes the shift in spectatorship, that is, the type of film that in the 1960s or 1970s appealed
to a select audience is now breaking box-office records (1999: 2–3).
In other words, without being 'popular' in the sense of the Hollywood blockbuster, these movies indeed have widespread appeal.
Whether the explanation is that spectators see themselves in these
films or that the democratic period has produced a different type of
viewer, these movies are far from élitist in either form or content.

The fact that a number of these movies demonstrate a strong
appeal to traditional family values as opposed to other lifestyle
choices that might be construed as marginal behaviour supports
Marvin D'Lugo's view of predilections in Spanish cinema that alter-
nate between preserving traditional principles against internal-
izing them (1997: 2). While some movies resonate with traditional
gender roles and an idealization of the *campo*, their open treatment
of female sexuality, reproduction and abortion acknowledges the
shift from sexual repression to the sexual expression that characterizes the democratic period. The often times one-dimensional conclusions of the cinematic denouement, however, gloss over the
embedded dialectic between cultural persuasion and the constant
negotiation for constructing alternative gender performances. During
the last twenty-five years, the re-evaluation of gender relationships in
both film and society has been a prominent feature of Spain's internal socio-political reorganization. Barry Jordan and Rikki Morgan-
Tamosunas claim that 'the role and status of women have been at the
epicentre of the social, economic and legislative changes which have

reverberated throughout contemporary Spanish society since the end of the dictatorship' (1998: 117). Nevertheless, the collapse of the Socialist government followed by the election of the Partido Popular in 1996 marks a political and, therefore, social shift to a more conservative discourse, a discourse that might treat the status of women in a way that re-installs a customary gender role paradigm. The belief that media 'exist close to the very core of identity production' (Stam and Shohat, 2000: 381) forces a constant evaluation of the capacity of movies to influence personal and social choices.

Solas, one of the movies cited by Evans above and the topic of this chapter, is a film that celebrates motherhood and represses active female sexuality in a way that is troubling. That the female protagonist is biologically compatible with or desirous of motherhood is not under scrutiny. Motherhood as the single path towards self-identification or relieving loneliness is the knotty premise that threatens to erase the sexual female, the working female and the independent female. While issues of materiality are primary to considerations of gender hegemony, sexuality – both reproductive and recreational – most often determines how women and men are signified into prescriptive or stereotypical behaviour. The rise in filmic images of sexuality was immediately evident in the years directly following the conclusion of Spain's military rule, ranging from the gratuitously explicit to the metaphorically political to the plainly banal. The very existence of performative sexuality and the purpose towards normalizing what these images represent signal the increased attention paid to the interpersonal relationship. Apart from the type of movie that considers relationships between men and women, the contravention of the traditional heterosexual archetype invests modern film-making with new social issues.

The analysis of *Solas* that follows is based on two principles: studying the film as a contested site between recovering conservative traditions and seeking broader definitions of sexual behaviour, and, second, viewing the film as a mechanism for constructing social precepts.

The paradigm of loneliness

In *Solas*, Benito Zambrano's directorial debut that earned five Goyas, the protagonist suffers from emotional privation and her return home is a self-saving act of survival. The plot is simple. Rosa

(María Galiana), mother of thirty-something daughter María (Ana Fernández), comes from the countryside to Seville where her husband is hospitalized. During her brief visit, this illiterate mother, who lacks the graces of the socially acceptable, is able to turn around her unwed pregnant daughter's wretched life in an act of healing love. This anecdote is played out in a process whereby María recognizes her loss and with profound nostalgia yearns for the sacred space of home and motherhood. While the handsome young doctor who cares for Rosa's husband is trained to treat physical illness, Rosa is the true healer in this film. *Solas* is plainly biased concerning sexuality and the traditional roles for both men and women within the social system. The sentimental and nostalgic influence of the film, couched in a mother's love for and redemption of her daughter, has enjoyed receptive audiences. The movie's emotional premise of a parent's uncompromising love that raises motherhood to idealized extremes is a compelling argument for family bonding and social morality in a society where, Paul Julian Smith points out, 'traditional family structures have collapsed with astonishing speed' (2001: 56).

Critics and audiences gravitated towards *Solas* for the protagonist's decisive rejection of her unhappy life; thus, a movie with a happy ending. While the female is unambiguously heterosexual, María's sexuality remains constricted since it is only through reproduction that her primary role is fulfilled. Thus the film is heavily inscribed with a retrograde posture regarding traditional notions of the male redeemer and the female redeemed. Bias concerning female and male sexuality in *Solas*, and the traditional role in society for both men and women, reflects the tension between the active presence of female sexuality in society and the restoration of the family by restricting female sexuality to reproduction. The emotional pull of the film, a mother's love for and redemption of her daughter, camouflages what otherwise might appear questionable about how the movie portrays female sexuality. Elena Sánchez Carretero writes that *Solas* 'hooks you from the beginning and leads you down a road of quiet but constant flow of emotion' (1999: 73). Her brief description in the weekly *Guía del Ocio*, designed to attract potential spectators, emphasizes the affective qualities that mark the film: 'Beautiful, moving, convincing, sincere, honest and positively surprising' (1999: 73), and Paloma Pedrero, contemporary feminist Spanish playwright, comments on the mother in her 1999 editorial: 'At the end of her life she laughs at the gods and finds a few drops of nectar to give to her suffering daughter' (1999: 14). Perhaps the comment of Pando, however, is the least restrained in denying cinema as an ideological apparatus. He celebrates that *Solas* 'has achieved the miracle of returning film to the edge of emotion where it belongs' (n.p.). All reviews implicitly and explicitly concur that the sentimental spirit of the film is powerful so that, ultimately, logic is obscured. The gift of any parent to soothe the troubled life of her offspring is indeed cause for triumphant passion, as was evidenced by the tearful audience at the 4.00 p.m. weekday matinee that I attended. The question remains: how much do the affective intonations soften the rigid codes of gender conformity that govern or obscure the explicit rebuke of sexual recreation?

The basic premise is that traditional roles for women and men, sometimes associated with the *campo* and Rosa, are good; female independence and sexuality, associated with María's life in the city, are bad. The fundamental conflict between innocence and ruin is played out through very basic but vital oppositions such as food versus want, darkness versus light, sexuality versus procreation, and the domestic sphere versus the social sphere. These oppositions are juxtaposed throughout the film to separate the spaces of loneliness and the city, and mother and the *campo*. For example, the opening frame of the movie depicts Rosa dressed in a white hospital coat standing before a window. We understand immediately the connotation of the scene: virtue, i.e. the innocence that the mother embodies, is godly and that she is blessed by nature's light.

These first few minutes of the film establish an irreconcilable difference. Rosa is cautious, polite, neatly clothed in an unpretentious blouse and skirt brought from home, her hair carefully and plainly styled – she is a simple woman from a simple town. María is resistant, casually dressed in pants and a loose jersey, her hair carelessly tied back; she wants to smoke and stops on the way home – to her mother's horror – for a drink in a bar full of men. Rather than look at the facile contrast between mother and daughter, I am examining the underlying polarity between the wife and mother from the country, a domestic sphere, set against the single woman in a big city, a public sphere. The dichotomy of the signification of these two spaces as indices of innocence and ruin is fundamental to the film's politics. In his analysis of *Jamón jamón* (Bigas Luna, 1992), Celestino Deleyto investigates 'the space of innocence' as laid out by Linda Williams: 'The melodramatic happy ending depends on the extent to which the characters can, at the end, return in a real or metaphorical form to this space of innocence. For this reason, melodrama is suffused with a nostalgia for the lost innocence associated with the rural and the maternal and is structured around the increasing awareness of this loss' (1999: 276). It is both startling and reasonable that Linda Williams' book-length study *Playing the Race Card: Melodramas of Black and White from Uncle Tom to O.J. Simpson* (2001), Celestino Deleyto's consideration of *Jamón jamón* and the present inquiry of *Solas* find a correlation with the sense of loss that each work treats. In one way or another, the safety of a paradise lost is served up as the ultimate goal and the only space of salvation.

In *Solas*, turning to the past is honoured and rewarded as the means for deliverance from a troubled present and improbable future. María re-creates herself in the image of the mother from the *campo*, signifier of a halcyonic state. The nostalgia that produces dissatisfaction and, therefore, the inability to problem-solve the present crisis is a deceptive emotion. Nancy Kline cites French writer Claudine Hermann in the voyage towards feminism: 'Women must not look backwards: they will be changed into pillars of salt. Let them reject nostalgia for primitive and already criminal societies. Nature and the past are their worst enemies. As women cannot turn to the past, they have to turn to the future and create their own and unexpected image' (1989: xviii).

The subjective camera

Formal properties, such as the use of colour, light and space as well as the story itself, demonstrate a design to return women to the domestic sphere. Signifying space is the preferred method for establishing the opposition of innocence and ruin to indoctrinate the spectator against marginal behaviour. The antithesis of city and country is instantly located not only in the difference between mother and daughter, but also in the contraposition between the mimetic space of the city and the diegetic space of the mother's home town. We *see* the city, whereas the *campo* is mythically and idealistically established through reference and inference until the close of the film when the *campo* is visually rendered as a paradise decidedly preferable to the dystopic city that María escapes. The city is an architectural nightmare of noise, clutter and sin. Some five minutes into the film, the two women get off the bus near the daughter's apartment. Without speaking a word, Rosa looks around her as the camera follows her view. She sees graffiti defacing the wall, a young man asleep in an old chair set out on the street for trash pick-up, a motorcycle roaring by and the temporary destruction of a construction site. These negative stimuli are both visual and aural. As spectators, we do not need to see or hear the *campo* physically in order to see on Rosa's face that she is viewing something unpleasant and unlike her hometown. The city where architectural spheres of moral squalor displace organic growth alienates the individual from life-giving traditions.

Regardless of the political or social issue at hand, the heavy-handed association of the city with evil and the country with virtue generates a flawed symbiosis that suffocates the prospect of meaningful resolution, or more to the point, that impedes judicious decoding by the spectator. In the case of *Solas*, the city versus the country model smoothly converts to a distinction of moral difference designated by spaces that censure female sexuality associated with independence and that honour female procreative sexuality associated with dependence. Ultimately, as Colin McArthur argues, 'the small town . . . operates as the binary antinomy not, strictly speaking, of the city itself but of "city values"' (1997: 24). Rather than denounce the city, *Solas* uses it to rebuke a woman in her mid-thirties who has yet to bear children, as though somehow living in the city has caused this neglect. Several spaces within the frame of the principal space of the city perpetuate the dichotomy separating the life that María has from the life that she could / should have. While the hospital as the first space we see may appear merely to function as a plot vehicle for explaining Rosa's trip to Seville, it serves up very specific metaphors. Above all, this space sets forth Rosa's association with healing and with the godlike father figure of the doctor who saves lives. Second, it establishes the brutality of Rosa's husband, María's father. The abusive husband / father and María's boyfriend are set against the handsome doctor and represent the stereotyping for all men in the movie who fall into one of these two categories. Third, the literal healing of the husband / father is subjugated to the moral and spiritual healing of the daughter. Although María's parents are in the city for the father's physical health, it is María's moral health that is her mother's concern. Towards the end of the film as María bids her mother goodbye in the hallway of the hospital, she receives her mother's healing blessing towards a better life.

A second space within the city, María's apartment, like its immediate surroundings, exteriorizes her shattered life. Even before we
enter the apartment, María's moral decay is reinforced. The long
hallway, one of several in which she is cast, leading to her front door
is darkened with off-camera sunlight creating shadows on the wall
to suggest her journey from a pit of darkness to a shelter of light.
María's apartment reeks of the loss of direction in her life and the
yearning for recovery. The purposeful use of light signifies choices
that are seemingly 'natural' versus choices that are inherently iniq-
uitous or unethical. The interior of María's apartment has little natural light so that the synthetic low lighting repeats her loss of
innocence. To establish her state of depravity, María's daily life is
condensed through brief vignettes that produce a negative impression of her existence in the city environment. The kitchen is clut-
tered and bereft of food – neither fruit nor milk, she tells her
mother. The shower stall, a space of cleanliness and purification is
mildewed and uninviting. Her mother sits quietly as María scurries
to straighten the untidy bedroom, an obvious metaphor for her
dishevelled lifestyle and sex life. In semi-darkness, María changes
her clothes to go out for the evening. The sight of her in panties as
she slips into a tight-fitting short skirt and low-cut, v-necked pull-
over top objectifies her image and explicitly identifies her as inap-
propriately sexual in contrast to her non-sexual, reproductive
mother. Yet it is within this murky arena of María's life that Rosa
insinuates the probable solution: a baby. A friend back home has
asked that María be godmother to her baby and as María looks at
the pictures of a happy mother with her baby, she begins the road to
reconciliation via her inexorable destiny as a female.

In contrast to María's disorderly life is the neatly ordered neighbour downstairs (Carlos Álvarez-Novoa), an older version of the
good doctor. There is food in his clean kitchen, plenty of light and
a window through which the neatly dressed sexagenarian peers out.
The neighbour's apartment is a space of order where tradition creates stability against the chaos of stepping outside the boundaries of
social norms. His grey, grandfatherly beard inscribes him as a loving
and gentle human being, and Rosa sets about formulating a bond
with him that she then bequeaths to her daughter. Essentially, Rosa
is not looking for a companion for either herself or her daughter,
nor does she have any intention of leaving her unhappy marriage;
rather she is seeking a father figure to take care of María. Rosa's

approach to the neighbour is one of maternal care. The motif of mother's milk as a source of spiritual succour occupies every aspect of Rosa's good deeds; in fact, her first encounter with the neighbour is at the market where she helps him select a fish that she later prepares for him. Rosa, in truth, is so busy knitting, cleaning, cooking, buying flowers and caring for her abusive husband, wayward daughter and the kind neighbour during her brief sojourn in Seville that she seems the very embodiment of salvation through sacrifice and good deeds.

María and her mother, as the title implies, suffer both from loneliness and from 'aloneness'. María's life is never threatened nor has she descended to the depths of decadence through immoral acts. While avoiding a marriage like her mother's that is an unending routine of duties, María has failed to find comfort and security with a male companion of, for example, the doctor's good nature. Her lifestyle – smoking, drinking and consorting with an undesirable male companion – provokes her mother's disapproval and, without the possibility of upward social mobility, María's static life is buried in the despair of low-paying, low-status jobs.

Alongside the shadowed lighting, blue lighting prejudices the spectator in scenes when María enters the long narrow hallway leading to her dreary apartment, as she sits on the toilet administering a pregnancy test, as she wearily mops a long corridor at work and as she weeps inconsolably in her own bed after her mother has medicated her blistered hands. All this bears a striking contrast to the natural sunlight in which María is bathed (baptized) as she evolves into her mother's role. These moments occur when she sits in the chair by the window in her father's hospital room, then in a rocking chair next to the window in her apartment, both places where we have seen her mother knit and sleep. The motherhood myth peaks during the last seven or eight minutes of the film. As María and her proxy father arrive at an agreement about María's pregnancy, the camera cuts to a close-up of Rosa sitting in a rocking chair back home in the countryside, dying peacefully before a radiant sunset. As the camera shifts to a medium long shot behind the rocker, the backlighting of the sunset frames her within a halo of beatific light. Rosa does not try to make her daughter 'honest' through marriage because *Solas* does not insist upon matrimony as a remedy. Such a solution would certainly cause the film to collapse into a 'nostalgic return to traditional and ocentric relations between men and women' as Susan Martin-Márquez characterizes Almodóvar's approach in *Kika* (1999: 40). Rather, the kind neighbour who longs to be a grandfather replaces any would-be suitor that María might find. The situation, therefore, is literally paternalistic.

In her 1998 study of Spanish film in the 1990s, *Mujer, amor y sexo*, Pilar Aguilar argues that many Spanish films continue to depict mothers who thrive on sacrificing themselves completely to their family at the cost of all personal goals (1998: 170). Clearly, Rosa has long since relinquished all hope of personal happiness; yet only a few months away from her own death, Rosa's final and purest victory in life is the rebirth of her daughter. Rosa, like her husband, is gravely ill and lives until she saves her daughter; María's 'sickness', however, is not physical. She needs someone to care for and to be cared for. Her lover is abusive and totally removed from the pregnancy, and her father is equally harsh and uncaring. In *Solas* female sexuality is neither destructive nor predatory; it does not lay waste to men who desire it; rather, it destroys motherhood. It is not that María is promiscuous; rather, her primary transgression is that her sexual activity is not directed towards motherhood. The spaces of sexuality and reproduction are the ultimate spaces that are opposed in *Solas*. The only loving relationship between a man and a woman in the movie is seen in the doctor whose off-screen wife is at home with a new baby. So, this becomes the model: the only consecrated sex is procreative sex, and the only means of happiness or moral prosperity is motherhood.

By the end of the film, María has moved from the shadowy darkness of ruin into the light of salvation by assuming the role of virgin mother. She has suspended all amorous relationships in favour of the kind elderly neighbour who has offered to spend his retirement income to care for her and her baby in the countryside. The neighbour rescues María, not as a husband but as a father figure, thereby restoring María to filial status even as she becomes a mother. Amid bright sunlight and accompanied by her infant daughter and surrogate father, María brings red roses to her mother's grave, then strolls away with her new family into the blissful greenery of nature. The only physical vista that we have of the countryside to which she has returned is a long take that slowly climbs to a slightly high-angle view of the beautiful, tree-filled park next to the cemetery, a perfect aesthetic context. The iconography of the Elysian-like gardens highlighted by a large cross signifies cleansing and the film-maker's attempt to centre the denotative and connotative inscriptions of a Spanish ideology in familiar symbols.

The emblematic cross at the cemetery re-asserts the primacy of Catholicism in Spanish culture. Aurora Morcillo Gómez traces the history of Church doctrine as an index of social identity where the family would nurture the soul (1999: 63). Once again, the family nurtures soul through women like Rosa who create a wistful memory for the present generation of young women who seek an ideal relationship. Through the use of religious iconography, the rural vistas and father figure as sources of renewal, *Solas* quietens modern alienation by preserving familiar patterns.

A feminist perspective

By associating procreation with innocence and failing to scrutinize the materiality that allows or denies freedom of choice, *Solas* restores the myth of motherhood. The 'dismantling [of] the ideology of motherhood by understanding its patriarchal roots' that Donna Bassin, Margaret Honey and Meryle Mahrer Kaplan explain occurred in the United States during the 1970s (1994: 3) is absent from contemporary Spanish history. Although María is the film's central character, the mother protagonizes the ostensible theme of moral prosperity via childbirth as the most valid sort of restitution and regeneration. Pilar Aguilar argues that few women achieve the status of protagonist since action associated with men almost singularly determines that quality (cited by Brooksbank Jones, 1997: 154). Action means the physical kind most often associated with some sort of violence so that its binary opposite, emotion (inaction?), is associated with women, and ultimately, the sentimental or 'woman's film', as theatre critic Juan Antonio Vizcaíno analyses, 'whose female protagonists tell all that they see and suffer in life' (2000: 27). The persistent retreat to a woman's affective or biological relationships as the driving force of her life confines the female protagonist to a very limited zone – albeit important – of human experience. As protagonists who seek subjectivity in a traditional society, both María and Rosa find transcendence through childbearing and nurturing rather than by means of social or political activism.

Solas does not fail, however, to break new ground by, as Smith points out, giving attention to the elderly and to domestic violence (2001: 56). Yet the primary socio-cultural icon to which a good number of these appealing recent releases refer is that of family, and who can challenge family and children? Indeed, Kinder concludes that audiences are forced to re-assess Spain's ethical compromise of 'replacing matadors and militants with hookers and dopers as the nation's privileged cultural icons' (1997: 20). The exploitation of Spain's cultural iconography, then, seems all the more insidious since it skirts the possibility of female roles that are not dominated by procreation, abusive men or loneliness. Due to the strong appeal that these movies possess (*Secretos del corazón*, *La buena estrella* and *Nadie hablará de nosotras cuando hayamos muerto*, for example), it would seem that audience members are lonely in the midst of what Laura Mulvey calls 'the seething mass of the urban environment' (1989: 70). This term, applied to late nineteenth-century England, corresponds to Elaine Showalter's study of the same period 'when all the laws that governed sexual identity and behavior seemed to be breaking down' (1991: 3). This perception of urban turmoil and 'sexual anarchy' characterizes our interpretation of present culture as though such a climate were new and unique to the late twentieth-century period. Modern, now postmodern, transitions in family, gender and sexual relationships have created social traumas that create a sense of emptiness. One way to deal with this alienation is to contrive an idealized version of tradition and 'family values', the very failure of which precipitated the postmodern cultural crisis.

Owing to the narration and politicization of sexuality in so many current Spanish movies, the performance of gender begs the question of national identity. To what extent do the recognizable 'forms of speech, movement and dress' on-screen correspond to cultural imperatives, social prescriptions and democratic promises? In his praise of *Solas* when screened at the Berlin Festival, Juan Pando reports that both critics and spectators found the female characters 'as authentic as life itself' (n.p.). The notion that the portrayal of women in *Solas* might somehow be 'authentic' seems to confuse neorealist cinema of social activism, such as Rossellini's *Open City* (1946) or De Sica's *The Bicycle Thief* (1949), with other productions of reality, a slippery concept in itself and the difference between simulacrum (miming) and representation (inscribing). *Solas*' acutely romantic ending, in both the anecdotal and visual narratives, undermines any pretence of authentic portrayals and, in fact, calls for careful analysis of its use of cultural realism. Pedro Almodóvar has been

Spain's chief engineer of a new cultural stereotype of 'transgressive sexuality' that is wrapped within deep-rooted cultural images inherent in Spanish tradition (Kinder, 1997: 13). His curious blend of the old and the new is further examined by Núria Triana-Toribio who shows that Almodóvar creates his movies by 'harnessing and mixing countless facets of Spanish society and culture' (1999: 227) like, for example, incorporating into his movies folkloric tradition, a staple genre of the Franco regime imposed to fabricate 'authentic' cultural representations (1999: 238). Kinder elaborates this duality by suggesting that not only Almodóvar's *La flor de mi secreto / The Flower of My Secret*, but also Alex de la Iglesia's *El día de la bestia / Day of the Beast* and Agustín Díaz Yanes' *Nadie hablará de nosotras cuando hayamos muerto / Nobody Will Talk About Us When We Are Dead*, all released in 1995, 'show a growing disillusionment with the libertarian ethos and an attempt to recuperate conservative traditions', yet they gain international attention by preserving 'a radical surface of outrageousness' (1997: 23).

Both Kinder and Triana-Toribio point out two vital components of present Spanish cinema that bear scrutiny. The return to traditionalism is a cinematic strategy that might explain the box-office appeal of films from the late 1990s. While film directors have raised the standards of Spain's film industry to capture international audiences, they have also catapulted renderings of Spanish culture onto the big screen that are familiar and endearing to audience members. Rather than reject elements of the conservative past as was anticipated in the new democracy, Triana-Toribio reports that audience members are soothed upon hearing music of the folkloric tradition in an Almodóvar film. She further suggests that such mellow remembrance of things past has healing powers within a ruptured society (1999: 238). Such seems to be the case with *Solas* whose small-town mother with her unconditional love brings peace and comfort in the midst of her daughter's chaotic and unfulfilling life. Rather than question the legitimacy of the portrayals, audience members welcome the ideal vision of harmony projected within an easily recognizable visual context. The problem of representation, whether it is the alleged authenticity of the female characters in *Solas* or of the folkloric tradition under Franco, is, as Brooksbank Jones concludes, that the images assists in conditioning reality through constructing the audience member (1997: 154). It is a film's very power to construct the spectator as well as its capacity to tease the distinction between art and nature that problematizes the representation of sexuality as a measure of personal autonomy or cultural deference. The soothing images of a mid-1930s María who has finally made the right choice is equally as manipulative and romantic as the folkloric tradition forced upon audiences several decades ago.

Bibliography

Aguilar, Pilar (1998) *Mujer amor sexo en el cine español de los 90*, Madrid: Editorial Fundamentos.

Bassin, Donna, Margaret Honey and Meryle Mahrer Kaplan (eds.) (1994) *Representations of Motherhood*, New Haven: Yale University Press.

Borau, José Luis (1999) 'Prologue', in Peter William Evans (ed.) *Spanish Cinema: the Auteurist Tradition*, Oxford: Oxford University Press, xvii–xxii.

Brooksbank Jones, Anny (1997) *Women in Contemporary Spain*, Manchester and New York: Manchester University Press.

Deleyto, Celestino (1999) 'Motherland: Space, Femininity, and Spanishness in *Jamón jamón* (Bigas Luna, 1992)', in Peter William Evans (ed.) *Spanish Cinema: the Auteurist Tradition*, Oxford: Oxford University Press, 270–85.

D'Lugo, Marvin (1997) *Guide to the Cinema of Spain*, Westport, CT: Greenwood Press.

Evans, Peter William (1999) 'Introduction', in Peter William Evans (ed.) *Spanish Cinema: the Auteurist Tradition*, Oxford: Oxford University Press, 1–7.

Jordan, Barry and Rikki Morgan-Tamosunas (1998) *Contemporary Spanish Cinema*, Manchester: Manchester University Press.

Kinder, Marsha (1997) 'Refiguring Socialist Spain: An Introduction', in Marsha Kinder (ed.) *Refiguring Spain*, Durham, NC: Duke University Press, 1–32.

Kline, Nancy (1989) 'Introduction', in Claudine Hermann (ed.) *The Tongue Snatchers*, Trans. Nancy Kline. Lincoln: University of Nebraska Press.

Martin-Márquez, Susan (1999) *Feminist Discourse and Spanish Cinema*, Oxford: Oxford University Press.

McArthur, Colin (1997) 'Chinese Boxes and Russian Dolls: Tracking the Elusive Cinematic City', in David B. Clarke (ed.) *The Cinematic City*, New York: Routledge, 19–45.

Morcillo Gómez, Aurora (1999) 'Shaping True Catholic Womanhood: Francoist Educational Discourse on Women', in Victoria Lorée Enders and Pamela Beth Radcliff (eds.) *Constructing Spanish Womanhood*, Albany: State University of New York, 51–69.

Mulvey Laura (1989) *Visual and Other Pleasures*, Bloomington: Indiana University Press.

Pando, Juan (1999) 'El largo túnel de la vida', *Metrópoli*, www.wlmundo. es/metropoli/paginas/estrenocin.html?nombre=p458a.

Payán, Miguel Juan (1993) *El cine español de los 90*, Madrid: Ediciones JC.

Pedrero, Paloma (1999) 'Solas', *La Razón*, 29: 14.

Sánchez Carretero, Elena (1999) 'Solas', *Guía del Ocio*, 1,224 (Viernes 28 al Jueves 3 de junio de 1999), 73.

Showalter, Elaine (1991) *Sexual Anarchy*, New York: Penguin Books.

Smith, Paul Julian (2001) 'Solas', *Sight and Sound*, 11: 7, 56.

Stam, Robert and Ella Habiba Shohat (2000) 'Film Theory and Spectatorship in the Age of the "Posts"', in Christine Gledhill and Linda Williams (eds.) *Reinventing Film Studies*, 381–401.

Talens, Jenaro and Santos Zunzunegui (1998) 'Introduction', in Jenaro Talens and Santos Zunzunegui (eds.) *Modes of Representation in Spanish Cinema*, Minnesota: University of Minnesota Press, 1–45.

Triana-Toribio, Núria (1999) '¿*Qué he hecho yo para merecer esto?* (Almodóvar, 1984)', in Peter William Evans (ed.) *Spanish Cinema: the Auteurist Tradition*, Oxford: Oxford University Press, 226–41.

Vizcaíno, Juan Antonio (2000) 'La gran paradoja de teatro', *Contrastes*, 9, 25–9.

14

From the margins to the mainstream: trends in recent Spanish horror cinema
Andrew Willis

This chapter focuses on horror films made in Spain or by Spanish film-makers since 1990. The recent revival of the genre within Spain has led to the production of a significant number of, broadly, horror films in recent years. Here, I want to identify different strands within this recent generic production. Certainly, after the international success of *The Others / Los otros* (Alejandro Amenábar, 2001), it is likely that there will be a significant number of films trying to repeat that production's huge international success over the next few years. Indeed, *The Others*, rather than being a catalyst for this cycle of horror production, can be seen as the peak of a general trend that saw a significant number of horror films made in Spain throughout the 1990s and into the early 21st century. Importantly, these ranged from short films to features. My aim is to come to an understanding of the trends within this cycle of generic production and, in particular, consider the ways in which these strands link to wider developments in the production of Spanish popular cinema.

Spanish horror in the 1990s

Before embarking on my analysis I feel it is useful to outline the development of horror cinema in Spain in the 1990s and to indicate the sorts of films that I am considering in this study. Without doubt, the horror genre has had a significant impact upon the Spanish film industry. The high point, at least in terms of numbers of productions and co-productions, of the late 1960s and early 1970s, saw horror films produced by a varied array of directors. These ranged from Vicente Aranda, who would later establish himself as an art-house staple, to Narciso Ibáñez Serrador, perhaps best known as the figure behind the successful television programme *Un, dos, tres*, to Javier Aguirre, who also created a reputation as an experimental film-maker in the early 1970s, without forgetting Paul Naschy, who became a key genre figure often playing the character of Daninsky the werewolf and would appear once again in the 2001 film *School Killer*. Some of these films received international exhibition in the 1970s in versions dubbed into various languages, often providing the lower halves of double bills in urban, exploitation-orientated cinemas. They often featured stock generic figures such as The Werewolf (*La noche de Walpurgis* / *The Werewolf's Shadow*, 1970), Dracula (*El gran amor del conde Dracula* / *Dracula's Great Love*, 1972) and The Mummy (*La venganza de la momia* / *The Mummy's Revenge*, 1973). However, following the loosening of censorship laws around Europe in the 1970s (marked in Spain by introduction of the S certificate after the restoration of democracy, see Kowalsky in this collection), many distributors looked for products that were more directly sex-orientated rather than the previously popular blend of horror and sex, sometimes labelled 'horrotica'. Following a shift into sex films some distinguished horror directors, such as Carlos Aured, who had made *Apocalipsis sexual* in 1982, found themselves forced economically into the ghetto of hardcore pornography as producers demanded more explicit scenes. From which many of them, due to their new 'bad reputations' would never be able to escape. However, while some of these horror films, such as Ibáñez Serrador's *La Residencia* / *The Finishing School* (1969) (for more on this see Lázaro-Reboll in this collection) were financially very successful, as a genre they would remain on the critical margins of Spanish film culture. This marginality was heightened when democracy was restored and critical interest began to focus on how film-makers would negotiate and engage with that historical moment. The horror film and its place in Spanish film history quickly became forgotten. Arguably, that would not change until the end of the 20th century.

This change began when, a generation on from the return to democracy, critics such as Carlos Aguilar (1999) began to reconsider the genre, firstly tracing its history and influence. This re-evaluation seemed even more significant as a number of young film-makers began to re-assess the value of working within the horror genre, many influenced as much by US and other European films as those previously produced in Spain. Importantly, Sitges and San Sebastián hosted well respected international horror and fantasy festivals, which allowed for a celebration of the genre and provided a place for young film-makers to screen their work. Many of those interested in the horror genre had been involved in the world of underground fanzines where obscure generic knowledge could be championed and celebrated. Film-makers such as Alex de la Iglesia with *Acción mutante* / *Mutant Action* (1993) and *El día de la bestia* / *Day of the Beast* (1995), Santiago Segura with the shorts *Evilio* (1992) and its sequel *El Purificador: Evilio vuelve* (1994), Nacho Cerdá with *Aftermath* (1994) and *Génesis* (1998), also short films, and Jaume Balagueró with his short *Días sin luz* (1996) and the very successful feature *Los sin nombre* / *The Nameless* (1999) produced works that were, in a variety of ways, engaged with the horror genre. However, they were significantly different in their approaches and simply classifying them generically as 'horror' is in some ways reductive. It is therefore important to discover a way of making distinctions within contemporary Spanish horror productions. One way of beginning to do this is by using work that has attempted to look at strands within contemporary genre film-making in other contexts.

Generic trends in the 1990s: irony and sincerity

One such work is Jim Collins' 1993 article 'Genericity in the nineties: eclectic irony and the new sincerity'. Here, Collins proposes that there were two main trends within Hollywood genre production in the 1990s. The first of his categories is based around what he terms 'an ironic hybridization', where traditional generic divisions are collapsed and films begin to playfully cross boundaries, creating weird and wonderful mixes. The second category, 'new sincerity', seeks to find a 'lost purity', in terms of genre, and eschews the irony that marks out the former. Both types of genre film have, according to Collins, 'emerged within the past decade as reactions to the same cultural milieu – namely, the media-saturated landscape of contemporary [American] culture' (1993: 243). He goes on to argue that the circulation of older generic texts and a growing awareness of patterns of distribution and the various mediums of exhibition have impacted upon recent genre products. With the rediscovery of Spanish horror over the past few years, in both Spain and beyond, it is possible to argue that this situation, that is one marked by an array of film-savvy producers and consumers, exists in relation to the production and consumption of these films. So while work that focuses on US film production might not address the specificity of Spanish cinema, it does offer approaches that can begin to inform our understanding of contemporary horror films. Here I want to argue that that similar trends to those outlined by Collins might usefully be acknowledged as existing in relation to recent Spanish horror productions, and that his analysis can assist in our understanding of Spanish genre production in a similar manner.

As noted, Collins labels one of the main trends in contemporary generic production as 'eclectic irony'. Marked by a jokey, irreverent take on genres and their codes and conventions, these films are playful in the extreme. His example is *Back to the Future III* (1990), within which, he argues, 'we enter a narrative universe defined by impertinent connections, no longer containable by one set of generic conventions' (1993: 249). In the context of popular Spanish cinema, this seems an excellent way of describing Alex de la Iglesia's *Acción mutante* (1993), a strange mixture of science fiction, slapstick comedy, the western and horror. In drawing from such a wide range of generic influences and styles this film, which one might describe as operating within Collins' framework for eclectic irony, highlights the diverse nature of these works. The resultant film might be explained by the rampantly 'cinefile' approach adopted by Alex de la Iglesia and his collaborators, where references to their favourite generic works and characters abound. However, this is not simply an exercise in creating in-jokes. I would argue that these self-reflexive aspects of such Spanish films mark a rejection of 'accepted' critical criteria, in particular of what makes a film worthy and of value, which of course really represents a very particular set of taste formations. The excess present within many of these films, in particular the 'horror' elements, seems designed to distance those concerned with 'good taste'. As Núria Triana-Toribio puts it 'Spanish critics who cherish fond memories of the days of Erice and Saura will sigh with despair . . . when they see such productions' (2003: 151). One of the main ways to upset such establishment film critics is to reject the traditional generic boundaries that they often hold so dear, thus leading them to reject new work and label films such as *Acción mutante* as incoherent. An irreverent, eclectic approach to genre is often seen as 'bad' film-making by commentators more used to well-established critical models of genre, ones that celebrate a sense of generic unity. While older audiences may have a desire for generic unity, younger audiences have no problem with the boundary-breaking and genre-mixing of such works. For example, *El día de la bestia* uses satanic horror as its starting point before throwing in slapstick comedy, conspiracy theories, chases, shoot-outs and hallucigenic drugs. Replete with in-jokes, grotesques and comedic excess, the film creates the impression of being made by an over-excited, over-stimulated group of fans who do not take genres seriously and choose to 'celebrate' their fandom on screen. Again, as Collins has argued, in doing so, they present an 'unmanageable textuality that refuses to play by the old rules' (1993: 250), creating works that, as financially successful films as well as generic hybrids, are successfully breaking down old boundaries and attacking traditional arguments about 'good' films and 'good' taste. These films are also part of a wider movement within Spanish cinema that celebrated excess, aiming clearly at a more youthful audience. In his comparison of critical responses to popular horror and 'worthy' horror films in the US, Jeffery Sconce has noted that what is at stake is often 'the taste of the "élite" audience of critics' (1993: 105), arguing that such writers feel culturally justified in dismissing 'lowbrow' fare, usually those films enjoyed by young audiences, as unsophisticated. As noted above, in Spain this has been evident in the mainstream critical rejection of massive popular box-office successes such as *Airbag* (Juanma Bajo Ulloa, 1997), *Torrente: el brazo tonto de la ley* / *Torrente: the Dumb Arm of the Law* (Santiago Segura, 1998), *Año mariano* (2000) and *Torrente 2: misión en Marbella* (Santiago Segura, 2001), films which in their excessive storylines, characterization and *mise-en-scène* seem to be 'self-consciously rejecting the Miró legislation model of "good films"' (Triana-Toribio, 2003: 151).

However, if we utilize Jim Collins' approach to such excessive, generically mixed, self-reflexive films it opens up a more interesting and rewarding way of thinking about them. Indeed, such films, rather than being incoherent, become a sophisticated and understandable response to contemporary media saturation. With a vast array of generic products, from a variety of contexts and historical moments, being much more easily available through a variety of sources such as DVD, video, the internet, as well as cinema, this eclectic irony seems an understandable response. Spanish films utilizing elements of horror, such as those of Alex de la Iglesia and Santiago Segura, can be seen as celebrations of the genre, and ones that are very conscious that much of their, predominantly young, audience are very generically aware as well. Segura's short films from the 1990s – *Evilio* (1992), *Perturbado* (1993) and *El purificador: Evilio vuelve* (1994) – revel in a high level of self-reflexivity that depends upon the audience sharing a sharp generic knowledge with the film-makers. As Andrew Tudor has noted in relation to contemporary horror, 'the use of pastiche and humour is seen as inviting the audience to be complicit and self-aware' (2002: 113). However, he goes on to argue that this playfulness has, according to some commentators, removed much of the genre's potential for subversion and critique (2002: 113). In the case of Santiago Segura's short films, however, the potential for subversion exists in relation to very specifically Spanish notions of what 'good' films are. Many of these are directly related, as noted above, to the period of the transition to democracy in the late 1970s and early 1980s and the cinema that was lauded at that time (for more detail see the introduction to this volume). Segura uses the horror genre, and an excessive take on its codes and conventions, as a way of rejecting these values, and the audience's knowledge and understanding as a way of celebrating that rejection and indeed opposition to the critical establishments sense of 'good taste'.

Evilio introduces a psychopathic killer who fits the generic stereotype: he wears a shabby overcoat and dirty T-shirt, he is unwashed and has unkempt hair and a dirty-looking beard. The film opens with him dragging three schoolgirls to his apartment den. He ties them to chairs and whilst hearing voices, getting headaches and singing to himself, brutally kills them one by one, blood spattering over a picture of Julio Iglesias pinned on the wall. In one of the film's self-consciously gore-drenched moments, Evilio feeds one of his victims ears to his pet mouse who is watching the proceedings from a sink in the corner of the room. After he has killed his three victims, Evilio leaves only to be attacked by three, Hitler T-shirt-wearing fascists. While they beat him in the street two middle-class youths spot what is going on and rather than stopping it join in, hitting Evilio with baseball bats. None of the five who beat him have any idea what he has done, they are therefore beating him because of what he looks like. The film through this ending asks us to consider who is the real evil, the fascists or the genre, the horror genre being one that has often been cited, due to its content, as the cause of aberrant behaviour in society. In a rather interesting way, then, Segura manages to use the genre to communicate ideas about the genre. An audience aware of the generic codes and conventions is likely to be aware of these discussions and therefore will appreciate the point being made. Those critical of the genre will just repeat the unease at the film's violent images, thus proving exactly the point Segura seems to want to make.

Segura followed this short film with another that played with generic knowledge: the Goya-winning *Perturbado*. This film is about a sex maniac and like *Evilio* much of the horror genre atmosphere comes from the score by José Luis Cid. However, here Segura blends horror elements with slapstick comedy. Driven insane by lust and pornography, the central character begins to see sexual innuendo in everything from handwash to chicken. The maniac is tipped over the edge by his misinterpretation of an innocent cartoon as highly sexual, resulting in his killing a woman with a cleaver. He is found clinically insane and committed to an asylum where a doctor tries to cure him. The cure fails and he is given shock treatment. The final shots of the film once again celebrate generic knowledge as the maniac sits alone in a room while a fly lands on his hand, repeating the end of *Psycho* (1960). Another joins it and they begin mating, his arousal revealing that he is far from cured. Here, the maniac is seen as the product of society, developing from a Benny Hill-like comic character, whose looking up women's dresses is supposedly innocent, into something more sinister. The audience is implicated in the earlier 'smut' by the knowing look given by Segura's central character to the audience as he comically looks at women as sex objects. We are invited to laugh along at this point but one wonders how far the audience are able to laugh by the end when he seedily tries to paw one of the nurses. Following the final credit sequence the maniac has escaped to enjoy the pleasures of the modern world once again. The excesses of the genre, and the audience's knowledge of them, are used to raise important issues in relation to representation within popular cinema, in particular, asking when images stop being 'funny' and become 'sinister'.

El purificador: Evilio vuelve marks the return of the Evilio character. The film opens with a typical middle-class family arguing as they drive through the night. They almost run over Evilio who asks them for some help and food. They reject him and drive out of the frame leaving Evilio in a mid-shot; he slowly turns to look directly at the camera (and the audience) and laughs in a sinister manner. His look and laughter inviting the audience to celebrate their generic knowledge, they know what horrific things are going to follow, and will be disappointed if they do not. What unfolds certainly delivers. It includes the family being killed one by one in a gory fashion, hands being cut off, nails being hammered into heads, sick being eaten and a little kitten's neck being snapped, each incident being more blood-drenched or outrageous than the previous one. Once again events are observed by Evilio's pet mouse who this time eats brains rather than ears. Segura's intention here is much more clearly to shock, particularly after the Goya success of his previous short. He seems to have aimed clearly at upsetting the taste of those who bestowed that particular honour upon him. Hence the inclusion of such images such as Evilio eating fresh sick and his tweaking a young girl's nipple with his knife. In many ways *El purificador* rehearses the outrageous 'bad' taste that marked his first feature *Torrente: el brazo tonto de la ley*, which led to so many liberal critics being uneasy with what they saw.

Jim Collins argues that other approaches to genre within contemporary film-making have spawned another trend. This he labels as a form of 'new sincerity'. One of the unifying aspects of Collins' two film-making trends is that generic knowledge is central and brought to bear by the directors and their collaborators as well as being acknowledged by the audience. Significantly, what Collins calls the 'new sincerity' films are much more easily assimilated into established critical perspectives and taste formations as they respect generic unity in their striving for a pure form. These films may therefore be seen as ultimately much more conservative than the eclectic films of Segura and de la Iglesia. For Collins the 'new sincerity', like 'eclectic irony', is also a response to the contemporary media world. However, here rather than creating works that seem over-stimulated and are clearly generic hybrids, what we have is an 'attempt to reject it altogether, purposely evading the media-saturated terrain of the present in pursuit of an almost forgotten authenticity, attainable only through a sincerity that avoids any sort of irony or eclecticism.' (1993: 257). Recent Spanish horror cinema has certainly produced a number of works that fit into this category. For example, *Aftermath*, the short film produced by Barcelona-based director Nacho Cerdá, is one such work. Based on the dark goings-on in an autopsy room, the film is excessive – it contains graphic scenes of body mutilation and necrophilia – and overwhelmingly serious. While the subject matter and excessive gore effects of *Aftermath* are clearly intended to challenge mainstream limits of what is acceptable, it is a film that offers a very sombre take on the horror genre. It certainly does not want to engage its audience on the level of in-joke quirkiness that marks the cinema of Segura and de la Iglesia. Cerdá himself has stated that 'I wanted to do a movie that was hard. I wanted it to be one of those films that you still think about once it's over. That's what I wanted to get across because it's a subject matter that is really, really important to me, and it's nothing to joke about or take lightly' (Totaro, 1997: 2). This approach clearly shows that in developing the project Cerdá saw the genre as a way to make a serious point. The film itself reflects this attitude from the outset. It begins with the off-screen sounds of a car crash as the credits run, followed by a shot of a dismembered dog. Over these images solemn classical music is played, the overall effect being very different from the Segura horror shorts of the same period. The shots of clinical rooms and equipment that are interspersed among the credits that follow the shot of the mutilated dog create a strong sense of foreboding. The credits end and we see a body being taken to the morgue. A crucifix has been removed and is handed to relatives echoing the shape made by the 't' in Cerdá's writing credit. The religious and spiritual undertones that will pervade the work are established at the outset, again, enhancing the feeling that this is a horror film that wants to be taken very seriously. There follows an FX-driven sequence where a body is cut up as part of an autopsy. The sequence is very graphic, the horror coming from the showing. This explicit display links Cerdá's work to a tradition of European horror films that have been very explicit in their bloody images and that attempted to use the genre and its potential for excess to challenge bourgeois morality, such as Franju's landmark, *Les yeux sans visage / Eyes Without a Face* (1959). Having established its horrific credentials at the outset, *Aftermath* goes further. Another body is brought to the autopsy room but the mysterious man who undertook the earlier work goes further here committing necrophilia as the corpse lies on the bench. Cerdá is clearly intent on going further than mainstream cinema could possibly go. This is something that many horror fans will desire and celebrate, their status as being able to 'stomach' such images all important within their own circles. Once again, however, Cerdá does not want his work to be simply seen as celebratory of its excess; here once more *Aftermath* is in sharp contrast to the bloodletting of Segura's shorts. Cerdá has stated that for him, 'this is not a film that condones violence, and it is not a bloodfeast movie. I want people to really think about it . . . I think it's a film against violence. It's a film against the manipulation of the human body, that's it. But in order to get that point across I had to show the true violence that was going on' (Totaro, 1997: 3).

Generic unity and realism

Perhaps the most interesting of the films that I would argue fall into the category of 'new sincerity' is Jaume Balagueró's *Los sin nombre / The Nameless*. On the surface the film contains a number of elements that seem new and 'trendy', in particular the stylized film- and sound-editing techniques, which might suggest a more ironic approach. However, underneath that surface it is a serious, almost old-fashioned, genre film. Adapted from a 1981 novel by British horror writer Ramsey Campbell, also called *The Nameless*, the film is an exercise in psychological terror. From the outset, with its dark lighting helping to create a suspense-filled *mise-en-scène*, the film is designed for the audience to take it seriously, which is essential to the way in which this particular type of 'sincere' horror works. If the audience is laughing and joking too much, they are not going to be unnerved or disturbed by the images in front of them. Certainly, *Los sin nombre* is a film that aims to unsettle its audience and, of course, this is traditionally the role of horror films. In this way, then, it is possible to argue that Balagueró wishes to return to a mythical generic purity of the type outlined by Collins. This aim is also reflected by his use of a novel that was nearly twenty years old as his source, revealing his commitment to the older values of the genre, updating, but also looking backwards to, the horror genre's past. Alongside this, Balagueró's *mise-en-scène*, which, as already noted, is shrouded with darkness, also contributes to the atmosphere and feeling of seriousness and unease. The overall effect of *Los sin nombre* is of a film that is sincere and genuine in its embracing of the horror genre. It is a film that accepts the boundaries of the psychological horror film and attempts to offer depth in order to say something about the human condition. In all of this the film seems to want to lay claim to being a 'pure' or 'authentic' version of the horror film. The world created in *Los sin nombre* is offered to the audience through accepted cinematic codes of realism, allowing the horror to exist in our world rather than the comic-book world of the ironic strand. While there might well be a supernatural element to the plot, the overwhelming choices in terms of the film's form focus on the creation of an overriding sense of realism. Formally, through a strong sense of temporal and spacial unity within the *mise-en-scène*, there is a clear logic to the world created. The eclectic irony strand does not work in this way; for example, *Acción mutante* continually works against unity with its shifting generic worlds that refuse the temporal and spacial logic of genre and narrative. The performance styles present in these films also reflect this difference. In *Los sin nombre* performance technique aims to create characters who are psychologically rounded, or 'realistic', with actors seeming to submerge themselves in their roles, foregrounding character rather than performance. In *Acción mutante* and the like, where the films are not striving for an overall effect of realism, actors are able to use performance styles that are much broader, self-conscious and comedic. Certainly, in *El día de la bestia*, dominant acting styles, based on 'believability', are rendered secondary to more excessive styles that are drawn from cinematic comedy traditions. Of course, when mainstream critics approach these varied 'horror'films they tend to champion those that stick to the generic rules as opposed to those that break them. Fanzine-based writers, however, are able to shift between the two as they have less invested in middlebrow notions of 'good cinema' and more in the various manifestations of 'horror'. Fanzines seem more able to accommodate and celebrate both tendencies alongside one another than the mainstream press. Notions of value based on 'good' taste are broken down in such publications where the vulgar or lowbrow sits comfortably with the sombre and serious.

The victory of the serious

2001 saw the release of two successful horror films, both of which I would argue fall into Collins' category of 'new sincerity'. Both *El espinazo del diablo / The Devil's Backbone* (Guillermo del Toro) and *Los otros* had a more international element than the other films discussed in this piece, the former by a Mexican director, the latter shot in English. Significantly, they were both made by directors who had already achieved some level of critical kudos with their previous works. In a sense this explains the films' critical acceptance, but, I

would argue, this is greatly accommodated by their perceived serious approach to the boundaries of the horror genre. Both films
reveal a new acceptance of horror, a previously marginalized genre,
in the mainstream. No longer simply the focus of fans and fanzines,
Spanish horror films have gone mainstream, winning awards internationally as well as filling cinemas. The international success of *The
Others*, in particular, has brought Spanish horror to a wider global
audience. Indeed, many of the films discussed in this chapter have
had a reasonably high level of financial success, if not in quite the
same league as Amenábar's work, which, according to *Screen International*, is the highest-grossing Spanish film of all time (Green,
2002). Whilst still not approaching anywhere near the volume of
output of the 1970s, the numbers of recent horror productions do
suggest that, far from existing in the margins of Spanish film production, horror films have now moved firmly into the mainstream.
Indeed, at the time of writing, this has been confirmed by the release
in Spain of Balagueró's follow-up to *Los sin nombre*, *Darkness*, with
300 prints, a large number for a Spanish film even in its home
market. *Darkness* has been produced by the Barcelona-based
Filmax's horror offshoot, The Fantastic Factory, whose aim is to
produce around six international products a year. The additional
fact that US mini-major Miramax weighed in with 40% of the final
$12m budget reveals that Spanish horror is no longer seen in terms
of national markets but potentially of global ones, particularly when
shot in English. The distribution patterns of some recent Spanish
horror, particularly those shot in English, show that they are now
handled as mainstream crossover products and no longer films that
will only appeal to cult audiences made up exclusively of horror
fans. Spanish horror has now truly moved from the margins to the
mainstream. How long it stays there may depend on the fickle tastes
of those mainstream moviegoers. The overwhelming success of
these films has meant that critics have had to address their prejudices
and find a way of discussing recent horror films. Interestingly, critical reception of *Los otros* and *El espinazo del diablo* has seen them
try. How they have done so is telling, as they have evoked the more
respectable gothic tradition within the genre – not surprising when
one considers that this is probably the most critically assimilated
part of the genre, due heavily to its literary sources and precedents.
For example, if one looks at the *Sight and Sound* reviews for *The
Devil's Backbone* and *The Others* (Smith, 2001a and 2001b), one

finds references to Hitchcock, Val Lewton, *The Innocents*, *Spirit of the Beehive*, *Vertigo* and the seventeenth-century artist Velázquez. Critically then, Spanish horror seems, increasingly, to be becoming assimilated into the world of serious cinema, or rather, one strand of Spanish horror cinema, the one that maintains the values of the critics who write about them. The assimilation of the 'purer' horror films of the recent revival continues to mark out the irreverent, excessive films of Segura, de la Iglesia and others as still, potentially, the most subversive as they remain outside accepted critical ideas of 'good taste'.

Bibliography

Aguilar, Carlos (ed.) (1999) *Cine fantástico y de terror español*, San Sebastián: Semana de Cine Fantástico y de Terror.

Collins, Jim (1993) 'Genericity in the Nineties: Eclectic Irony and the New Sincerity', in Jim Collins, Hilary Radner and Ava Preacher Collins (eds.) *Film Theory Goes to the Movies*, London: Routledge, 242–64.

Green, Jennifer (2002) 'Spanish House of Horror', *Screen International*, September 27, 12.

Naschy, Paul (2000) *Memoirs of a Wolfman*, New York: Midnight Marquee.

Sconce, Jeffrey (1993) 'Spectacles of death: Identification, Reflexivity, and Contemporary Horror', in Jim Collins, Hilary Radner and Ava Preacher Collins (eds.) *Film Theory Goes to the Movies*, London: Routledge, 103–19.

Smith, Paul Julian (2001a) 'The Others', *Sight and Sound*, November, 54.

—— (2001b) 'The Devil's Backbone', *Sight and Sound*, December, 38–9.

Totaro, Donato (1997) 'Nacho Cerdá Interview', *Off Screen*, www.horschamp.qc.ca/offscreen/nacho.html (accessed 23 February 2002).

Triana-Toribio, Núria (2003) *Spanish National Cinema*, London: Routledge.

Tudor, Andrew (2002) 'From Paranoia to Postmodernism? The horror Movie in Late Modern Society', in Steve Neale (ed.) *Genre and Contemporary Hollywood*, London: British Film Institute.

Index